RUNNING: ME RUNNING EU

RUNNING: ME RUNNING EU

Stephen Doswell

*To Marianne,
Keep on running!
Steve D.*

mot juste

PUBLISHED BY MOT JUSTE

First published in the United Kingdom in 2024 by Mot Juste.

Copyright © Stephen Doswell 2024.

The moral right of Stephen Doswell to be identified as the author of this book has been asserted by him in accordance with the Copyright, Designs and Patents Act of 1988.

All rights reserved. Without limiting the rights of copyright reserved above, no part of this publication may be reproduced, stored or introduced into a retrieval system, or transmitted, in any form or by any means (electronic, mechanical, photocopying, recording or otherwise), without the prior written permission of both the copyright owner and the publisher of this book.

ISBN 978-0-9569670-7-7

Cover design by Spencer Roberts
Book design by Peter Erftemeijer, Mot Juste
Printed in the UK by Hobbs the Printers Ltd

For my aunt Doris, who embraced adventure, defied convention and calmly served her country, living life her way.

Contents

Introduction 001

1 The Why before the What
1. The smoker you drink, the runner you get 005
2. The Great Dave 007
3. A proper runner after all (aka sh*t gets real) 011
4. A parkrunner and a Harrier 013
5. That's it. We're out: the 2016 Referendum 017
6. A death, ten good years and the October Man 021
7. Give it a name and run about it – Aha! 025

2 The Actual Running Part aka the What, the When, the How
1. The challenge begins – Spain 033
2. France: a kind of club run and friends reunited 037
3. (Not so) United Kingdom: running's own Glastonbury 043
4. Italy: Upacchi Tibers and Tuscan Hills 061
5. Belgium: Gent Running Team and the torchlight embrace 065
6. Germany: running in another language 069
7. Portugal: to the Tagus 073
8. Slovenia: a late entry and a warm welcome 077
9. The Netherlands: seven hills and a dead leg 087
10–11. Denmark and Sweden: two parkruns and The Bridge 095
12. Croatia: And quiet flows the Drava 109
13. Ireland: the Curragh, the Curragh! 123

Stages 14–18 – five days, five countries: a short tour of the Habsburg Lands in Hokas

14. Vienna: a frosty reception 131
15. Győr, city of rivers 135
16. Don't panic, it's just the Paneláky of Petržalka 139
17. Brno – checking out Czechia's second city 145
18. Poland, parkrun and pointed hats: 153

Final weeks: seeing the whole jigsaw at last 161

19. The Maltese mishap 163

	Stages 20–23 Lithuania, Latvia, Estonia, Finland	
	(Baltic Week): snow, ice and a yoga warmdown	175
20	Kaunus: another second city	175
21	Latvia: the sudden pleasure of a crowd	183
22	Estonia: the beauty of Tallinn	191
23	Finland: a ship, more ice and a parkrun	197
24	Cyprus: at last, some warmth	209
25	Romania and the RoboRun	219
26	Another frontier: 'what the f*** am I doing in Bulgaria?'	227
27	Luxembourg: into the ravine, the journey's almost done	235
28	Greece: Acropolis now	241

Postscript	253
Map of the 28 stages of RUNNING: ME RUNNING EU	256

Introduction

This is the story that ends one evening in Athens in a blaze of honey light reflected on the flag stones at the Acropolis. It ends with the fulfilment of a heart-felt, intensely personal, year-long challenge to run in every country of the European Union by 29 March 2019. It ends amid the knots of tourists as they exit the well-trodden grounds at the Parthenon's fenced perimeter, where a 61-year-old Englishman, rather incongruous in running shorts and top, stands proud and smiling as they pass.

Where the story begins, though, well, that's less clear-cut. The simple answer is one year earlier on a Mediterranean island, with a ten-mile run from a holiday villa through flower-scented country lanes and around the sandy vistas of a beach-lined bay, to a small summer seaside resort. Another answer would be on the day in late 2017 when that Englishman came up with a name for his challenge, because once things have a name, they become real, at least for me (and this is my story). Or perhaps even before that, when the shock at the June 2016 vote to leave the EU gave way to an effort to come to terms with the result. I voted to remain, but don't worry, this story isn't remotely political.

As I was pondering the uncertain times we were living through and what the next year would bring, a thought came to mind: "I can't do anything about the referendum, but I can run about it…" It was an odd phrase. What did it mean? What *could* it mean? Humans are an adaptive species. When we come across sudden, unexpected changes in our environment, at first we may be puzzled, cautious, possibly worried, even stunned. But sooner or later we adjust. If something happens and we don't like it, we can try to change it, we can ignore it or we can find a way of living with it. I took "… I can run about it…" as a sub-conscious signal to get on and find my own individual way of living with the reality of leaving the EU. Later in the story I'll reveal why it was such a big deal to me personally. No political messages, though, I promise. This is a tale about running, making connections with people, achieving ambitions and learning something about oneself along the way. It's personal, naturally. It's also about the joy of travelling and discovering first-hand some of the sheer variety to be found in 28 European countries. If that's enough for you to keep me company beyond this point, then let's go back to where the story of RUNNING: ME RUNNING EU really started.

PART 1

The Why Before the What

RUNNING: ME RUNNING EU

CHAPTER 1

The smoker you drink, the runner you get

I've always been a runner, even when I was meant to walk. A reminder of this came to light one day in 2017, around the time that that odd phrase "I can *run* about it" had popped into my head. My father died in April that year and as I sorted through a multitude of suitcases, bags and boxes in my late parents' house I found a long-forgotten, now-grainy newspaper cutting with a photo of a bunch of schoolkids in south London preparing to take part in a charity event for The Spastics Society. The event was the 1967 Round Dulwich Walk, a five-mile jaunt around the leafy London suburb where I grew up, and I was one of those kids. I still have a modest trophy for coming third that year, an achievement only secured by running most of the way. It was to be my first and only 'running' trophy (so far – there's still time, at least I like to think so) but the thrill of winning something probably sparked connections deep in my psyche that linked running and reward forever.

Since then, I've probably amassed half my bodyweight in finisher's medals for 'proper' running events although I've never been remotely fast enough to take a podium place, not through a conscious lack of effort, simply a lack of serious pace. Neither slow, nor fast, just somewhere in the mass of mid-paced runners.

It's been said that we Brits excel at sports where we can sit down (rowing, equestrian, motorsports, sailing). I've never tried those. In fact when younger I showed no great ability in any sport. Our grammar school was divided into six houses, with 15 boys in each house from my year-group. Even with 11-a-side in football I struggled to make the house team and didn't represent my school in any competitive activity, except chess – yes, also sitting down but hardly a sport – and cross-country running, and even then only as a squad member. But still, running…

Virtually every year from schooldays onwards, I would sign up for a 10K here or a half marathon there, train a little before each event, enjoy the whole occasion, collect my medal and then grant my running shoes a further period of extended leave until a fresh event caught my eye. So I ran – intermittently – but would never describe myself as a runner back then. A party animal, maybe. For me since the mid-70s, a good time was recorded not in minutes on a stopwatch but in pubs, gigs, clubs and anywhere else where my 'performance' could be measured in music, booze and making merry.

A year into a new decade and there was no reason to assume that I'd ever want to stop the party. Until one day at the start of January 1981 when I lined up for a 10K. It was barely 48 hours after a New Year's Eve spent drinking and (hard to imagine now) smoking. The race began and I struggled from the start. In fact I felt dreadful and found it hard to breathe, the lack of preparation made worse by a five-year nicotine habit that had billowed from the odd fag on the way home from school to a pack of cigarettes every other day. The moment when I could cross the line couldn't come soon enough. By the time it did (I have no record of the result, which is probably just as well) I knew that for me cigarettes and running were completely incompatible and would have to go their separate ways. I'd always known this, of course, but I've often had to learn home truths the hard way, through raw personal experience. Still wreathed in immediate post-run sweat and wheezing heavily, I resolved to quit smoking, cut down on other excesses and run more often. If ever there were a couple of New Year's resolutions worth sticking to, it was those and it was then, in 1981. I was 24 and as Neil Young, one of my musical heroes then and now sang "Twen'ny-four an' there's SO much more…".

PART 1 | THE WHY BEFORE THE WHAT

CHAPTER 2

The Great Dave

As marathon historians know, 1981 was also the year when the London Marathon began. One of those who took part in that first year was Dave Bedford, distance runner and my personal running hero. In an era of clean-cut images among athletes, Dave Bedford stood out as a bit of a rock'n'roll character. He had long, curly hair and a droopy Zapata moustache and he ran with a swagger (and sometimes, in a more regimented time when even a minor flourish of individuality would get you noticed, red socks). Years earlier, partly because of being a compliant child in a strict household with no prospect of ever being allowed to grow my hair long, I'd taken a vicarious shine to this runner with a rebel pose and as a 14-year-old just getting used to the growing freedoms of adolescence, I plucked up the courage to travel on my own to Crystal Palace stadium to see the great Dave Bedford run in the 3,000 metres steeplechase, which he won at a canter. He went on to break the world 10,000 metre record in 1973 and was national cross-country champion at various times.

True to that rock'n'roll image, legend suggests that Dave hadn't prepared for the inaugural London Marathon in 1981, had only entered as a bet and had apparently 'trained' in a night club the evening before. There was a parallel with my own lack of preparation for that 10K a few months before, but only in my most delusionary dreams! Dave Bedford went on to become one of the key figures behind the phenomenal growth of the London Marathon, serving in various roles from the 1980s and as race director for 12 years until 2012. He was awarded an OBE in 2014 for services to athletics and charitable fundraising.

We're at 2014 already. Time to rewind again. Ten years earlier I made my own debut appearance in the starters' pen for the London Marathon. I'd been training well. Having always run on my own when I did any running at all – these were still the days of two or three annual events with a bit of intermittent training before each one – it had been an enjoyable novelty to discover the pleasure of running with a partner. This was not my *partner* – Liz, my wife. Liz and I had quickly discovered during the one run we'd made together in the early 80s that the ingredients in the glue of our relationship would not include running. It simply isn't her thing. While the streets, towpaths, parks and trails of the great outdoors are my domain, the gym is hers. Instead, my 2004 marathon training partner was Judy, a neighbour and a practising GP. Here was someone with a training plan and the discipline to stick to it.

At that time, my work hours were flexible. For a GP, though, practice hours are fixed. So we would run in the early hours before work. This was a rude awakening for me, one of life's owls, used to staying up late to get things done and not accustomed to being up with the larks to make an early start. But if getting up and out at a cold, ungodly hour was hard, little by little the payback became apparent. Slopes I'd struggle to run up at first became ever less of a challenge and my mileage began to grow. At first, I'd feel like the late comedian Spike Milligan who once wrote of his reaction to a new early morning running routine during military life: "Ten miles?! There is no such distance!" Route lengths I'd once thought of as unimaginable for a single run – 14, 16, 18 miles and more – now became an expected part of our weekly programme. I found that I was able not just to embrace the idea of being on my feet running for three hours and more but actually managing to *run* those distances.

So when Judy said, "Next weekend we're stepping up to 20", I had fewer misgivings than I would have done just a few weeks before. That's the thing about distance training – it builds your fitness, certainly, but just as importantly it prepares you mentally so you can tell yourself that you've already broken past your own previous limits and you can do so again, that 20 is just a couple of miles more than 18, and so on. As all distance runners know, as the mile markers pass, more and more of the running is done in your head.

Come the morning of the London Marathon and I was there in Greenwich Park if not bright then at least early. Not as early, though, as Judy, who'd stayed in a hotel that had promoted itself by offering to bus its marathon guests to the start. And it did – but way too early, leaving Judy and others out in the cold and feeling disgruntled with hours to kill before things got going. She was in a different starting pen and we didn't meet on the day. We both had aspirations to finish in under four hours. When my own wave finally started I was dismayed to be hemmed in by the sheer number of other runners. This was my first big city marathon and I hadn't allowed for the congestion. What do seasoned marathoners do in those circumstances? Be patient, go with it, stay calm and step up to target pace once the numbers begin to thin out. What did I do? Got frustrated, started weaving in and out of the pack, speeding up to get past slower runners and throwing myself out of all race rhythm.

With mental preparation now out of the window I carried on forcing the pace in the early miles. At this point I can picture experienced distance runners shaking their heads – but I wasn't an experienced big city eventer and there I was running almost as naively as it's possible to run. So what came next was probably inevitable. Heading towards Tower Bridge I started to lose energy. Only ten miles in? That was ridiculous. It was way too early to start feeling as tired as I was at this point. Yet after crossing the bridge and heading out towards Docklands I knew that I had to do something. If not, I wasn't going to finish. But if one personal flaw had disrupted my marathon bid, now another trait, a tendency to improvise, came to my rescue.

I saw a filling station by the roadside with a forecourt shop. I stopped running, stepped off the course, went in and bought a bag of Jelly Babies and the largest version I could find of that gooey, nutty chocolate bar formerly known as a Marathon, which I downed at speed. I stepped back onto the road and began to run again, chowing down handfuls of Jelly Babies along the way until I'd quickly finished half the pack. As fuelling regimes go it was pretty crude, but it worked. For the moment, though, I'd probably lost at least five minutes but by this point I'd adjusted my expectations. The target had now changed. However badly I'd managed the race to this point, I had put hours and hours of early mornings, freezing conditions and miles of hoofing into this. I'd worked hard to earn the strength and stamina to get a marathon medal. Forget sub-4, now I simply wanted to finish.

By the time I reached Canary Wharf I felt energised again and this made me feel that I could go further, but still without being able to imagine getting to the finish line. I kept going and headed back towards the City. I struggled across the cobbles at the Tower of London and after more mental digging-in and moving forward, I was on the Thames embankment, running alongside the river. By this time I was hoisting up whatever willpower was left from the depths. The well was running distinctly dry as I passed Blackfriars Bridge and I had to promise myself that I would stop at the next bridge – so long as I kept going towards it. Once I got to

Waterloo Bridge, I made the same bargain again with myself to keep going to the next bridge. Couldn't manage it a third time, though so I dropped bridge-by-bridge in favour of lamp-post by lamp-post. It was at this point, somewhere near Charing Cross Station that I recall passing a group of middle-aged women belly-dancing. It was an odd and unexpected sight. Especially when I tried to find out afterwards who they were and where they came from and realised that no-one else had seen them.

To this day I've never been sure if they'd really been there or had just been the imagined product of a by-now confused mind, struggling with exhaustion and the more pressing reality of running the final few hundred yards into Westminster and around to The Mall. "Come on, don't stop, you're almost there," a voice shouted as I neared the turn into Parliament Square. How many times have I heard that since then in other races? And yet the words of encouragement do help. I didn't stop and I was almost there. I rounded the corner. Big Ben. Now, finally, and only at this point, I believed that I was going to finish. With the finish gantry in view, a pair of runners dressed as the childhood storybook characters the Flowerpot Men inched past me. Just a few metres remained but here was a new challenge: I'd been overtaken by Bill but I was damned if Ben would beat me, too! I summoned the final spurt needed to separate them and crossed the line after 4 hours, 26 minutes and 55 seconds.

PART 1 | THE WHY BEFORE THE WHAT

CHAPTER 3

A proper runner after all?

(AKA SH*T GETS REAL)

I'd run the London Marathon. It felt like a 'coming of age' experience, something that marked people out as a 'proper' runner. Maybe not proper like Dave Bedford, but still... Years later as I write this, I release that I think very differently now. If a person runs a 5K parkrun on a Saturday morning, they're a runner. If they've joined their local running club's beginners' course or they're following a couch-to-5K programme via an app on their phone, they're running, so they're a runner.

Back then on that day in April 2004, I felt that I'd crossed some unspoken threshold and was now 'a runner' in a way I hadn't quite been before. This had been my first London Marathon and, I told myself, there would be others. In fact it would be three years before I next had a place in the Marathon (London, of course – where else would I want to run one…?). It was March 2007 and this time the training had been intermittent. I was back running on my own again, but as before, I'd managed to build up the mileage until a month out from the big day when I was out on my longest pre-marathon training run. It was meant to be a 20-miler. I'd run from my home in south Birmingham and out onto the Stratford canal, through the outer suburbs and into the countryside. I planned to keep going beyond the point where the M42 motorway steps noisily over the canal on a concrete viaduct. Trouble was, I'd felt a pain in my right Achilles tendon earlier. I should have stopped immediately. But it was only pain, after all... I kept going.

By the time I heard the roar of motorway traffic my ankle was really sore. I reached the flyover's giant pillars and decided to turn round and 'fly home on one engine' (I was working at aircraft engine manufacturer Rolls-Royce at that time and the analogy came easily to mind). It was a long and painful trek back. The run reduced to a jog, then to a walk and finally a hobble, until a point when I couldn't put any more pressure on my right ankle at all. I laboured up a ramp from the canal towpath, limped into a pub car park and called Liz. A few minutes later her car appeared and

I climbed in, dejected by the realisation that, whatever was causing this pain wasn't going to go away quickly. As a physiotherapist confirmed two days later, my right Achilles was inflamed. She measured the tendon and showed me that it had swollen to more than double the size of the healthy left Achilles. I mentioned the marathon. She laughed, not unkindly, and shook her head. "I'm sorry, Steve, that's absolutely out of the question."

It would take a few weeks of massage, twice-daily stretching exercises, wearing a raised insole and a complete six-week break from running before I could even consider going for a short, gentle run. I followed her advice, despite the temptation to get back out running again once the immediate pain went away. But something else had also happened. I'd begun to feel that perhaps my damaged Achilles heel would figuratively speaking become my own permanent 'Achilles heel', a recurring weakness that would curb my ability to run long-distance again. Maybe it would be better not to take the chance. More positively, I was beginning to realise that running was important to me. Perhaps I should take better care of myself. I certainly didn't want to experience another lengthy lay-off. In fact I did start running again after quarantining my running shoes for the six weeks prescribed by the physio – but it would be another nine years before I would line up again for a second attempt at 26.2 miles. For the next few years I convinced myself that half-marathons would be my limit. It was yet another example of how much the mind determines what you can or can't achieve, in running as in all other endeavours.

PART 1 | THE WHY BEFORE THE WHAT

CHAPTER 4

A parkrunner and a Harrier

During the years that followed I went back to a familiar pattern – the odd 10K and a half marathon every now and then. And then one day I saw a story in the Birmingham Post that would change everything. Just one paragraph in a single column under the simplest of headlines: Leafy 10K, it announced a race organised by the Bournville Harriers running club. As a child in London, I'd grown up knowing Bournville only as a brand of dark chocolate. Moving to Birmingham years later I discovered it was the name of a pleasant district of the city that was the home of Cadbury's and in which the Quaker Cadbury family had built their model community for workers and their families. It's certainly a green and leafy area.

I didn't register in advance but signed up on the morning of the race. I enjoyed the run and knew a couple of the people who seemed to be involved with the club. To my surprise there were a few stalls at the end with some excellent home-made cakes and lots of conversation. It felt like a friendly club and I resolved to join it once I had a car again (I'd given up my car during a business downturn when work dried up following the 2008 financial near-crash). After I'd raced the Leafy 10K and while rewarding my exertions with coffee and carrot cake, someone mentioned a 'park run' in Cannon Hill, my local park. Turned out it was something regular that took place every Saturday morning and it was free. I checked it out the very next weekend and a long-term love affair began. From that point on, I swapped the Saturday lie-in for the weekly rendezvous with fellow parkrunners.

In those early days, some 150 people or so would meet for the weekly run. I got to recognise some faces, and friendships began to form, normally fuelled with mugs of tea and chat in the park café. I was quickly hooked by the elegant simplicity of the parkrun formula. I registered once with a few personal details, printed the personal barcode assigned to me and then just turned up in time for the 9am start. No need for running numbers or registration on the day. No registration fee and no overt commercial pressures, either. It seems almost too good to be true, but for once in life, with parkrun, what you get is exactly what you see. And some time later on Saturday, the parkrun organisers would post that morning's results – Name, Time, Number of parkruns run altogether and personal best time. Ah yes, the PB, the most coveted acronym in running. That weekly quest to outdo one's own previous PB became one of the guiding motivations that would get me out and trotting down the hill to Cannon Hill week after week. But not the only one.

The beauty of parkrun for me is that beyond the simplicity of the set-up, it's a highly social pop-up community. People gather from about 8.30, they listen to announcements, applaud the volunteers who turn out every week to time the finishers, scan barcodes and marshal the course, then run at 9am for just over 3 miles (5K), taking anything from 15 to 60 minutes. The weekly parkrun's for everyone. It's a run or even a walk and certainly not a race. Although clearly some do push themselves hard, people take it entirely at their own pace with no pressure to perform. Once it's over, stories are swapped, personal performances compared and perhaps a little like the après-piste social aspect of skiing (not that I've ever been skiing, although I did once model some ski-wear on a dry ski slope for a local newspaper, but that's an entirely different story), that post-parkrun moment fragments into a myriad conversations, before eventually the crowd starts to thin again and parkrun marker tapes, cones and signage are put away for another week. By about 10.30am the park has returned to normal and no-one passing after that time would ever have known that an event had just taken place involving hundreds of people (because my local parkrun's popularity can now be measured in the upper hundreds, even exceeding a thousand on a couple of occasions).

Of course, this is now old news for a growing number of people, and certainly for runners. In my mind, some time in the late 2010s, the Saturday morning institution known as parkrun fully entered public consciousness. It went mainstream. It was no longer 'merely' a mass movement. It had left its cult status behind several years earlier, but in the words of a story headline in one of the national newspapers, We Are All Parkrunners Now. Of course, that isn't strictly true – many people remain 'on the couch' and a long way from viewing running 5K as a perfectly reasonable way to start their Saturday, many others do all kinds of other things to get their weekend started, others still simply don't have the luxury of going for a 3.1 mile run on a Saturday morning because of work, family or other responsibilities. But for a fast-growing minority, parkrun has become an institution and a routine activity. Before it became mainstream, parkrunners could fairly assume that people they met would know nothing of parkrun, so if the topic came up at all, they might preface their conversation by explaining what it was, unless it was one of those rare occasions when they discovered a fellow parkrun believer. Now, increasingly, a knowledge of parkrun can be assumed and the need to explain it when meeting people is becoming rarer. They may never have run one but they know what it is.

Winding back to the end of 2011, parkrun had become a personal Saturday morning fixture, and an anchor point on which my life gained a welcome and friendly extra mooring. Come 2012, I found myself with wheels again – nothing exciting, just a red Fiat Punto, once laughably disparaged by the leader of a project I worked on as 'not manly enough' (he drove a Land Rover Defender, presumably adapted to run on pure testosterone) – and almost immediately set off to join Bournville Harriers Running Club. It changed my life.

Already knowing a couple of faces at the club from parkrun, I quickly fell into the warm company and weekly routines of my new-found fellow runners. Monday nights were club nights where announcements (club notices, race times and stand-out performances) were shared and the running pack headed off on one of a handful of regular local routes. At first it took time to recognise people from one week to the next. I'd joined during the winter season, it was dark when we assembled and, running alongside people, I saw them mainly in profile for the 50 minutes or so that it took to run the typical six mile route around Bournville and surrounding south Birmingham suburbs. Once the evenings became lighter I began to see more of people's faces, plus I'd stay for a drink at the bar at Rowheath Pavilion. The pavilion is an amenity created in 1924 by the Cadbury family, benevolent employers who were mindful of the health and leisure of factory workers and their families living in the company's model Bournville community. Rowheath is still a thriving sports and community hub a century later, though now run independently. As a community created by Quakers, to this day, Bournville has no pub as such, but the pavilion now has a bar, popular with locals as well as members of the various sports clubs who call the pavilion their home. And so belonging to Bournville Harriers helped me feel a part of life in Birmingham that was different to the way I'd felt during the previous 20 years in the city.

I remember talking about this one day after a weekend race, probably one of the many 10Ks that take place in pleasant shire towns around Birmingham. For 20 years I'd felt that I was in Birmingham, but not really part of it. Now, thanks to becoming involved with two running communities (parkrun and Bournville Harriers), I felt more rooted than ever before. In the following years, as the institution of parkrun began to spread to towns and cities across the UK and beyond, I would start to venture out to discover other parkruns both locally and further afield. Indeed some of my memorable RUNNING: ME RUNNING EU moments were to come when I was parkrunning in other countries. But Cannon Hill parkrun, or CHP as we know it, remained my home run. It still is.

There's a lot I'd like to say about races run and good times enjoyed during the first half of the 20 teens, while proudly wearing the distinctive club colour teal (don't call it blue, or green, and certainly not turquoise...) of Bournville Harriers, but it's time now to wind forward to the event that inspired RUNNING: ME RUNNING EU.

PART 1 | THE WHY BEFORE THE WHAT

CHAPTER 5

That's it. We're out: the 2016 Referendum

The EU referendum result was a shock for many people, however they voted. It was for me. In elections, people cast their vote to express a great many things. It's always struck me as odd that voters have to respond to a whole tangle of parties, policies, priorities and personalities and yet they are given such a crude limited tool with which to record their personal preferences: just an X in a box with a short, stubby pencil. The 2016 Referendum campaign left voters with a similar tangle to unpick with that pencil. However, unlike with an election, there was one simple question on the voting paper: Leave or Remain?

It's said that one of the issues in many people's mind as they voted was identity. I've always seen myself as a native Londoner (with my vowel sounds, how could I not be?), an adoptive Brummie, English, British *and* European. Confused? Not really. I know lots of people who feel this way. Think of a Russian doll, or the way someone can be a son or daughter, sibling, parent, spouse or partner, colleague, parkrunner, charity volunteer and other things all at the same time. In my case, I'd grown up in south London and also lived for a year in France, learned to speak French and, later, a couple of other languages (albeit with no great ability), and while working in France made friends with a German and a Spaniard, Reinhard and Esteban, who like me were strangers in a foreign city and who are still close friends to this day. In particular, Reinhard and I were conscious of our personal good fortune in being part of a generation who had grown up in peace-time, in an era of reconciliation and shared destiny between European nations which had been intermittently at war with each other and shedding each other's blood on European soil over several hundred years.

My grandfather had been wounded on the western front in the 'Great War', my father had been a child evacuee escaping from the Blitz of German bombs one generation later, while my aunt had driven army trucks and staff cars behind the front line as the Allied army pushed

Hitler's collapsing regime back into Germany. During that same war, Reinhard's father (a kind and generous man whom I met often during visits to Reinhard's family home near Mönchengladbach) had been part of the German army of occupation in France, a short drive from where his son was now a language teaching assistant in a French school, as I was, too.

In later years, work had taken me to various European towns and cities, just as summer holidays as an adult had been mainly spent in Europe's warmer climes (unlike those of childhood, almost always spent around the UK's shores. The warmth of the Mediterranean at the age of 18 had been an exotic discovery when 'normal' for the younger me was a dip in the chill of the North Sea or at best a more southerly wetting in Weymouth's cool waters).

Much later, turning 50, my 'midlife crisis' if ever I'd had one, had been resolved not in the front seat of an E Type or on a Triumph 'Bonny' but in a university classroom in Birmingham studying how countries club together – and sometimes fall apart. I studied the workings of the European Union, the velvet divorce of Czechoslovakia, the tragic, bloody collapse of Yugoslavia and Slovenia's determined re-birth as an independent country and member of NATO and the EU. Not very rock'n'roll, perhaps, but because of where I'd been, what I'd seen, the history I'd read and the people I knew, it's probably no surprise that I voted to remain in the EU, although I understand why many others didn't.

Just at the point where you may be wondering how far this story is going to stray from running, let me quickly use a running term and say that this is just an out-and-back stretch of the story's course with some background scenery along the way.

In the early weeks and months following the Referendum it took me a while to settle my own thoughts and feelings. I did a lot of talking and even took part in a TV panel discussion on the BBC current affairs programme Panorama, being interviewed by Adrian Chiles in a pub in West Bromwich, along with fellow runner Barbara and a few other people who'd woken up on the morning of 24th June 2016 having voted one way when a majority in the West Midlands had voted the other way. Despite having my say on Panorama, I felt powerless and downcast, under a heavy weight of emotion. I also knew that it wasn't healthy to carry on feeling burdened in this way. I'd grown up in a family where mental health problems had overshadowed so much. Fortunately, I tend not to dwell on negative thoughts for long.

My sense of unease about the 'Out' vote was palpable and real but I was able to think myself out of this negative state of mind by recognising that I could be as unhappy with the Referendum result as I wanted but it would make absolutely no difference. Worry for the future, lose sleep, fine – it alters nothing. Those who are familiar with the 'change curve' will recognise this as me adjusting to new circumstances. Shock, grief, denial, anger – according to the change curve theory, we go through all of these stages to some degree when we experience a loss of a loved one or anything else that we perceive as a radical change in our circumstances.

It may seem odd to speak the language of bereavement here but that's how it felt at the time. Less than a year later, though, I experienced an actual close family bereavement. It served as a stark reminder that time is precious and there's no sense in waiting passively for life to take you places. And that was a further spur that led directly to RUNNING: ME RUNNING EU.

RUNNING: ME RUNNING EU

CHAPTER 6

A death, ten good years and the October Man

In January 2017 my 86-year-old widower father had fallen ill and, his only child, I went to his house in Kent to look after him. On a wall was his retirement certificate, marking 50 years as a railwayman. He had been a war child, his school career interrupted by the Blitz, and like so many hundreds of thousands of city children at that time, he was evacuated, three times in his case, to Devon, to Sussex and the Rhondda valley, south Wales. He was bright but the frequent upheaval had broken the rhythm of his education and he left school at 14. He joined the Southern Railway which became British Railways and later Railtrack. He married at 25 and within two years was a father. Thanks to the perk of discounted rail travel, and before cheap package deals brought the lure of the Mediterranean within easy reach of working family budgets, he took my mother and I on holiday by train across France, Belgium and Germany to Austria. There were also school trips by train and ferry, crossing borders to Germany and Switzerland. These long journeys first opened my eyes to 'abroad', to the differences (food, language, climate, landscape) and similarities (people had families, raised children, went to work, played football). Those early continental holidays kindled an excitement for travel that has never left me.

During those January days, my father rallied but within weeks went into a rapid decline. This time he did not recover but died in April. Amid the grief, I recognised that my father had seen some adventure in his life – National Service and time spent in Egypt; even the war years themselves had offered some excitement to a child entering his teens, despite the repeated trauma of family separation. By contrast his retirement years had brought him little in the way of adventure or excitement; instead, he'd been scarred by my mother's premature death, loneliness, ill-health and perhaps inevitably a loss of a zest for life. His death was a watershed moment for me; at the time its significance was less clear as I dealt with conflicting feelings: a sharp, immediate sense of loss, also relief that his suffering was over. But during those bleak days of bereavement as

I settled his affairs, I began to think about how I wanted to spend my own remaining years.

A few weeks later in June 2017, barely a year after the Referendum, I turned 60. It was another moment for reflection. I was – and felt – healthy and fit, and, to borrow a phrase, I had all my own teeth (despite a fairly extravagant chocolate 'habit'). By the standards of my grandfather's day, 60 would have put me on the threshold of being 'old'. With improvements in public health and life expectancy and changing attitudes, 'old' now starts considerably later, at least in my mind. A group of my friends and I have been together since school days. During the course of 2016-17 we celebrated each other's landmarks, pleased to a man (it was a boy's school) to have made it this far intact and blessed with good health and happiness. One, Alan (who would later become one of my sponsors for RUNNING: ME RUNNING EU), spoke of 'ten more good years', that on average we could expect to hang on to our present exalted state of good health until our next round of landmark birthdays, when we were 70. It was a slightly sobering thought (which was just as well, given the number of bottles popped during our various birthday celebrations). Age is just a number but, like a New Year, the big round birthdays can also be moments of reflection and fresh resolution. For me, in the aftermath of the Referendum and the very recent death of my father, turning 60 was certainly one of those moments.

One final perspective on this: I have a slightly older friend, Tony, who's a singer-songwriter. Tony recorded and released an album in 2019. That isn't the kind of venture that my grandfather or maybe even the younger me would ever have imagined a man in his late 60s to be getting into. Tony called the album October Man, the title reflecting his sense of the page he'd reached on his own life's calendar (Me? I'll only admit to being somewhere in late August. It's still summer!). Tony's album didn't just happen, though. He made it happen. Back at the point of my landmark birthday, I sensed something similar; that it was easy to become complacent, to take things for granted: health, income, mobility. I'd already had some adventures in life, I knew that my circumstances (home, family, friends, work) were fortunate and I could have more adventures of my own, but they wouldn't simply come to me, I'd need to make them happen.

Something was happening with time, too. As a child, as a teenager, time had been infinite. Even as a twentysomething, its limits were understood but impossible to feel. Now, I began to see time as a precious resource that, like water, could be used and enjoyed but if neglected and wasted, would simply seep away. Just like health, just like fitness. Just like energy and the zest to do things: use them or lose them.

As with all shocks, whether private and personal like a bereavement or public and wide-scale like the biggest political change in a generation, it takes time to absorb the impact. Some people struggle to come to terms with unexpected change – but I like to think that eventually most of us find we can and do adjust to a changed future. We thought it would always be like this but now it's like that instead – so we adjust our expectations and we deal with it. Or, to put it more simply in the context of this story, when the going gets tough, runners get running...

RUNNING: ME RUNNING EU

CHAPTER 7

Give it a name and run about it – Aha!

I can't change the referendum – but I can run about it. I remember a day in late 2017 when these words popped into my mind. They didn't make sense, at least not in a tangible way, but at the same time, they did. I'd done with the dark thoughts, now it was time to lighten up and do something positive and channel my feelings in a constructive way. *I can run about it…* I didn't know what that meant but I liked the idea of action behind it, that running could in some way give me a way of dealing with this momentous national leap into the unknown. It felt positive and decisive. It wasn't about running away but running *for* a reason or a cause… or a charity. I kept on whittling away until the idea became clear, at least in outline: a running challenge for charity with a link to the EU.

Throughout my career I've been a writer, whether it's commercial content, company news, editorial features, annual reports, translations, restaurant reviews, an academic dissertation, even the odd poem. Rearrange my initials S R and surname DOSWELL and you get SELL WORDS. It's how I pay my bills and how I've been able to express myself over the years. And I've always been aware of the power of words as the names of things. I tend to do pretty well in quizzes where general knowledge is important. I don't have the kind of mind that shines with its powers of logic and deduction and I may not always know how things work, but I often know what those things are called. When something has a name it's as if someone's taken a felt-tip marker to it, given it a clear outline and added some colour.

So as I turned this idea for a running challenge over in my mind I began toying with what to call it. Once I'd given it a name it would be real. The name had to reflect running and Europe. I wanted it to tell people that it was my challenge. Above all, it had to be memorable. Anyone who enjoys crosswords will know that if you write down the letters you have for a particular clue and leave blanks for the missing ones, the right word will often jump out at you. And that's exactly how I found RUNNING: ME RUNNING EU. The name practically star-jumped off my page of hand-scrawled alternatives. Clearly running in the footsteps of ABBA and Alan Partridge (or Steve Coogan), this was indeed an a-ha! moment. I now had a name for it and the challenge was real.

The remaining features then came quickly. By this point, on the national stage the government was working towards a date when Britain would leave the EU: Friday 29 March at 11pm. So I decided that I would run in every country of the European Union with that time and date as the deadline.

I also decided to double up on the number of charities to support. I chose the Birmingham-based RSVP (Rape & Sexual Violence Project) and the small national charity Changing Faces for reasons that I set out at the time I created the fundraising page on BTMyDonate:

> I'm enthusiastic about running, European politics, history and communication. I'm also aware of the devastating effects of rape and sexual violence as weapons of war, notably during the collapse of Germany in WW2 and in the Balkans during the disintegration of Yugoslavia in the 1990s. And as a 'professional' communicator I understand how important the face is to convey meaning, emotion and identity and consequently how impairing it must be to live with facial disfigurement. These disparate interests and insights come together with RUNNING ME RUNNING EU, my attempt to do some good for RSVP and Changing Faces. These two small but vital charities are each led by inspiring individuals who in turn have inspired me to create this challenge. Thank you for supporting me.

During the late 1990s I'd worked with Changing Faces on behalf of a client company who supported the charity at the time. I'd met the founder James Partridge and been impressed by him as an individual. By creating Changing Faces and the services it provided, James had been able to channel a devastating personal experience for the good of many other people living with facial disfigurement. I vowed at that time that one day I would do something of my own to support Changing Faces directly. In fact James and I did explore the idea of a small project together in the early noughties and didn't pursue it then. From time to time over the years, the idea would return of doing something to support Changing Faces. So when I conceived the notion of RUNNING: ME RUNNING EU, the decision to select Changing Faces was easy. Now, writing this, I'm pleased to have finally been able to contribute to the work of James Partridge and the charity he founded.

My path to RSVP was different, although, again, an impressive individual was involved. First, some history. Having read a lot about European conflicts, I was familiar with – and at the first time of reading, shocked by – the systematic rape of German women and girls during the closing stages of the Second World War. The maltreatment of German women was one among countless brutal chapters of that war, perhaps less well-known than others. The Nazi regime was guilty of terrible war crimes. This was also a crime of war, and, like all the other atrocities inflicted and suffered during that war, it had been carried out within living memory of older members of my family. But that was then. By the 1990s we had come to think that war on European soil was unthinkable, that we had systems and institutions that would bind destinies together and resolve all disputes a long way short of war. We were wrong. The collapse of Yugoslavia brought war, and further war crimes, including rape.

At my running club, Bournville Harriers, I met a fellow member, Lisa Thompson, chief executive and tireless fundraiser for RSVP, a small West Midlands charity providing support and services for survivors of rape and sexual violence. Lisa's an ultra-runner, tackling challenges that it just isn't in my own personal make-up to even want to contemplate. Whether she's running from coast to coast in the north of England or urging herself forward to complete a 170-mile multi-marathon in Arizona, Lisa's always raising money for RSVP. I'd previously offered to help the charity in some way but we'd never settled on the details. Now, with RUNNING: ME RUNNING EU, here was an opportunity to fulfil the offer. From the moment when I first broached the idea of the challenge with Lisa, she was enthusiastic, full of gratitude, and promised to support me however she could. And indeed, once RUNNING: ME RUNNING EU was under way, it was Lisa who I always knew I could rely on for encouragement on Twitter and Facebook. Her support was constant.

Incidentally, I chose to use BTMyDonate for fundraising rather than one of the better-known platforms because it allowed fundraisers to select two or more charities to support without having to create separate fundraising pages for each one. It served me well during the 12 months that I was active with RUNNING: ME RUNNING EU and thanks to the fact that it was fee-free I was able to make sure that 100% of all donations were split 50-50 between the two charities, who received the money in regular tranches a few days after each donation. BT discontinued BTMyDonate later in 2019.

Things were falling into place. The challenge had a name, a purpose and a destination (several, 28 in fact). While working out the detail, I decided early on that part of the rationale for Running: Me Running EU was to run with other Europeans, and in some way to demonstrate by personal example that, while the UK as a whole had voted to leave the EU, many of us felt and continued to feel part of the great family of European people. It wasn't purely about the physical act of running on the territory of the other 27 EU member-states plus Britain (we were still a member-state at this point, after all); I also wanted to find opportunities to speak to people, to find out about them and also to tell them about me, about Bournville Harriers, about Changing Faces and RSVP, about Britain. And if – and only if – they brought it up first, about Brexit, too.

This last point might strike some people as odd. After all, wasn't this whole challenge an elaborate reaction to the Brexit vote? Well, yes but also, no. Two things to say here. Firstly, when I created Running: Me Running EU, at no point in the description on the fundraising page or in any of the many tweets and Facebook posts that I wrote during the 12 months of the challenge, did I ever use the word 'Brexit'. I knew people, runners and others, who saw Europe and the world through eyes and filters (because we all have filters) that were different to my own, and who had voted to leave the EU. I wanted everyone to feel they could support me as I undertook my challenge and that they could donate to the two charities without compromising their own beliefs. Secondly, I didn't want to wander around Europe like the Ancient Mariner with an albatross around his neck spreading a tale of woe. Whatever the background to the challenge, with Running: Me Running EU I'd managed to fashion something positive, constructive and engaging. What I was about to embark on inspired me and I certainly wanted it to inspire other people.

So I was clear about why I was running, who I wanted to run for, in the broadest sense who with, and by when. I certainly knew which countries to run in, if not yet the precise locations. I'd also been thinking about the kind of running I'd do and where. A couple of factors came into play here. In January 2017 I swapped my normal independent consultancy work pattern for a full-time role as an employee for a small energy company. As an independent, I'd always had flexibility over where I work and when. As an employee again, I had to adjust my expectations about free time. However, the company had operations in Poland and Germany and in my role I would need to go to both countries. I had also retained one freelance work commitment with a long-standing client based in Belgium. Holidays were planned in Spain and Italy and I would take advantage of those, too. So if I could tailor RUNNING: ME RUNNING EU to fit with those work and holiday trips, that would save time and money.

This was important because RUNNING: ME RUNNING EU was 100% self-funded. Every penny of train, plane, ferry, coach and metro fares, restaurant and café bills and hotel charges, would come from my own pocket. I've always been a reader of maps and browser of train timetables. Over time, I would become a master at finding and timetabling low-cost options to eat, sleep, run and travel around the 28 countries of the EU. Despite all these opportunities to economise, though, money had to come from somewhere, so to be working full-time with a guaranteed monthly income at the start of the challenge was a godsend.

I decided that I wouldn't run a marathon at any point during RUNNING: ME RUNNING EU. The training regime required to prepare for a marathon and the time needed to recover after running 26.2 miles were unlikely to fit well with the needs of the challenge. Someone else might disagree but I know my own body, stamina and injury record. At this point I'd run five marathons and trained for a sixth. I was conscious of the greatly increased chances of a calf- or other muscle tear or of inflaming a tendon with the intense high mileage of marathon training. My Achilles heel had literally proved to be my Achilles heel while over-training for a marathon ten years earlier. That had put me out of the 2007 London marathon and off the road completely for six weeks and I wouldn't be able to afford to lose so much time from a running schedule that was always likely to tighten like a cramping muscle towards the latter stages of the challenge.

I'd look around for events of 10K or longer, up to a maximum half-marathon (13.1 miles or 21K) but no further. I would also look at parkruns, because several EU countries had now become part of the growing global parkrun family. True, these would be 5K events only but distance wasn't the primary issue. Running in each EU country was the main objective, and running in the company of others was another consideration. As the challenge progressed, my most satisfying social experiences often arose where I was able to communicate directly with other runners in the smaller events or even in informal groups, and I would discover this for the first time in France. But much more about those encounters later. Finally, when I wasn't able to arrange to run with others, I was prepared to run alone where circumstances made that the best choice to fit in with my itinerary. And wherever running solo was the most practical solution, my goal would be to run for 10K or about an hour, more if time permitted, less if circumstances made it necessary. Sometimes the running would need to be structured, at other times I would simply go with the flow.

It was time. March 2018. I'd created the challenge, worked out the format, obtained the support of the two charities and told everyone else what I was going to do and when I'd do it by. I'd given myself a year and set the timescale, aided by the British government's decision to fix 11pm 29 March 2019 as the time and date for the UK's withdrawal from the EU. We know now how that turned out – it proved to be a movable feast – but that would make no difference to Running: Me Running EU. I'd set myself a deadline. It was time to get on and do it.

PART 2

The Actual Running Part

AKA THE WHAT, THE WHEN, THE HOW

RUNNING: ME RUNNING EU

STAGE 1

Mallorca, Spain: "It was a warm, breezy afternoon when the actual running part of RUNNING: ME RUNNING EU began."

PART 2 | THE ACTUAL RUNNING PART

STAGE 1

The challenge begins

SPAIN, APRIL 2018 – 360 DAYS TO GO

It was a warm, breezy afternoon when the actual running part of RUNNING: ME RUNNING EU began. For reasons of time, money, convenience and sheer practicality, I'd decided early on to incorporate the challenge into any existing plans I had to travel to any of the EU countries. And Stage 1 was the first example. Following an often wet, grey Midlands winter, Liz and I were in Mallorca for what had become a regular early spring reminder that other climates were also available! A few days in and around Pollensa at the foot of the Tramuntana mountain range that crosses the north of the island had become part of an almost-annual Easter routine since the days when our children, Gemma and Luke, long since grown-up, would spend hours in the pool of whatever villa we'd rented in the area that year. There's a cycle-cum-running track along the side of the busy road that links Port de Pollensa and Pollensa town. I'd run to the sea and back along the track a few times on previous trips when we'd been staying in holiday lets on the eastern edge of Pollensa.

This year, in April 2018, we'd gone back to stay at a large-ish house with lush subtropical gardens out in the country off a back road between Pollensa and Alcúdia Bay. Unlike the main road with its purpose-built lane for two-wheeled or two-legged traffic, this road twisted its way between a long rambling chain of small properties and gardens and the occasional field and was lined with hedges, walls and fences, often with little or no verge and occasionally just enough space for two cars to inch past each other. Since a fair proportion of local traffic at Easter is of recently-landed Brits getting used to driving left-hand drive hire cars, the passing is often done gingerly, in a very cautious fashion. So, as runners reading this will already be thinking, not the easiest of running routes.

Before setting out on the Stage 1 run itself, I'd run a couple of times along these narrow, twisting lanes from the house to the sea and then along a short stretch of dilapidated tarmac – the remains of a stretch of road made redundant by a bypass and now mainly used as a parking area by shoreline strollers – before stepping onto the start of the paved, tree-lined sea-front promenade that curves around to the centre of Port de Pollensa. So here it was, Stage 1 of a plan, an ambition, a statement – the completion of which seemed so far away, so remote, and even hard to imagine. Anyone who's run a marathon and even more so an ultra will know this feeling, just as they would probably then say, "Better get started, then!" So I did.

These were the first steps of what would become the biggest running challenge I'd ever undertaken and without doubt the greatest adventure of my life (so far, anyway – there's still time…). At this point, though, it seemed… modest, to the extent that I felt almost embarrassed to be running at no great pace through Mallorcan lanes, while carrying with me this great pretension that I was embarking on a weighty enterprise. But there I was, propelling a not-so-weighty 80 kilos of London-bred, Birmingham-dwelling intent around a pocket of countryside on an island off the coast of Spain at the start of a personal quest. No one was forcing me, no one needed me to do it, no one would be any the wiser if I didn't, and yet here I was.

The air felt close in the lanes that afternoon, and frequent farmyard animal smells wafted over the road, which kept me aware of my rural surroundings, while bilingual road signs and private notices in Spanish and Mallorquín (the local variant of Catalan heard constantly in local shops around this corner of the island) provided occasional food for thought, bringing me back out of the semi-meditative state that regular runners withdraw into as their minds fall into step with their breathing rhythm.

Eventually, up ahead on a long straight stretch of road, a small square of blue at eye level began to grow from a mere notch below the sky, opening out to reveal more and more of the sea until I reached the bay of Alcúdia. Turning right, I would have reached the town of Alcúdia. To the left, the bay curved away towards the calm, low-rise family resort of Port de Pollensa which was to be my turn-round point. But first I crossed the bay road onto the beach to take a breather and enjoy the view.

As a family, we'd been drawn to this part of Mallorca over a succession of Easter holidays when Gemma and Luke had been much younger. Luke in particular had happily joined in with the games of local children in the square, tagging uninvited but unselfconsciously along as they played, streaming in a line across the flagstones, past café terrace chairs and tables, leaving parents grateful for some adult time in the relative evening cool. With Gemma and Luke themselves now adults, Liz and I now returned alone to enjoy the warm breezes, lush landscapes and profusion of flowers that made this calm corner of the Balearics such a pleasure in spring.

I resumed my run, stopping only to take a picture at the road sign marking my entrance into Port de Pollensa. I passed the first, sparsely separated houses at the edge of the built-up area and focused on the sea, the sand, the curvature of the bay, the still semi-distant but approaching town centre and, beyond it, the rise of land towards the Formentor peninsula. It was warm but the promenade approach was tree-lined, offering welcome shade. I ran to the centre of Port de Pollensa, past the tourist mini-markets, past the Spar, the jewellers, the displays of sunhats and beach-balls, until I reached the marina entrance at the very heart of town. Here, the sounds of traffic mingled with the distinct flat semi-ring of halter-ropes fluttering against the masts of yachts in the breeze. A brief water break here and then I turned to head back around the bay, this time with the sun loungers, parasols and glinting sea to my left, beyond the edge of town, back along the long straight lane, round the curves and eventually returning to the villa. Ten miles out and back. Low-key, no fanfare, but I'd run in Spain. Stage 1 was over.

RUNNING: ME RUNNING EU

PART 2 | THE ACTUAL RUNNING PART

STAGE 2

France: a kind of club run and friends united

12 MAY 2018 – 323 DAYS TO GO

I'd planned most of the early stages around existing trips, whether for work or holidays. I'd always known that when it came to the French stage, I would run in Nantes. Hearing the name, people often say, where's that? Or ask if I mean Nancy. It's possibly one of France's less well-known cities but that relative anonymity belies its size and history as France's sixth largest city with just over 300,000 people. It stands on the western Loire, 30km from the Atlantic. Historically, it was the former capital of Brittany and also, like Bristol, a major port for the triangular trade between France, Africa and the Americas – in other words a centre of the slave trade – on which much of its prosperity was built. That's a very unpalatable heritage seen through a contemporary lens and one which the city openly acknowledges, perhaps to an even greater extent than Bristol (at least, until the wave of protest and re-evaluation of the slavery heritage in 2020 brought the effigy of British slaver Edward Colston crashing down into the waters of Bristol Harbour). But I knew nothing of this back in 1978 when I first set foot in Nantes.

To say that the city of Nantes features in my personal history is an understatement. In September 1978 I arrived, a nervous, excited 21-year-old Londoner, at the entrance of the Lycée Clemenceau, the grammar school where renowned author Jules Verne and French war hero Georges Clemenceau (and also, long after my time there, a certain Héloïse Letissier, better-known as Christine and the Queens, or simply Chris) had once studied. And there I was, dishevelled and damp with perspiration in a red sweatshirt and backpack, barely able to speak French and yet about to join the teaching staff at this illustrious place and spend a year there as a language assistant. Preposterous!

Today, with our heightened post-millennial awareness of mental health, we talk about imposter syndrome. On that hot September day in 1978, there was no syndrome, I *was* an imposter. So much so that, once I had been ushered to my accommodation for the year, a plain, corner room on an upper floor in this Napoleonic school, roasting behind two large windows that had been left locked and unshuttered for an entire summer vacation and with a parquet floor and window sills strewn with the carcasses of long-dead flies, trapped behind glass from which there could be no escape, I decided that I had made a terrible mistake and resolved to leave as soon as possible. It was an unpromising start to the year that made me.

I sat on the bed, wondering how quickly I could get away, brimming with emotion, I turned the roneo-copied pages of the Lycée Clemenceau yearbook for the next school year, listing the teaching and ancillary staff in order of seniority and status. There almost at the back (after the teachers and just before the catering and maintenance staff), I suddenly saw my name: Monsieur DOSWELL, Stephen – Assistant d'anglais. And as quickly as I'd decided to turn round on the spot and return home, I realised that I had a role and a responsibility and that the school was relying on me to be its English language assistant. I still have that guide and there's a small mark just discernible more than 40 years later – a tear stain. As I came to terms with the realisation that I couldn't just up sticks and go, I heard a knock at the door. I opened it. There stood a stranger of my age, tall, smiling, holding a distinct dimple-shaped bottle containing a peaty fluid. "Hello, I'm Reinhard. I'm the German assistant. Do you drink whisky?"

And with those words a friendship was born that endures to this day. Our Spanish colleague-to-be, Esteban, was in hospital (kidney stones) but once recovered, he joined us and together we began a year of discovery, experience, fun and friendship that changed us forever. It helped me to shed my residual but often still-limiting shyness and replacing it with a measure of confidence and also gave me a taste for adventure that would eventually lead me to embark on RUNNING: ME RUNNING EU. It was also a year in which I discovered my Englishness and got to understand aspects of being British that we describe as our national character.

When I realised this soon after returning home, it seemed perverse that one could get this kind of self-knowledge by being *away* from one's own country. Years later, I see that there was nothing perverse or in any way odd at all about it. It's precisely by leaving our own cosy, familiar environment that we truly get to understand just what's so, well, cosy and familiar about it. When we meet other people, sample other cultures, we get some points of comparison and from that we can evaluate what aspects of our own society might be better and what others might do better than us.

After all, didn't the Apollo space mission astronauts get an insight into the beauty and wonder of their home planet by leaving Earth's orbit and observing it from space? During our current century's turbulent 'teenage' years of divisive referendums and ever more contested national identities, I've sometimes recalled Kipling's lament, "What do they know of England who only England know?" I haven't travelled extensively around the world, but I have learned to find my way around Britain's own backyard and over the years I've made an effort to understand Europe's history and politics and Britain's sometimes intimate, sometimes distant, but always intertwined relationships with our nearest neighbours.

Back in Nantes during that exceptional year 1978-79, I lived and worked as a teacher (well, a language assistant, at least), living a French life with Reinhard, a German and Esteban, a Spaniard. We neither paraded our 'Europeanness', nor did we question it. However, our parents had all lived through war or dictatorship or both. At Reinhard's age, his father had served in the German army of occupation barely 30 miles from where we were now working together. My father had been sent away three times as an evacuee to escape the Blitz. Esteban's parents had lived through the Guerra Civil in Spain. The three of us were acutely aware (I know, because we discussed it) that we were lucky to be alive and together at a time of peace, and when all of our countries had a sense of mutual gains to be had from working together.

So I can certainly say that my own inner European Union was conceived and nurtured spiritually and emotionally in that year. That faith remains with me and I feel no less English or British for it. On the contrary. Europe is a place where I can be British – and when I crank out a few sentences in another European language, no one could possibly doubt my Britishness!

Just re-reading these last paragraphs it's clear that I've headed once more into the undergrowth and well off the running trail. Time to head back, but I hope it helps everyone who's still with me on this journey to understand why, when it came to RUNNING: ME RUNNING EU, the French stage had to be in Nantes.

So I had two reasons to be back in Nantes. Firstly, this was to be a 40th anniversary reunion of 'les trois Clemencaires', the Englishman, German and Spaniard who once used to walk around Nantes' famous botanic gardens the Jardin des Plantes every lunchtime after their daily meal at the school across the road, speaking their common language of French together in three strange and unrelated accents that must have struck any passing local people as odd, even comical, to hear. Now we would be back there again, albeit with considerably less hair than in the 1970s, especially in my case.

And Nantes would be the setting for Stage 2 of RUNNING: ME RUNNING EU. With the calendar date moving closer, I Googled local running clubs and found FAN, or FreeAthletes de Nantes. I discovered that they met every Saturday morning at a particular park. In what would become a standard pattern for how to run with local runners during the challenge, I sent an email to introduce myself and ask if I could join them on the Saturday of my visit. I was slightly disappointed to receive no reply – happily, this was to be an exception – but figured that I would find the park, turn up anyway and run with whoever was there. And worst case, if no one was there, I'd run alone. It would be Saturday, or parkrunday for the millions of parkrunners worldwide. So at least I would find a park to run in.

I flew from Birmingham to Nantes. It would be a short flight. Or at least that was the plan. Somewhere over Normandy came the announcement that no one expects to hear except in a cinema: "Ladies and Gentlemen, is there anyone on board today with medical training of any kind?" Heads began to turn, to reveal a passenger laid out in the aisle. Just ahead, a woman declared that she was an industrial nurse, unclipped her seatbelt and went back to tend the stricken man. It became apparent that he had suffered an anaphylactic shock and was in need of immediate medical intervention. The plane diverted to the nearest hospital and within minutes the contours of the island of Jersey grew large and map-like below us as we descended to land. Paramedics came on board and after examining the man, stretchered him off the plane. Eventually the plane resumed its planned journey and before much longer I was back in Nantes.

Suffice to add that the reunion with Reinhard and Esteban was everything that I'd anticipated and hoped for and it gave me a great, satisfying sense of reconnection. On the morning of the run, I ran from our modest hotel in the city centre out to the mid-suburbs and found the park entrance. There were a few people around but no discernible group of runners. Eventually a younger woman who introduced herself as Emilie approached me and asked if I was there to run with FAN. I said yes, explained why I was there and after a couple of minutes we decided to run together. Just as we began to track the park perimeter to make sure we weren't in the wrong place we were joined by another woman, Nathalie, also there for the run with FAN. And so we ran together around the Parc de Procé, crossing into its sister park at some point along the way. Beyond the formal landscaped sections the terrain became one of woodland, so that we could have been in the Wyre Forest or a similar rural setting, except that we were in fact running well within the city suburbs. I knew that Birmingham had many such woodland trails within its boundaries and that must be true of so many other cities for anyone with the time and inclination – and, ideally, the trail running shoes – to explore.

Speaking French again was enjoyable, not exactly like slipping into an old pair of comfortable slippers, more like putting on once much-loved clothes that no longer fit as well as they used to but which remain fit for purpose, if lacking a certain cut and elegance! Somewhere during the run and in mid-conversation I asked Emilie and Nathalie if I could take a photo of us together (it's best never to assume…) and we did so outside an abandoned – and allegedly haunted – house in a clearing within the woods. Our run continued and after an hour and a gentle 8K or so we found ourselves back at the park gate where we'd started. Here we met another small group of FAN runners who'd set out earlier. More greetings and a group picture taken for the FAN Facebook page and then coffee in a parkside café. Nathalie who was from Nantes showed interest in my story of the 40th anniversary reunion and also the idea of running 'about' the referendum and raising funds for charity. We had the first of what for me would become many conversations about Europe, about Britain and Brexit, about running. When we said our goodbyes I trotted back to the hotel, very satisfied that I'd met and run with local people, told them my story, been given a good reception and made to feel welcome. Again, this was to be repeated time and again wherever I went. For now, though, I'd run Stage 2. It was time to return to the reunion.

STAGE 3

Catton Park Passing Camp Bournville at Thunder Run, a 24-hour relay race for teams. I ran as part of Bournville Harrier's 'Fruit'n'Nutters' team. Each one of us would set out to complete the Thunder Run's hilly 10K circuit. According to the rules of Thunder Run we had to have a member of our team on the course throughout the 24-hour event.

PART 2 | THE ACTUAL RUNNING PART

STAGE 3

(Not so) United Kingdom: running's own Glastonbury

19-21 JULY – 253 DAYS TO GO

When I began to consider which running format to choose for the UK stage, it was appealing to take the opportunity of being at home and run in a conventional race, with a start and finish line, numbers, some pzazz and running bling and lots of other runners. As the year would turn out, not all – and in some cases, none – of these features would be available in some of the future stages. Running the 'home' stage would also enable me to complete it without the logistical challenges of the later runs abroad. I had to make RUNNING: ME RUNNING EU work for me. Nonetheless, I wanted the UK stage to be challenging. The event I finally selected met all the criteria. It was one I'd run before, one that has an almost mythical appeal for many of my Birmingham running buddies, as it does for thousands of runners from all over the country. There are runs, and then there's... Thunder Run.

Imagine a country estate in the heart of England divided horizontally, one half a mostly flat but uneven stretch of grassy pastures, the other half a long bank climbing into wooded hills to a ridge offering fine views across three counties. Now picture the lower, grassy stretch covered with a pop-up encampment of tents, marquees, awnings, a few camper vans and flags, and several blocks of portaloos, stretching for several hundred metres ahead from a country road to the tree-line and for half a mile left and right. Welcome to Catton Park on the Derbyshire/Staffordshire borders, not far from Lichfield and just a mile from the National Arboretum. For one weekend in mid-July, Catton Park became a festival, a rally for the running tribe, a testing place for stamina and resolve and the setting for what many runners regard as an intense, fulfilling highlight of their year, summed up in two words: Thunder Run.

The event itself centres on a 24-hour competition in which relay teams of typically 5-8 and a small hardcore of solo runners, attempt to run as many laps of a 10K course as possible, individually and collectively, from 12 noon Saturday to 12 noon Sunday. Demand for entries is high and it's a case of fastest finger first from the moment that entries open on a given day for that year's Thunder Run. Places at each year's event normally sell out in minutes. Delay or dither guarantees disappointment but be ready instead with the cursor poised and you stand a chance of entering yourself and your team into one of the great domestic running experiences.

I'd already taken part in previous Thunder Runs, to the extent that it was now one of the first fixtures in my own annual race calendar. On our first appearance four years earlier as a mixed team of eight men and women, the Bournville Fruit'n'Nutters team had been my running club Bournville Harriers' only representatives at Thunder Run. But our photos and anecdotes had left an impression on the rest of the club, and by the time the 2018 event came around, our representation had grown so that we had five teams of eight plus two solo runners to add to the thousands of other runners from clubs and groups from around the country.

It's hard for members of Bournville Harriers not to think about chocolate when we can smell the aroma of chocolate being made just down the road from the club HQ, at Cadbury's famous Bournville factory. So it was unsurprising to read the list of Thunder Run team names this year and see the chocolate-inspired Bournville Heroes, Marvellous Creations, TealTeasers and Bournvillains, alongside our own Fruit'n'Nutters. One mid-July Friday morning a small convoy of vehicles eased away from the club's base at Rowheath Pavilion. The convoy headed east from Birmingham to Catton Hall, arriving early in order to secure our favoured spot on the eastern edge of the camping grounds, where the 10K course emerges from the trees and from where the residents of what becomes 'Camp Bournville' can clap, cheer, ring cow-bells and offer words of encouragement to the stream of passing runners during the long hours of Thunder Run.

Since the actual running doesn't start until the next day, Friday is about setting-up, settling in and attuning to the no-frills simplicities of camping again. It's also about checking out the event arena where the running starts and finishes and where the Thunder Run HQ, First Aid, catering and running-related retail outlets and shower cabins are set up. Another regular (and popular) feature was an original red London Routemaster bus now living a new converted life as a bar. Once the running is done for the weekend, it had become one of the Fruit'n'Nutter team's wind-down rituals to haul our weary legs up the Routemaster's back steps and chill out on the top deck for a while, exhausted but exhilarated, before calling time on Thunder Run for another year. It would happen again this year, too, but first we had some running to do.

For a handful of Harriers who'd made the 30-mile journey from Bournville to Catton Park, the running on Thunder Run weekend would begin almost perversely with me driving us away from the camp that we'd only reached the previous day, to head for a few miles around the twisting country lanes to the National Forest centre at Rosliston. Why? Simple. We may have had a 24-hour running event ahead of us, but this was Saturday morning and that meant parkrun. I've already said plenty about parkrun and what it means for tens and now hundreds of thousands of people around the globe, from Evesham to Esbjerg to Eswatini. For our group, parkrun had certainly become a Saturday ritual and the imminent prospect of Thunder Run wasn't enough to distract us from one of the near-sacred weekly rites of running. We weren't alone in that view, either. Others had also made the four-mile journey that morning from Catton Park to the National Forest to run on Rosliston's woodland trails, so that by the time the final finisher had crossed the line, the typical average weekly attendance of 150-175 runners had doubled to 339. Happily the volunteer event team at Rosliston are used to the annual upsurge in numbers on Thunder Run weekend and they plan for it. In fact several of the volunteers were themselves Thunder Runners who had generously chosen to marshal the Rosliston course rather than run.

Each parkrun course is different, although the format is same: a free, weekly, timed event set up and marshalled by volunteers and run by a mix of loyal locals who turn out to their nearest parkrun each week, and parkrun 'tourists' who travel the country and beyond – distance no object – to run different parkruns and add to their total. Back in July 2018 I'd already run on a couple of dozen English parkrun courses, although most of my parkruns had been at my local Cannon Hill Park in the shadow of Warwickshire County Cricket Club's imposing Edgbaston stadium. Standing that Saturday morning by the National Forest visitor centre at Rosliston, I didn't know it at the time (because at this stage I really hadn't planned far ahead) but by the end of RUNNING: ME RUNNING EU I would run parkruns in five more countries.

The weekly parkrun experience usually involves lingering conversations in a nearby café after the run but on this Saturday morning we clearly had other plans and a deadline. We allowed ourselves a quick coffee on site but were keen to get back before the gates of Thunder Run's car park for competitors were sealed.

Back at Catton Park, we confirmed which leg each Fruit'n'Nutters member would run. Each one of us would set out to complete Thunder Run's hilly 10K circuit which promised several steep inclines, dozens of exposed tree roots, plenty of sharp turns and a variety of surfaces from stony tracks to slick, tussocky grass – and we would do so more than once. According to the rules of Thunder Run we had to have a member of our team on the course throughout the 24-hour event. So, with our individual finish times expected to span from 50 minutes to just over an hour, on average, each of our team of eight runners would probably need to run the course three times. Everything would slow down once night fell and we were less sure-footed and reliant for light on head-torches and an occasional shaft of moonlight. We would also have to factor in the risk of slips, tumbles, turned ankles and full-on face-plants, day or night. Between us, we'd earned a metaphorical badge for each of those at previous Thunder Runs.

Sadly, by the end of this year's event one member of our team, Linda, would amass the full set of badges by herself. I still wince now at the haunting memory of her bruised and blood-spattered face and a 'Why me?' expression, signalling shock and sadness that her Thunder Run had come to an abrupt, unwelcome end on her first run in the woods, as paramedics dressed her wounds in an ambulance before taking her to a nearby A&E. I won't mention further details here to spare her feelings and because the memory is distressing. There was another, practical impact of losing Linda from our roster: being one team member down would also mean that someone might have to run an extra lap. On that Friday before any of this happened, I hadn't yet discovered that that someone would be me.

None of this was in our minds that evening, full of expectation for the weekend ahead. We knew the hazards, but risks are risks, to be noted and managed but not feared. We were there to enjoy Thunder Run, not to worry about the downside. I wasn't just ready to run, I was excited – and eager to get going. But I'd have to wait a while. I was running fifth leg and wouldn't be starting until around 4pm. Conditions were dry and bright, with temperatures in the low 20s, fairly typical for mid-July in the English Midlands. After we'd gone as a team to the arena to see the start of Thunder Run and cheer on the first-leg runners, I walked around the

PART 2 | THE ACTUAL RUNNING PART

camp, taking in the atmosphere and reading the running club flags that revealed how far runners had come to be part of Thunder Run.

As a lover of maps, travel, place names and accents, it always fascinates me to see the flags and hear how changing geography alters speech, expanding southern vowels, flattening them in the east, taking a Londoner's semi-neglected r sound and turning it into a rich rolling mouthful by the time it reaches Scotland. Nasal twangs, sing-song intonation, different stresses – each one creates a sense of place and together they reveal how far we can stretch the language this way and that, and yet we can still understand each other. Overhearing snippets of chat from members of clubs as variously distant from each other as Chorlton Runners, Steel City Striders, Lliswerry Runners or Mornington Chasers, along with the predominantly Birmingham accents within our own Camp Bournville, stirred a pleasure in me at how we can retain the features of our distinct identities, our club colours, where we're from and how we speak, and everyone respects that, because we have this shared passion – running – and a shared purpose – to run the course, enjoy the atmosphere and be part of Thunder Run, something bigger than ourselves but to which we all contribute something. I'll admit to feeling a warm glow, a sense that all was well with the world, at least on this big grassy estate at that mid-July moment in the Thunder Run bubble.

Because it was so familiar to me, it took place just an hour from my home and it was something I did every year, Thunder Run would be the least 'exotic' of all of RUNNING: ME RUNNING EU's 28 stages. Yet in one sense I can draw a certain parallel between Thunder Run where running clubs come together and the European Union of member states. Both are about a large community of smaller entities that retain their independent characteristics and traditions but which agree to work together and operate to some common rules. By doing so we create something of great value that's bigger than ourselves without losing our own individual identities as clubs or countries. Sometimes we compete, sometimes we collaborate but ultimately we find room for expression and we get what we want from being part of it.

I can sense reactions from "Well, ye-es, up to a point..." to "NO!" Only a naïve idealist with the pinkest of tinted specs would take the analogy any further. A 70-year-old international economic system with some features of a state is slightly more complex than a weekend running challenge held once a year with a bit of camping thrown in. I know that with size and complexity comes tension and contention – no community is perfect and even small clubs with shared goals can become divided; families, too. Besides, I also knew well that a fair chunk of the people around me, who'd chosen to share this field with fellow runners at Catton Park, may have put their x in the opposite referendum voting box to the one I'd chosen just two years before. Anyway, analogies can only take you so far and I've probably over-stretched this one already. At Thunder Run it was time to head back to Camp Bournville and get ready to run.

With shadows starting to lengthen and the temperature beginning to fall from its peak but still promising a low bake on the course, I set out for my first leg shortly before 5pm. Down at the start, I waited in the holding pen a good 15 minutes before our previous runner Jude was due in. I didn't expect her to exceed her own estimated time by a quarter of an hour – although Jude is faster and more competitive than me – but I wanted to be ready and in place long before she came in to view to snap the team's relay baton around my wrist. As a reforming procrastinator (one deadline at a time…) I have frequently cut it fine in the past, but being late is stressful enough and my stress tolerance for time pressure reduces with each passing year, which is just as well.

I had another reason for being timely. The first year we took part in Thunder Run, I'd been rather casual about getting down to the start line for my overnight run. Imagine my embarrassment at hearing "Steve! Where the **** are you?!" coming out of the semi-darkness when I reached the handover pen. I'd miscalculated. Team-mate Mark had run the arduous course in challenging night-time conditions, wanting nothing more than to pass on the baton, get off the course, shower and sleep. The last thing he needed was to finish, only to discover that I wasn't there and then to run back and forth along the shadowy holding pen, peering into the dark mass of assembled runners, shouting my name into the gloom. But there I was – missing, as the old joke goes. It would be fair to say that in that moment he wasn't best pleased. A shower and a few hours' sleep later and Mark was able to smile about it. It took me longer to forget, though, and I would still cringe at the memory months later. My born-again punctuality probably dates from that moment, although it takes time to slough off a lifetime of late-coming and there are still occasional lapses. But not at Thunder Run.

I spotted Jude. As she ran the final steps towards the finish I moved through the waiting crowd of next-leggers and waved so she could see me. With a snap she coiled the baton around my wrist and I was off, running out onto the grassy course and soon tracking along the base of the wooded bank. A few hundred metres later the course turned abruptly right and immediately I was climbing steeply into the trees, the path switching back and forth, the incline challenging, the packed earth underfoot uneven but firm. Later it would loosen, slick with night dew. For now, though, it gave enough grip to get me up the hill until the land began to level out.

The run was arduous. There are several inclines, plenty of sharp turns, the surface either tussocky, energy-sapping grass or stony trails. Exposed tree roots lay in wait, sometimes one after the other, the ground constantly threatening to trip unwary runners with its thick, dark, wooden varicose veins that often left little or no space for feet to fall comfortably. In running parlance this is a 'technical' course, demanding good technique and constant vigilance in order for runners to stay on their feet. Good footwear is also essential. I'd naively turned up in road shoes in previous years – fine for city streets but offering little protection against the hazards on the Thunder Run course. I'd got away with it the first year because conditions that year were dry. The second year found me sliding all over the place, at one point clinging to whatever bushes I could find to inch my way along a 200 metre earthen path that humidity, rain and constant churning by a horde of runners had reduced to a slick, glistening caramel slop. I'd bought my first trail shoes immediately on returning home to Birmingham. By the time of the 2018 Thunder Run I was on my second pair of Inov 8 trail shoes. I found them rather rigid and harsh on the big toes but they cased the feet well and they were well up to the rigours of Thunder Run.

The course dropped back down from the hills along part of the perimeter of the campsite. I saw the camping stoves, the trestle tables laid out with home-bakes and multi-packs of crisps, resting runners sitting back in foldaway chairs. There were a few claps, a few words of encouragement as I passed. I knew I'd be approaching our own 'Camp Bournville' soon and that there would be noisy support. As a club, we pride ourselves on what I'd once dubbed the Bournville Wall of Sound, setting up a cheering station whenever the route of big races brings runners out to our home territory in south Birmingham, especially the annual Birmingham Half Marathon. When you're running into Bournville, expect a cacophony of shouts, cheers and the raucous ringing of cow-bells. And it's much the same at Thunder Run, except that the noise level only climbs when

Bournville Harriers are spotted and the rest of the time is kept to a considerate clapping for other passing runners. It's a campsite after all.

When I tell other people – runners or not – about Thunder Run, I sometimes describe it (analogy alert…) as the Woodstock or Glastonbury of running. Most people will understand the allusion: a festival, a campsite, a huge pop-up community devoted to something we love, but in this case one where there's no music, except a few runner-friendly records on the arena's PA or whatever people have streaming on headsets or personal speakers for their own pleasure. As for drugs, there's alcohol from the bar plus whatever booze people have brought with them. But the main stimulants are the adrenalin of getting ready to run, the micro-doses of dopamine every time there's a clap or a "Well done, mate. Keep going" on the course, and the post-run 'swimming with endorphins' effect when mind and body relax, nothing's a problem and everything's well with the world. After the build-up and the start of Thunder Run, the camp settles into a kind of calm routine of waiting, watching and getting ready for your next turn to run.

Back on my run, I'd passed Camp Bournville and a little further on, the encampment where other familiar faces from Cannon Hill parkrun had seen me and whose words of support had hung briefly as I headed back out onto a long straight uneven farm track thick with grass. The encouragement was appreciated. At the same time, I was happy to be away from the camp again, to settle into my own rhythm, still in view of other Thunder Runners but largely unobserved as each runner concentrated on their own breathing, pace and – especially – footfalls: at Thunder Run you're rarely more than a misplaced step away from a slip, a trip, a tumble or a sprained ankle.

Another turn and I began to climb again, still on thick, demanding grass. I saw the distinctive red race numbers of a different kind of competitor, who was not running Thunder Run as a member of a relay team – as I was – but who had taken on a much greater challenge. Three times round an arduous 10K course over 24 hours was exertion enough for me but the red-number runners had taken on a whole other level of ordeal. These were soloists. No handover point for them. They do the whole of Thunder Run on their own, taking breaks when they want to, but generally going round the course over and over again, hill-climbs, tree-roots, tussocky grass, stony paths, twisty trails, 10K after 10K, from 12 noon Saturday until 12 noon Sunday. This year, the winning soloist would complete a barely conceivable 19 circuits. I like a challenge but simply could not conjure up the personal stamina, the dig-deep resilience required to run or walk 190K (118 miles) in just 24 hours.

Mutual appreciation is guaranteed at Thunder Run and it's impossible to run the course without collecting a few dozen or more "Well dones" along the way. It becomes automatic and a natural courtesy to do the same, in much the same way that everyone thanks the driver when they get off a bus in Birmingham (as a native Londoner used to more brusque manners in the capital, that took some getting used to during my early days in the second city). But when it comes to soloists there's a pecking order of admiration. A simple "Well done, Solo," muttered – because the rest of us mortals in teams still have our own exertions to cope with and energy to save – but sincere, becomes an automatic response whenever we pass a soloist. Increasingly as time passes and night falls, the red numbers become harder to spot and it's the body language alone – the hunch, the trudge, the hunkering down – that marks someone just ahead as a soloist.

As the hours pass, the soloists' responses become shorter, fainter, merely a grunt and sometimes simply silence. But that's OK. Distance runners are familiar with that feeling of withdrawing to an inner space inside themselves as the miles mount up and their bodies come under increasing stress. I certainly recognise it in the soloists. Whenever I see them out on the course in the early hours, I know that many will by now be hard to reach as they shelter in their spiritual 'safe room', conserving energy and coping with the extreme test of endurance as they move ever forwards. Given the scale of their personal challenge, a reply may not be forthcoming. But we get it. Sometimes overt communication is unnecessary.

At the 5K mark there's a water station and during the night runs, some very welcome floodlights, too. The next two kilometres I find to be among the most demanding of the course, with stones embedded in the trail, switchbacks, and exposed tree roots at every turn. Here in the woods we are enclosed and in the late afternoon heat the air is thick and soupy. The land rises again, eventually falling back before another climb and this time there's an opening ahead, getting brighter, until finally we're out of the trees and up on the ridge – open land, wider vistas, and the presence of the Sutton Coldfield TV transmitter, a reminder that we're not in some parallel world but ploughing along in the Midlands countryside not far from the city. Emerging onto the ridge is the high point of Thunder Run, and not only in terms of elevation. The land levels out and as the hillside falls away to the right, we know that the hardest part is complete, at least this time round. True, we'll have to do it all over again in a few hours, and then once, maybe twice more, but for this circuit, the major challenges are now behind us.

I passed the 8K marker and almost immediately turned sharp right to head down the slope along a very narrow trail, through an entrance gate and then left down a steep grassy bank, taking care not to fall, before running along two sides of a boggy lake, turning right for a few hundred metres, and then left, back into the camp. One kilometre to go. Here the camp was lined with club flags, awnings, runners relaxing. There was music, food smells, children playing. After the solitary rigours of navigating the treacherous woods and being up on the ridge, this was like a return to civilisation. With plenty of claps and words of encouragement to feed off, I reached the short, final, stony climb, dropped back down, skirted the side of a ploughed field and entered the arena. With a final right turn and the finish arch ahead, I removed and straightened the bracelet-baton ready to pass it on. I spotted Simon waving from the holding pen and ran up, snapped the baton firmly around his wrist and watched him disappear back into the pen to head out. I left the course, hot and sweat-streaked but happy to have stopped running. Several glasses of water later from the arena's mobile tanker, I returned to our camp like a warrior returning from battle (if only in my own head). After more "Well dones" and enquiries about how the run had gone, I wrote my finish time on the team chart, collected my bag and headed down to the shower block. It was time to clean up and then eat.

I wasn't due to run my next leg until much later, around 10.30pm. Well before then, our plans changed. Linda had fallen in the woods, I'd seen her in the ambulance and she was now at the hospital. We were one team member down and I decided to run an extra lap, as others had done in previous years when we'd lost runners through injury. There was no pressure on me – it simply felt like my turn. But I would do it by running two legs back-to-back, with no handover in between. Although it would be tiring and tough, I preferred to do this and avoid yet another round of toing and froing to the camp and back between runs. There's only a certain number of times that you can go through the Groundhog Day experience of queuing for the shower before the novelty wears off.

As evening fell and the light faded, the campsite's darkness was broken by the soft glow of lights strung around tent openings and awnings. There was now another kind of light: narrow, piercing beams from headtorches – a Thunder Run requirement after sunset – as people walked around the camp. As time passed, the animated chatter and laughter from earlier died down to a level of quiet exchanges in low tones. On the course perimeter as it passed the camp, several Bournville Harriers gazed in semi-silence from an assorted line of camping chairs, contemplating the darkness of the woods just feet away on the other side of the course, occasionally offering brief encouragement to passing soloists as they emerged from the trees. Numbers dwindled as individuals bedded down for a couple of hours' rest, while others fastened timing chips, pinned running numbers and picked up hoodies to wear while waiting to begin their own next leg.

Overnight, after each of us completed our latest run (and this time, in my case, a double leg), we had a system: on returning to camp, we would make sure the next runner was awake and would be ready to get down to the handover pen in good time to pick up the baton from the current runner. In the middle of the night, it isn't easy to stand by the side of a tent and whisper "Nicola… are you awake?" without disturbing the whole camp. But no-one enters Thunder Run expecting to enjoy a night's uninterrupted sleep. Even though people do their best to keep noise levels at a minimum, the camp is a hive and there's always someone on the move.

Sleep is broken in a dozen ways – a snore, a hooting owl, a barking dog, a motorbike at full throttle on a country lane. Or – uncommon but it happens – a rude awakening as a returning runner trips blindly over an invisible guy rope and lands on a tent. If the stumble itself doesn't produce enough decibels to tear someone from their forty winks then the expletive that follows will do the trick. It's hard enough to sleep when you know you have to be up again in a couple of hours. When I've finished my run, showered and changed, my mind and body are still bright with adrenalin and exhilaration, even more so when it's already getting light again as I'm just zipping the tent closed.

But I was in a pitch-dark sleep when I heard a disembodied voice: "Steve… Jude is out there… You've got 40 minutes". Shaking off the mental fog I switched on the LED camping light and fumbled around trying to change into my next set of running kit while still lying down in a ludicrously tiny pop-up tent which only ever sees the light of day (or the dark of night) once a year, at Thunder Run. I unzipped the tent as quietly as I could (it still sounded like a long, loud continuous rip in the night's fabric), poked my feet out of the tent and squeezed into my trail shoes.

They felt ill-fitting but would have to do. One day I would find better shoes. I stood unsteadily, not feeling remotely ready to run, adjusted my eyes to the light of my own head-torch and went to check the team timing chart. Some of the entries were now smeared and hard to read but I could see that, as expected, the later legs were taking everyone longer as darkness, night dew and fatigue made an impact. On the course one or two runners puffed past, this time with no one to see them but me. The row of chairs was empty. I had time for a quick snack: a chocolate brioche and a long swig of water sufficed, and I headed down to the arena.

Things had cooled down and I was glad of my hoodie, which I would give to Jude to take back to camp. There were fewer people around but the handover pen itself was several deep with waiting runners. One had an inflatable flamingo, another a stick with multi-coloured tassels that could easily have done duty in a Morris dance. But this wasn't fancy dress. These were for the incoming runners on their teams to spot in the crowded pen. We Fruit'n'Nutters use a less sophisticated technique of keeping watch, moving quickly to the guard rail when we spot our team-mate and waving wildly. Sometimes incoming runners of less-established teams would forget who they were handing over to and would vainly shout a name without reply, only to discover that they'd got it wrong or that the team order had changed. This usually provokes a few smiles and the odd chuckle from within the pen. I kept my gaze fixed on the corner where approaching runners come into view. We all have our own distinctive way of running and we're often able to recognise someone from their gait long before we can see their face. It's like a signature. A runner turned the corner and I knew it was Jude.

We swapped my hoodie for the baton and I was off again. Same course as earlier, only darker. Much darker. The first ascent was steep and strenuous and my feet slipped awkwardly in my shoes as the trail climbed and twisted, the ground now softer in the moist night air. Although conditions were generally good – it hadn't rained – vision was much reduced, even with light from the head-torch. I felt less steady on the more technical (aka hazardous) parts of the course and stumbled a couple of times but managed to stay upright, picking my footfalls very carefully over and between the tree roots. Descending from the hills for the first time on this overnight leg, I found that the campsite had become a Marie Celeste of tents and awnings. Plates and mugs lay on tables where they had been left but there were few signs of life. The lights were on but no one was watching. People were either asleep, out on the course or down at the arena, showering or waiting to run. Back up in the woods at the halfway point the water station was bathed by floodlights. Even at this hour, here and at various outposts along the course, marshals were awake and keeping watch, some still with energy enough to offer words of support. At this time, after midnight in the dark woods, I found that reassuring.

Coming out onto the ridge at night is uplifting, especially in moonlight. The best time is just as dawn is breaking. I ran the pre-dawn leg once, reaching the ridge in time to see the very beginning of a new day as the vaguest pink tear slowly opened across a seamless blue-black night. At such moments it can feel like a privilege simply to be alive. Even without communing with the cosmos on this particular run, I was very happy at this point to be out on the ridge. And happier still at exactly the same spot an hour later, this time knowing that the night-time double leg would soon be over.

Back at the arena, with my handover to the next runner Nicola completed, I gulped down some water from the tanker, headed back to the camp and made sure our following runner, Helen, was awake. I picked up a bag that I'd prepared in advance in an unusual display of forethought, and returned to the shower block. The showers at Thunder Run are small, portable cabins which offer piping hot water, a small seat, a shelf and a hook. They can get a bit grungy underfoot as runners remove an accumulation of mud and grass but generally I've found them to be serviceable and far from unpleasant. True, I once had a sense of humour failure when, after my overnight run, I'd gone for a shower to discover that the water had run out and that it would be a while before they reconnected the supply, an unwelcome scenario at four in the morning. This time there was no such problem, apart from a losing battle spent trying to towel myself dry in a steamy shower cabin with all the humidity of Hong Kong in April.

What's to be found when you're freshly scrubbed and famished in a Staffordshire field and it's almost 4am? Happily, the answer was coffee and a jacket potato with a chilli topping. The normal diurnal rhythms and routines – eat by day, sleep by night – were completely abandoned by this stage. I knew I would pay for it later once the fatigue kicked in but at that moment I felt refuelled and refreshed, and I revelled in the experience of being up and about while streaks of a new day's light began to broaden overhead and colour returned to the sky. Back at Camp Bournville a couple of people were up, hoods up, blankets around their shoulders, steaming mugs of tea beside them. I chatted briefly but made myself return to my tent. Even just an hour or so of rest and sleep would help. At least it would be worth the attempt.

I managed a semi-slumber but all too quickly the customary sounds of morning on a campsite began to grow in number and very quickly in volume, too. Other Thunder Runners stirring, the unzipping of tents, a muffled metallic clank of pots and kettles on camping stoves, rustling packets, low-toned conversation and, from another club's pitch, a radio. I heard a peal of merriment: Rich, another Bournville Harrier, always ready to laugh. It was Rich who had brought our stricken team-mate Linda down from the woods. He'd been visibly affected by what had happened to her, so it was good to hear his good humour restored. That was it, the camp was up, my tent was full of daylight. Sleep was over. Six more hours of Thunder Run to go.

As the months passed I would speak about my plan to run in every country of the EU by the end of March 2019 to whoever was willing to listen. But on that mid-July 2018 morning, the challenge seemed almost incidental. We were here for Thunder Run and choosing it as the UK stage of the challenge felt almost arbitrary. The few people I'd told so far about the challenge had been enthusiastic and supportive. But at this point it must have sounded like a vague ambition rather than an inspiring project that was firmly under way. I certainly wasn't wandering around the camp with a collection tin for RSVP and Changing Faces. With hindsight, someone reading this may say, well, why didn't you? A fair question. All I can say is that so much of RUNNING: ME RUNNING EU was driven by instinct. Its momentum would gather over time and Bournville Harriers – and others – would later show themselves to be generous supporters of the two charities by sponsoring the challenge. Right now, in a field in the middle of England during the final hours of Thunder Run, it just didn't feel right to buttonhole people about it.

I ran my fourth and final leg at half past ten. By this stage any aches and blisters were harder to ignore. Quads and calves get sore and Achilles strained with the repeated running, twisting and turning on unforgiving surfaces. The risk of mis-steps and tripping grows as bodies ache and minds begin to tire. But I was OK. It was warm but the air was fresher than during my first run.

There's a kind of pleasure that comes with knowing that you're near the end of a race. Relief forms part of it, and with that comes an added confidence that you have enough will and strength left to see it through. That becomes important in endurance running – marathons and ultras, when mental strength plays a crucial role. Experience teaches you a whole curriculum of tricks and mind-games, things to tell yourself about how well you're doing, ways to frame the distance run already and the miles left to run, all calculated to tune you out from the present pain of exertion and minimise the remaining distance in your mind. I don't normally need to dip too far into the mental medicine chest for a fairly routine 10K race. Even so, the knowledge that you have to run three 10Ks (or four in this case) in 24 hours sometimes needs a dose of mental preparation. At Thunder Run, I normally have to steel myself for the initial climb into the woods, which really is quite steep and twisty and hazardous when conditions are wet. After that, I can take each subsequent challenge as it comes. Reaching the half-way point in any race tends to boost the spirits and dispels any remaining uncertainties about one's ability to complete the course. Certainly the 5K marker at Thunder Run is a welcome sight, and by the time I emerged from the trees and ran along the ridge from 7K to 8K for the fourth and final time, I was feeling more than happy. The hard part of Thunder Run was almost over and soon we could celebrate. Heading into the arena once again I spotted Simon at the front of the pen, snapped the yellow baton around his wrist and trudged off the course.

The familiar routine followed: water at the tanker, walk back to camp, collect the bag, return, shower (after a waiting in a queue), refuel (crepe and a coffee), and back to camp again. This time, though, there would be a quick turn-round before returning to the arena yet again, with the rest of the Fruit'n'Nutters team, so that we could be ready to meet Sharon a few hundred metres from the finish as she ran the team's final leg. It was time for what's become part of the ritual at the end of Thunder Run. Near the end of the course we waited alongside a straight, grassy stretch of the course as a succession of other runners passed, and peered ahead. I heard the shout: "There she is!" and saw Sharon approaching. We clambered up the final stony slope and waited. Sharon reached us and we all began to run together in a slightly strung out group, until the course widened as we entered the arena. We linked hands – all eight Fruit'n'Nutters running together, with Sharon in the middle.

And that's how we crossed the line in a ceremonial display of team unity. The transponder beeped as it detected Sharon's velcro'd ankle chip. The rest of us had all removed our own chips once we'd finished and had left them well away from the course perimeter so as not to confuse the timing mechanism. Thunder Run was over. At least the hard part. What then followed was the sense of jubilation. We handed in our timing chips and collected our medals. With this latest piece of running 'bling' around our necks we eased our way through the mass of Thunder Runners who by now were filling the arena for their own celebrations and waited our turn for team photos on the podium. There was now just one more part left of the end-of-Thunder-Run ritual, and one I'd most been looking forward to. It was time to get on the red bus. Drinks in hand we climbed the stairs and took our seats on the top deck, toasting another happy weekend of running and bonhomie for the Bournville Harriers Fruit'n'Nutters.

Back down amid the throng in the arena I saw two familiar faces. The first was Mark, who I'd kept waiting at the handover point in the middle of the night a few years earlier. All of that was now forgotten. This year, Mark had been a red-number runner, a soloist, completing a startling nine circuits – 90K, 56 miles – during the 24 hours of Thunder Run. The other was another Bournville Harrier soloist, Antony, who'd managed even more with 11 laps. Both were surprisingly chipper. As empty fuel tanks go, both were probably operating on fumes by this point although they didn't show it. Kudos to them both.

Back at the camp, tents and awnings were already being packed away, chairs and tables folded, surviving home-bakes shared out and bags of rubbish ferried to the refuse dumpsters. I've always felt a mild sadness at this point. Arduous and challenging though it is to be part of Thunder Run, I've always enjoyed that feeling of entering the camp on the Friday and feeling enveloped in a warm, happy, comforting (if not exactly comfortable) bubble for the next two days, enjoying the challenge, the atmosphere and simply being with friends from Bournville Harriers and, beyond our immediate camp, appreciating the presence of other clubs from the wider running community, all together for a weekend, insulated from domestic duties and the world's concerns. I was sorry that for Linda, Thunder Run had ended so abruptly and painfully. But this year there had been 42 people from BvH at Thunder Run – five teams of eight and the two soloists, nearly a quarter of the club's current membership. It's on occasions like these that my sense of being part of a strong, welcoming community is at its strongest.

Thunder Run is a kind of pop-up spa resort for the spirit and senses. Physically it's also an intense and challenging boot-camp and by the end I was exhausted. As always, the final sting in the tail was a hazardous drive home as my eyes flickered more than once with deep fatigue on the A38 back to Birmingham. I didn't have the strength to think any more about Running: Me Running EU but I would be back to it soon enough. Stage 3 had been an intense, bustling festival of running concentrated into 48 hours. Stage 4 would be very different.

STAGE 4

Valtiberina, Italy With Karen and Tony on the Tuscan Hills 8-day 5K Challenge: "The temperature is typically in the upper 20s and can even be over 30 degrees by 8.30am. Shade is a blessing and we greet the wooded stretches with something approaching joy."

PART 2 | THE ACTUAL RUNNING PART

STAGE 4

Italy: Upacchi Tibers and Tuscan Hills

8-DAY 5K CHALLENGE: 10–18 AUGUST – 225 DAYS TO GO

The next stage of the challenge came hard on the heels (I like to avoid clichés but for runners that one was a shoo-in…) of the last one. And later, the schedule would become ever more hectic the closer the calendar took me towards my ultimate deadline. Yet these early stages of Running: Me Running EU were generally intermittent, sometimes with gaps of several weeks between them, partly because I'd planned several of these stages around existing trips and partly because I didn't yet feel the pressure of the deadline. Mainly it was because I was working full time. I knew that there would come a time when I'd need to be more systematic, when I'd have to treat the challenge like a grown-up work project in order to get it done, but in the middle of summer 2018 I hadn't yet reached that point.

For doomsday scenario planners who are always mindful of what can go wrong and can name every pitfall in the most watertight plan, that may sound complacent to the point of neglect and I recognise that procrastination is a personal trait. And yet, I've led a life of stumbling upon solutions and I've rarely been in a hole deep enough that I couldn't see daylight. In short, things will work out. 11pm on 29 March 2019 was the other side of Christmas. True, I couldn't yet chart my path from here to there but I wasn't worried. I only knew one thing: I would complete Running: Me Running EU. Of that I had no doubt.

In that spirit of vague but buoyant optimism, I headed off with Liz on holiday to stay with friends Karen and Tony in a quiet fold of the Tuscan hills in the Valtiberina, the Tiber valley, where Tuscany meets Umbria, to the fields of wild flowers, the scented profusion of herbs – rosemary, bay, basil, sage and mint – or 'wild mojito' as we would name it when the burning mid-afternoon heat began to ease and the lengthening shadows called for cocktails. We'd been summer guests for several years and Tony, Karen and I had taken to running a 5K course every morning, setting out by 8am before the heat turned it into a trial by ordeal. We'd drive from the house perched on the valley side along the bumpy, hilly, pitted track (powerful low gears are essential) out onto a crudely tarmacked road that connects a sparse string of farms and houses to the outside world and the remote hamlet of Upacchi at the top of the valley to the fine historic village of Anghiari, our nearest centre of civilisation, for which read a small supermarket, bars, restaurants, a visiting market, summer music performances in the small town square and occasionally time-trialled cycle sprints that climb an impossibly steep incline from the Tiber plain below, offering a bizarre spectacle of sweat and endurance on the part of the competing *ciclisti* that's entertaining enough to draw crowds of locals and visitors alike away – if only briefly – from their evening Campari, Cinghiali (wild boar) and Chianti.

Typically we'd descend the valley a little, park by bushes and start running downhill, each at his or her own pace, coping with the flies and heat, registering the change of grip underfoot as the rough, pitted tarmac gave way to an uneven surface of stones and dust which catches the throat and nostrils when the rare passing car or moped leaves chalky clouds in its wake. Occasionally the land levels out but the overall direction of travel is persistently downwards until after a series of curves the road passes a small stand of trees where we make a U-turn and begin the return ascent – a classic out-and-back. Although we set out early, it's still very hot – the temperature is typically in the upper 20s and can even be over 30 degrees by 8.30am. This makes the climb back up even more of a challenge. By now the heat is already intense enough for us to welcome even the momentary respite of a tree shadow.

Shade is a blessing and we greet the wooded stretches with something approaching joy. After willing our car to re-appear where we'd left it we negotiate a curve and finally there it is, a final 50 metres ahead that seem to take an age to run. Gasping for water, dripping with sweat, we find our bottles and drink deeply, fending off the flies by now well-focused on the panting trio of mammals whose slick, exposed limbs are just there to be bitten. We compare times, reflect on today's conditions, hotter than the previous day, make allowances, congratulate each other on another hard effort and quietly determine to shave a few more seconds off the next day. Tomorrow comes and we do it all over again. And again. And again. And that's why I decided before our holiday that the Italian stage of RUNNING: ME RUNNING EU would be what I named as the Tuscan Hills 8-Day 5K Challenge.

The previous year I'd finally put a long-held idea into action and spent a few hours on Google selecting images of wild boar, cypress trees and Mediterranean hills combined with a suitably Latin-style typeface and put it all together on PowerPoint to design the 'official' running vests of the 'Upacchi Tibers Pop-Up Running & Cycling Club'. Happy with the design, I had them made to order at Printigo, my local go-to bespoke running garment printer near home in Birmingham, presented them to Karen and Tony when we arrived in Italy and kept one for myself.

And this year, for Stage 4 of RUNNING: ME RUNNING EU, the Upacchi Tibers were back. Over the eight days of 5K runs and gruelling heat, choking dust and demanding inclines I recorded times between 26:51 and 26:21 minutes, shaving off a few seconds here and there but never coming close to a break-through performance in those conditions. Not that it mattered. The silly selfies we took at the end of each run were a fun way of punctuating each day's effort. Of course there was much more to the holiday. Karen and Tony are the world's best hosts, the summer weeks we've spent with them have been among the most enjoyable of any holiday, and I simply find Italy the easiest of countries to spend time in. But for the purposes of this story of RUNNING: ME RUNNING EU, Stage 4 was completed on the eighth day of the 5K challenge. And within hours we were packed and heading back home.

STAGE 5

Gent Running Team
September 13, 2018

Internationaal bezoek! Steve Doswell uit Birmingham heeft gisteren gekozen om met T4 van Gent Running Team de Belgische tak van zijn 'RUNNING: ME RUNNING EU' project te voltooien! Steve wil voor eind maart 2019 in alle 28 landen van de Europese unie gelopen hebben! Keep up informed of your progress Steve!

Ghent, Belgium "And what then happened led to possibly my favourite picture from the entire 28-country challenge. Around 20 GRT runners gathered round, placed me in the middle and shone their torches towards me. It was a warm, happy moment, a collective embrace for a fellow runner and someone trying to demonstrate that at least some Brits still felt part of the wider European family."

PART 2 | THE ACTUAL RUNNING PART

STAGE 5

Belgium: Gent Running Team and the torchlight embrace

8-DAY 5K CHALLENGE: 10–18 AUGUST – 225 DAYS TO GO

I'd never been to Ghent (Gent in Dutch). I knew of it only from its football club, one of the best in Belgium and which features frequently in European competition, and because of an epic poem distantly remembered from a childhood anthology, Robert Browning's "How They Brought The Good News From Ghent to Aix". My own good news from Ghent was that, a few days before my trip there, an introductory email I'd recently sent to local running club the Gent Running Team had been answered promptly, if a little tersely: "Yes, run with us next Wednesday. 7.30pm from the yacht club. Don't be late." This was to be another stage of RUNNING: ME RUNNING EU where the location was influenced by a work trip. I'd been running (a doubly appropriate word for it in this story…) workshops for euRobotics, a European membership association for the European robotics sector, for a few years. This year, the robotics department at Ghent University had offered to host the annual workshop for national event coordinators for European Robotics Week.

I have no professional background in robotics but I do know something about getting people talking, sharing ideas, making decisions and solving problems together – sometimes called collaboration skills. And that's why euRobotics had been using my services regularly as a workshop 'moderator' in recent years. The workshops are an environment where people from across Europe come together, pooling their ideas and experiences about organising events, about robotics education and about capturing local media and public interest. I'd got to know a few of the regular attendees, Lia from Madrid, Artur from Barcelona, Ana from Bucharest, Krzysztof from Poznań, and somehow over time I'd also became one of the familiar faces representing the annual pan-European meeting place for this cross-section of robotics professionals. I took Eurostar to Brussels and changed for the half-hour onward journey to Gent St-Pieters, arriving shortly after 5pm. The workshop would be the next day. Meanwhile, my plan for the evening was simple: find my guest house accommodation, change into running gear and head to the edge of the city to hook up with Gent Running Team and run Stage 5 of RUNNING: ME RUNNING EU. I'd worry about where to eat later.

It took time to find the guest house. I'd opted to walk. Travelling on a shoe-string means that taxis are an absolute last resort and, while a great fan of public transport, I didn't want to lose time trying to figure out which bus route would get me to the right part of town, from which bus stop and when, how to pay, etc. As time-saving goes, it proved to be a false economy (note to self: learn the lesson). Eventually, hot and slightly concerned about missing my rendezvous with Gent Running Team ("...7.30pm. Don't be late..."), I rang the guest-house bell and was shown to my room. Within ten minutes, after a rapid costume change, I was back on the street, Google Maps open, and orienteering my way towards the city perimeter and my encounter with the local club. As the time ticked away to 7.30pm I increased my speed from a jog to a saunter and then to a pace more typical of a Monday night club run, hoping I wouldn't have to resort to a final sprint. Finally, with water and yacht masts in view, I crossed a road to join a large mass of runners.

I heard a hubbub of Flemish conversations. As I approached, the runners began to split into groups and a few started running. Although confident enough to join the Gent Running Team for one evening as a stranger and a foreigner, I didn't want to become an unknown and possibly slightly suspicious figure just tagging along without invitation or introduction, so I spoke to the nearest runner. Hearing my English, she directed me to one of the organisers. I introduced myself and was invited to join a moderate paced group who would be running about 9K. We formed a circle on the car park tarmac and a warm-up session began, using what to me seemed unfamiliar but no doubt effective stretching exercises. To be honest, I'd never been as disciplined as I should about warming up, so these techniques would do as well as any. There were a few interested and vaguely friendly glances in my direction as I took part. And then we were off, running into the wooded park along the waterway in what was once part of Ghent's inland port. The light was fading by this point and I was conscious of being virtually the only runner in the group without a head-torch. I mentally cursed: as a regular Thunder Runner, I should have thought of that.

Staying mid-pack I got talking to a couple of runners, a very athletic-looking woman who introduced herself as Els and a younger guy whose name I didn't catch. Els was a coach, keen tri-athlete and qualified sports masseuse. I mentioned the lack of a head-torch. Else simply smiled and said that within the pack there would be light enough for everyone. We all quickly fell into an easy conversation about aspects of running just as I would expect to do with fellow Bournville Harriers on a Monday club run. I realised that this was further evidence to support my hunch that, British, Belgian or whatever, our mutual love of running unites us and that, regardless of other national differences, we were all Europeans in wickable running gear together.

Every couple of minutes as the pack advanced through the woods and out into the open, someone would shout a warning – "'Fietsers!" or "Lopers!" – as bikes or other runners appeared out of the gloom and came towards us. I tentatively asked Els if she thought the group would mind being part of a photo at the end. "Not at all!" she said and took charge as we finally returned to the yacht club car park. Els quickly explained that 'Steve' was 'Engels', an Englishman running in every country of the EU for charity, who wanted a picture to prove that he'd been running in Belgium with the Gent Running Team.

And what then happened led to possibly my favourite picture from the entire 28-country challenge. Around 20 GRT runners gathered round, placed me in the middle and shone their torches towards me. Someone took my phone and took some pictures. It was a warm, happy moment, a collective embrace for a fellow runner and someone trying to demonstrate that at least some Brits still felt part of the wider European family. I found my way back to the guest house, showered, changed and ate a good meal at an almost-deserted restaurant across the road. Stage 5 had been a very happy experience.

STAGE 6

Hamburg, Germany I joined the Hamburger Laufladen regular Tuesday evening session. Some wore the distinctive Hamburger Laufladen-branded running top and during the evening I'd been admiring its simple blue retro design. After the session we all took a drink back at the store, where Jens Gauger handed me a Hamburger Laufladen top in my size: "A souvenir of your evening with the Hamburger Laufladen Tuesday group – and a gift."

PART 2 | THE ACTUAL RUNNING PART

STAGE 6

Germany: Running in another language

TUESDAY 16 OCTOBER – 166 DAYS TO GO

I'd never been to Hamburg. That wasn't strictly true. I'd once changed trains at the Hauptbahnhof, the large central station at the heart of the city. That had been another kind of adventure altogether: the escape from Copenhagen after an Icelandic volcano had spewed lava ash into the atmosphere in such a vast quantity that it had closed northern European airspace for several days, stranding hundreds of thousands of travellers including me, forcing us to make long unforeseen journeys back home by other means – no planes but trains and automobiles. I'll come back to that later.

A few months after that fateful referendum an existing client made me an offer of employment that I chose not to refuse. Having worked for myself for nearly 25 years, I valued my independence and hadn't rushed back into salaried life when the opportunity had arisen. But I'd got to know this particular client – a one-time start-up business in the energy sector that had grown rapidly – and I enjoyed working with them. The chance of a secure income was also attractive after a period when work opportunities had become intermittent. So when asked at the tail-end of 2016 if I knew anyone in my network who might be interested in a senior communication role I said "Actually, I do. Me…"

I joined the company a few weeks into the new year, my start date delayed when my father fell ill and I spent time looking after him. He recovered at first but sadly this was to prove temporary. Within weeks he was admitted to hospital. It was gut-wrenching to see him so frail and diminished and for me it delivered a searing, indelible lesson about life's decline. I remembered the tall, strong man of my childhood, a firm but kind father with a ready laugh and a natural intelligence. I was greatly saddened by the way his loneliness following the loss of my mother through ill-health several years earlier and his own declining health had severely reduced his horizons as time passed. We'd once been close, less so in later years. I knew that the clock was ticking and yet I'd imagined after his recovery earlier in the year that he would rally again, but not this time. He died in April.

My new employers were fantastic. I'd barely been with them any time at all and yet they allowed me the time off to do what was necessary without a quibble. Returning to work after this sad episode, I got to grips with the job as best I could. The company had been founded ten years earlier. After getting the fledgling business on its feet, the owner-founders built up a management team and largely left the running of the company to them. As the year progressed, though, they began to get actively involved again. The company exited the shared premises it had been using as its HQ and decanted virtually all UK employees (around a thousand people) into one building. Part of the 'sell' to the people who were relocating was that the new site would have adequate car parking for everyone.

Without fully believing that the company would go for it, I'd proposed that, as part of the banked landscaping around the new car park perimeter, a running track should be created along the top as a new employee amenity. I had visions of popular lunchtime running sessions. To my surprise and pleasure, the 'trim trail' was approved. It was (for me) one of those rare moments when work and running 'careers' came together. We would later inaugurate the trail with a coached warm-up session thanks to officials from Coventry Godiva Harriers running club, based at the University of Warwick's campus nearby. So most employees were now located together in one building. That left a few in central London, an office in Poland and a couple of dozen staff in airy surroundings in a leafy Hamburg suburb. My job made a Hamburg visit likely and, once I'd come up with RUNNING: ME RUNNING EU, Hamburg became my target destination for the German leg of the challenge.

By this point quite a few Bournville Harriers knew of the challenge. They also knew that I wanted to make contact with fellow runners around Europe and run with groups on their own scheduled club runs. When I mentioned Hamburg, one of the founders of Bournville Harriers, Martin, passed me a name, Jens Gauger of Hamburger Laufladen (Hamburg Running Store). "Get in touch with Jens," said Martin. "He's a mate of mine." So I did. The work trip was arranged and I headed to Hamburg. The company had arranged for the work group I'd travelled with to stay at an opulent hotel. Trouble was, it was in a fairly inaccessible place, far from the nearest metro station and seemingly only reachable by taxi.

I wanted to be both within easy reach of the running group and walking distance from the company's office where we were to work the following morning. On both counts for practical purposes it made little sense (to me at least) to be so far away.

Although the company's chosen hotel offered plumped-up luxury and 24-hour service should that be needed, I declined the comfort and booked in to a simple two-star hotel which better suited my objectives that night and which I paid for myself. On an unexpectedly mild October evening the day before the office visit I trotted out from my very modest low-budget accommodation and let Google Maps navigate me to the Hamburger Laufladen. It was after hours and the store was closed for sales but the lights were on, the interior busy with movement as a dozen or more of the Laufladen's regular Tuesday running group gathered for the evening's session. I found Jens and made what quickly became a tactically questionable decision by introducing myself to the group in German. Jens immediately invited me to tell the others why I was there (he already knew) and I cranked out my scantly rehearsed patter about RUNNING: ME RUNNING EU, about running in all 28 countries of the EU by the significant deadline and about the two charities. It wasn't the best speech ever given in German by an Englishman but they understood enough to get the idea behind RUNNING: ME RUNNING EU – and enough to know that if they approached me and spoke in their clearly superior English, we'd probably all have a much better conversation! Several directed friendly smiles towards me and I felt that I'd made the right decision by joining Jens's group that evening. And with that we headed out. I wasn't sure where or how far we were going but it didn't matter. Stage 6 was under way and I was in good company.

Jens began to talk to me in German. My own use of the language must have been convincing enough to make him think that I could sustain a conversation. To be truthful, I understood maybe 60% of what he said – and I was reminded of my life as a young language assistant in Nantes when I'd resigned myself to never having the subtlety of tone or phrase in French to express exactly what I wanted to say, still less of understanding every nuance. That year, my command of French improved enormously over time. Here in Hamburg, on this one single evening, my limitations in German hardly mattered. This was all about the challenge and it was going well. We ran for about 8K around the boundaries of parks, along roads and avenues until we entered a small athletics stadium. We stopped. Jens explained (and I understood the gist of what he said) that we would practise pacing around the track in a series of short 100m or 200m bursts, some at a tempo (mid-speed) pace and some at an all-out sprint. Most of the Laufladen runners left me trailing, Jens included, and I was impressed by his pace.

After about 20 minutes we then reformed in a line along the track edge for a series of calf and hamstring stretching exercises that left me gasping (and wincing). Holding an excruciating pose for half a minute at a time, Jens had us each counting up or down in order, in German. The exertion was so great that I had difficulty concentrating and remembering the right numbers (counting down, what the hell comes after *siebenundzwanzig* when you're knackered and panting for breath?!), which didn't earn me many Laufladen admirers when all everyone else wanted to do was to count down as quickly as possible so we could STOP! Happily the tables were turned when Jens switched to English and now it was everyone else's turn to stumble over the numbers. At last it was over, we took a breather and then trotted back to the store.

Several of the regular runners wore the same distinctive Hamburger Laufladen-branded running top and during the evening I'd been admiring its simple blue retro design. As the session ended and we all took a drink back at the store, Jens disappeared briefly, to return holding a Hamburger Laufladen top in my size: "A souvenir of your evening with the Hamburger Laufladen Tuesday group – and a gift." I was delighted – and I've been proud to wear it on a handful of occasions during club runs back home with Bournville Harriers. More than happy with the evening, I trotted back to the hotel. By the time I returned, in need of a shower, it was after 9pm. I forewent dinner. The hotel offered no catering beyond breakfast and there was nowhere open nearby. But one missed meal was no price at all for what had turned out to be another fantastic evening on the RUNNING: ME RUNNING EU adventure. The next morning I headed to the office, grateful that the work trip had given me a chance to piggyback a stage of the challenge onto it.

PART 2 | THE ACTUAL RUNNING PART

STAGE 7

Portugal: to the Tagus

SATURDAY 20 OCTOBER – 170 DAYS TO GO

Six stages complete, 22 left. Five months remaining. I was aware of the deadline I'd set myself to complete the challenge. It wasn't yet looming and as a not-yet-recovering career procrastinator, I happily refused to visualise the cliff-edge of time. It was around this time that one of my closest running friends and fellow Bournville Harrier Stacey asked me a question which I knew someone would eventually ask and which I'd managed to avoid up to that point: "Do you have an actual plan so you know when and where you're going to be running in each country?" I thought quickly about the various ways to express "No". Stacey had been a resourceful, organised and very effective chair of our club. She gets things done. I'd first told Stacey about my idea for a running challenge and my reasons for wanting to embark on it before it even had a name. She'd been hugely encouraging from the very start. I didn't want her to doubt either my sincerity in wanting to complete the challenge or my ability to see it through. There was a pause as her question hung in the air. Eventually I answered. "Not – as such…" (Whatever she was thinking at that point, her face gave nothing away) "…but I know I'll get it done." I said that with complete conviction and it was true, because I'd always *known*. I just didn't know *how* yet. I didn't have the path mapped out but I knew how I wanted to feel at the end. For now, for me, that was enough.

The next stage came quickly. That same week, I was off to Lisbon. It was another work trip. I'd agreed to be an awards competition judge on behalf of a professional institute I'd been a member of for almost 30 years. It was a voluntary role (so unpaid but the travel and accommodation were covered) but I'd always found these judging gigs to be hugely rewarding – the appreciation given and the friendships formed, the company of fellow communication pros from across Europe, the chance to see how organisations in other countries communicate about the organisational issues of the day and, always, the pleasure of discovering a foreign city. In this case we were being hosted by our Portuguese colleagues in Lisbon once again. The hotel was modern and stylish, but for me, there would be little time to spend admiring it.

These judging sessions typically take place over three days – Friday to Sunday – and are pretty intensive, with a huge number of entries to look at and little time to dwell on each one. Impressions have to be gathered and conclusions drawn quickly, arguments made as to why this magazine is worthy of an award or why that electronic newsletter is strong on style, less so on substance, why these colours and this relaxed imagery may work for a Danish audience but could be considered unprofessional in parts of southern Europe. We often keep going well into the evening before breaking off at 7-8pm, eyes blurred, weary, and brain in shut-down.

On this trip, I'd also given myself the added challenge of completing a report for the energy company I worked for by midnight on the day I flew into Lisbon (communicators just love a deadline…). So I forewent the organised welcome meal for the 'pan-European jury' and spent those first hours of my time in the famous 'white city', so called for its architecture, cocooned in my hotel room. I completed the report and sent it off, happy to have got that part of the weekend's work done. I was hungry but too tired to venture out. There was just time for a quick solo meal before the hotel kitchen closed. Fatigue weighed on me suddenly like a heavy blanket. I barely noticed what I was eating. I had enough charge left in my brain to make a mental note that I'd kept putting off writing that report. My predicament was entirely self-inflicted. The procrastination had to stop. I'd need to find a cure tomorrow or maybe the day after… (a joke at my own expense).

That night my mind would not rest and I slept fitfully. Somehow in this ridiculously tight schedule I would also need to find time to run Stage 7 of RUNNING: ME RUNNING EU. Of all the stages where I'd combined the running challenge with a pre-planned trip for work or holidays, Lisbon was the one where it felt as if I was trying to shoe-horn a size 10.5 foot into a size 9 road shoe. After skipping the hosted dinner on the first evening I didn't want to miss out again. Nor did I wish to seem unsociable towards our hosts. After a full day of judging with an early start, they'd arranged for us to visit a local restaurant as a group and, since much of the pleasure of these trips came from the chance to eat, drink, talk and be merry with some fellow Europeans, I wasn't going to miss out. Judging finished at about 6pm that evening and we were due to meet in the hotel lobby at 7.30pm. There was just time to get back to my room, change into running gear, head out for a short run, return, cool down a bit, shower and change. The dinner wasn't going to be formal but as all runners know, you can't just run and then jump straight into a shower. Time was going to be tight.

I headed out of the hotel and straight down into a pedestrianised quarter of restaurants and theatres just as it began to throng with Lisbon's evening crowd, locals and tourists alike. The run became a slalom as I veered left and right to avoid the knots of people criss-crossing my path ahead. There were no other runners and it was apparent that this wasn't an area where runners routinely came. I felt out of place and at first my prospects for the run were unpromising. It felt like an exercise in simply getting it done. But soon I left the lights of the restaurant district and entered a huge, more sparsely lit and monumental square close to the waterfront. Lisbon stands on the wide waters of the Tagus and I turned right to follow the water side, past the small Cascais do Sodre terminus station and continued for several hundred metres. Here in the semi-gloom I could make out the dark figures of a few other runners – not many, but enough to reduce my sense of being a complete oddity in this part of the city. And there, across the water on the south side of the city, distant and illuminated in sharp contrast to its surroundings above the night-dark cliff on the south shore, stood Cristo Rei, the statue of Christ, a reduced-scale reimagining of Rio de Janeiro's emblematic Christ the Redeemer.

I remembered the words, "I am the light of the world…," an appropriate line of scripture for this distant but impressive vision across the water. There was no time to linger, though. I had to get back. I retraced my route, this time skirting around the busy theatre district by following a wide boulevard before cutting through a couple of side streets to return to the hotel. I must have presented a sweaty and dishevelled spectacle to members of our group who were already gathering in the lobby. In haste I returned to my room, quickly showered (no time to cool down first), changed and within minutes was back in the lobby, not as composed as I wanted and still sweating but at least I was on time. I explained the reasons for my run, as much to account for the fact that, frankly, I must clearly have looked a bit of a mess.

The Lisbon run was one of the less satisfying stages of the challenge, simply because of having to squeeze it in and rush it. I even thought briefly about maybe returning to Portugal just for RUNNING: ME RUNNING EU but discounted it as expensive in time and money. I may not have been being paid for this trip but the cost of travel and accommodation was covered. Plus I'd have to carve more time out of what was likely to be a busy period. I was still working for the energy company and I had the rest of the challenge to complete. Returning to Lisbon would be impractical. And I didn't need to. I'd set the rules for this challenge and I'd always been pragmatic about it. I wasn't wealthy, at that point I didn't have a lot of free time and I had to make the most of the resources available to me. I was in Portugal and I'd just run about 6K. It would have to do. Other stages would be more elaborate. Here in Lisbon the job was done.

PART 2 | THE ACTUAL RUNNING PART

STAGE 8

Slovenia: a late entry and a warm welcome

SUNDAY 28 OCTOBER – 159 DAYS TO GO

I returned home on Sunday evening. Back to work on Monday, leaving no time to ponder about anything apart from the next stage of RUNNING: ME RUNNING EU. By Thursday I was back in the air again, this time to Slovenia. No improvised solo running this time. Instead, a chance to take part in what has become my favourite running event in the capital, Ljubljana, one of my favourite cities, in a country for which an early fascination has developed into something close to a passion. I'd booked the flight some time in advance, and my friend Stanka had very generously offered me the use of her neat, tiny flat in the very heart of Ljubljana for the weekend. Barely five minutes from the start line, it could hardly have been better placed. So for once everything had been planned well in advance. For the Slovenian stage it was always going to be the Volkswagen Ljubljanski Maraton, or at least the half marathon. The city really puts on a show for what is effectively a weekend running showcase. It's a big city event in a small central European city of 279,000 people, a size of population that ranks it between those of Southampton or Nottingham but with less bustle than either. It has a beautiful historic centre that sits on the Ljubljanica river, with parklands that begin in central Ljubljana and extend over wooded hills that roll out into the surrounding countryside, a joy for runners and hikers, especially when its abundance of trees is decked in autumn colour. The city centre itself is flat, many parts are pedestrianised and it's easy to get around on foot, by bike or bus.

Slovenia is a relatively new country, having only become an independent state in 1992 after the collapse of Yugoslavia. I'd always been interested in Yugoslavia, this communist country that wasn't behind the iron curtain, and whose citizens could travel freely. Liz and I had Serbian friends who lived in London and we'd sensed their turmoil as their country of origin began to fall apart. I'd known little about Slovenia itself, though, until

I first came to Ljubljana on a work trip in the early 2000s. Further meetings in Slovenia followed, Slovenian work colleagues became friends and I've been returning ever since.

A few years after that first visit, at the 'dangerous' age of 50 I'd chosen not to buy a motorbike or a sports car or do any of those other things that immediately conjure up a neon sign flashing the words 'midlife crisis'. Instead, I took a different direction, regressed to my studious, slightly nerdy younger self and went back to university to study European politics, while still working. For much of the two-year part-time Master's course at the University of Birmingham I studied Slovenia's success story, emerging very quickly from the wreckage of Yugoslavia to become a very successful member of the European Union. In 2010 I'd spent time carrying out interviews in Ljubljana for my dissertation, a marathon of research and writing at the end of my MA course.

So that year I now had work connections, friends and academic interests in Slovenia but still no thoughts yet about running in Ljubljana. That came four years later. By then I'd heard about the city's highly regarded marathon and half-marathon, the two races combined. There's also a 10K which takes place earlier on the morning of the main event and the day before there's a series of 'Lumpi-Runs' for children of different age groups. In fact during the final weekend in October each year, the heart of Ljubljana is virtually given over to a festival of running. In 2014 I ran the half marathon for the first time. The organisation was impressive and so was the way that the whole city seemed to come out to support the event and cheer people on. In 2016 I returned, this time with some fellow Bournville Harriers, and ran the full marathon. Now it was 2018 and I was back again, this time embarked on RUNNING: ME RUNNING EU.

Of all the organised races that I'd planned to run during the challenge, Ljubljana had been a fixture in my mind from the very beginning. I had the flight, I had the accommodation. Everything was in place. Almost everything... Having run six of seven stages so far either solo or in an informal club or group setting, I'd only once needed to go through the formalities of entering a race. By September I'd already set up the logistics for Ljubljana but with barely a month to go I realised with a lurch that I hadn't actually registered for the race itself! I checked the website and as feared, I'd missed the deadline. I did various searches. I emailed the organisers. No response. At this point many people reading this (assuming any people will ever read this...) may imagine that that neon sign really would be flashing 'crisis' and that panic would have set in. I have to say that, even though to panic would have been a natural response, I didn't.

A couple of thoughts here: well, three. Firstly, I tend to see the world through an optimist's rose-tinted mirror-shades. Sometimes it's an unwarranted optimism, a sense that things will turn out fine when all the evidence suggests that they won't. The second is my conviction that you can usually get what you want by working your way around a problem. Not always, but often enough to give me confidence that if a door is locked there's very possibly another way in if I look for it hard enough. I remember going to a local music festival, where I'd been given a wristband to wear over the weekend and, not knowing how these things work, I'd removed it, assuming that they'd give me another one for the second day. At the gate I was refused admission, even though I had the original wristband with me (with its plastic toggle broken). The rule was simple – remove the wristband and you won't get back in. I asked, and argued, and pleaded, politely but persistently, making my case to a succession of festival staff as I was handed up the line of command. I wasn't going to give in, they weren't going to let me in. Someone was going to have to give way.

I knew by then that I was in the wrong, and that they might simply end it abruptly by calling the door staff. I kept my tone respectful but persistent. Eventually they gave me a new wristband and let me in. I'd been lucky, but maybe I'd helped to make my own luck. The third thought that kept panic at bay was a sense that RUNNING: ME RUNNING EU was a kind of 'Zen' experience, a journey in which there would be highs and lows, obstacles and achievements, frustration and satisfaction, and that each of these features was simply part of the journey. Here was an obstacle. Entries for the Ljubljana Marathon were closed, yet I was confident that I could still reach my goal, and optimistic that a solution could be found. So I didn't panic. Instead, I tweeted Valerio, a friend in Ljubljana, who I will introduce shortly.

> "Hi Valerio – Can you help me? 1/4
>
> I missed the entry deadline for the Ljubljana Half Marathon. The contact page on the website doesn't accept messages. 2/4
>
> I'm desperate to run in Lju this year. I'm running in every EU country before Brexit for two charities. I call it RUNNING: ME RUNNING EU. 3/4

> Do you know anyone at Ljubljanski-Maraton HQ. If you do, can you ask? If not, don't worry. Had to ask… 4/4"

Later that day Valerio replied. It was an encouraging message…

> "Hi Steve! I will not be running myself this year but I can help, or at least try. […] The head of our running group is a very active fellow, who is very good at networking, so I think it's safe to say that you have more than decent chances to succeed. But you have to play it by ear until then…"

Since 2018, whenever anyone asks (ironically, of course…) "What did the Romans ever do for us?" I think back to this moment. Valerio was a Roman living in Ljubljana, married to a Slovenian woman, Saša, with an adorable child, possibly the only toddler at that time to be seen running around a square in Ljubljana wearing an AS Roma beanie hat, reflecting the football loyalties of his father (the child now has a sibling, no doubt with a similar AS Roma inheritance). I'd first met Valerio in London a few years earlier when a mutual contact had introduced us by email and asked me to help Valerio find his feet (an appropriate metaphor in this story) in my home city. With work interests and a love of football and Slovenia in common, we'd hit it off and stayed in touch after Valerio returned to Ljubljana.

And now here he was putting me in touch with someone who might just possibly rescue my plan for the Slovenian stage of the challenge. As I soon discovered, that someone was indeed 'a very active fellow' – Urban Praprotnik, Slovenia's famous running coach. Together, Urban and his wife Jasmina are a powerhouse of activity – authors, journalists, broadcasters, ultra-marathoners, organisers of running and hiking expeditions and also of Slovenia's largest recreational running club – Urbani Tekači (Urban Runners – a neat wordplay for a club based in Slovenia's capital city). Urban told me to meet him at the running fair on the day before the Ljubljana Marathon and together we would sort out my entry. The running fair took place at the city's small exhibition centre just beyond the city centre on the days leading up to the marathon.

The fair, simply called *Tečem* ("I run" in Slovene) serves two purposes. It's the event base where registered runners pick up their running numbers, branded bags, running tops and accompanying documentation (including a ticket for entry to the free 'pasta party', a good, honest serving of pasta and Bolognese to build runners' carbohydrate levels before the big race,

PART 2 | THE ACTUAL RUNNING PART

STAGE 8

Ljubljana, Slovenia
Interview with Jasmina Praprotnik. "I had the flight, I had the accommodation. Everything was in place. Almost everything… With barely a month to go I realised that I hadn't actually registered for the race itself!" Fortunately Slovenia's running guru Urban Praprotnik managed to get me signed up for the Ljubljana Half Marathon. And then he said "Let's meet my wife, Jasmina. She will interview you for our YouTube channel."

available in a large catering hall underneath the exhibition centre). It's also a place where running apparel brands sell their shoes, tops, shorts, socks, compression stockings, belts and whatever else runners need or want to wear. Ditto sports nutritionists with a variety of gels, cereal bars and supplements. Also merchandise from previous Ljubljana Marathons – there's always a choice of well-designed sports gear from holdalls to tops to buffs and headbands.

There are also presentations from a small stage about aspects of running – perhaps a book launch or tips about mental preparation. The year after this event (because Ljubljana is now a fixture in my personal running calendar) I saw Jasmina present her latest book, about an 80-year old marathon runner, from this same stage. And dotted around the fair are stands promoting other race events in the region, whether Trieste in Italy, Split in Croatia or Banja Luka in Bosnia. This is also a reminder that in Slovenia, you're never far from another country, with the Austrian, Italian and Croatian borders each less than 50 miles away from the exhibition centre where this running fair was taking place.

Urban was as good as his word. We met at the entrance to the fair. He led me into the number collection hall and within two minutes I was registered and holding my 2018 Ljubljana Marathon number and chip, bag, running top, event instructions, various leaflets and a ticket to the pasta party. I was good to go. Urban was interested in RUNNING: ME RUNNING EU. "Let's meet my wife. She will interview you for our YouTube channel." And that's how, a few minutes later, I met Jasmina for the first time and very much enjoyed recording my first interview of the RUNNING: ME RUNNING EU adventure. I was relieved. It was the Ljubljana Marathon (in my case the Half, although it's one overall event) and I was in.

That night back in Stanka's apartment I laid out my kit ready for the next morning. I was excited about the day to come but also relaxed, with everything finally in place and the start line barely five minutes from where I was settling down to sleep. But the next morning I wasn't going straight to Slovenska Cesta, the main road through the centre where the start gantry was set up and the race would start. Jasmina had mentioned a group warm-up session before the start and had invited me to join them. The rendezvous was a smart, glass-fronted fitness centre just around the corner from Stanka's flat. I made my way there to find 30-40 runners, male and female, young, middle-aged and older – just as for any race back home – pinning on running numbers, drinking final coffees or hydrating with sports drinks, adjusting caps, visors, sweat-bands, some laughing and joking, others talking earnestly, some alone, browsing messages or just quietly enveloped in their thoughts, perhaps some with pre-race nerves and others clearing their minds to prepare for what is as much a mental test as it is of physical endurance. That's certainly true of marathon running and, to a lesser extent, it's also true for half marathons, too.

From what I could gather, Urban and Jasmina's group were about 50-50 for the full and half marathon. Urban called the group together and began to speak in Slovene. I've been learning the language but I understood little – it takes time to tune in to the pace of spoken language, certainly more time than I'd spent in Ljubljana that week. Then I heard my name mentioned and 'Velika Britanija' (Great Britain) and realised that Urban was introducing me and the running challenge. I understood a reference to the 28 countries of the EU and heard 'Brexit'. Spontaneously the assembled Urban Runners began clapping. Clearly they approved of the idea of RUNNING: ME RUNNING EU (I assumed they weren't clapping for Brexit! I hadn't met anyone outside the UK who was in favour of it – and I wouldn't in the future, either). For me, it was a moment of pride and further affirmation that there was something 'right' about having embarked on this challenge.

With a signal from Urban, the group moved towards the exit. As soon as we were outside we began to run in a long tail behind Urban down to the Prešeren statue, Slovenia's most famous poet looking on as we headed up the right bank of the Ljubljanica river and around to the first of several pedestrian squares in this part of town. Here, Urban led us in a series of warm-up exercises before we continued at a jogging pace to the next square. There we jumped en masse for a photo, formed a large circle, turned and massaged each other's shoulders, then held hands, broke the ring and ran in a line across the square for another photo opportunity that ended in laughter. With a few final words of encouragement from Urban, we then wished each other luck and ran to Slovenska Cesta to find our respective starting pens based on expected finish times. I'd opted for the 1:50 – 2:00 hour pen. These days I expect to complete a flat half-marathon in about 1:50 and for RUNNING: ME RUNNING EU it was all about the participation and certainly not about pushing for a target time.

The Ljubljana Marathon always has a fantastic sound system at the start and it would be hard not to feel pumped up by the time the start signal was given. You certainly don't need to speak Slovene to find the start line. The word START in huge letters on a rigid banner above the road is all the Slovene you need! Around the corner on Congress Square, all the paraphernalia for the finish line is capped with an equally huge banner marked CILJ (Finish), which also has the meaning of target or goal. It seems an appropriate word to mark the end of what for so many runners is a significant achievement. After running many races over the years including dozens of half marathons and (for me at that time) five marathons, it's easy to become blasé and think that it isn't that big a deal, that ultra-running (30 miles or more) is where the new challenge lies. But for so many people in the start pens at Ljubljana on that morning in October 2018, this *was* a big deal. It may have been their first half marathon or their first full 42K event. They may have been running for a target time, for charity, in memory of a lost loved one or as a test of recovery from a major illness, maybe as a benchmark in a programme of weight loss, or as part of a journey of personal discovery. It may have been their first race in a foreign country – and Ljubljana certainly attracts runners from all of Slovenia's immediate surrounding countries as well as a fair few Brits and a smattering of Germans. And for all the reasons behind RUNNING: ME RUNNING EU and because this is my favourite event, in a city I've grown to love, and perhaps also because this year I almost didn't get to enter at all, it was a big deal for me.

And so the race began. As always, the city had turned out to watch and to cheer, to wave banners with the names of runners, and to shout "Don't give up!" and "You can do it!", and later "Še mal!" (just a bit further – even when there was a lot further to go!). There were bands and drummers, every 5K there were refreshment stations, each one a more welcome sight than the last, offering water, sports drinks, chocolate squares and orange segments. Heading north along one of the main exit roads from the city centre, we eventually turned left and followed a railway track where passing trains hooted their encouragement. By now we were in the leafy outer suburbs. And still the crowds lined the streets. We passed through the pocket of countryside beyond the Tivoli Park. Support was sparser here but no less warm and appreciative from those who did stand vigil to clap and offer encouraging words. By this point I was glad that the atmosphere was calmer.

During marathons, as the miles pass and I hunker down, still aware of my surroundings but also increasingly embedded in an inner space, I prefer it when the crowd recedes and the running takes on a meditative quality. It's in this state that I often experience what I've described, only slightly tongue-in-cheek, as 'seven seconds of nirvana', a few fleeting moments in which there's an intense sense of wellbeing, in which the running and the breathing and what's inside me and what's outside in the surroundings, all meld momentarily into one. It feels good. I know virtually nothing about Zen but it's what I imagine as a 'Zen moment'. Those who practise techniques of mindfulness may recognise this as 'being in the moment'. There, that's three sets of words in inverted commas, which just illustrates how hard it is to capture the feeling precisely in words. And as quickly as it's there, it's gone. Once again I'm suddenly sharply aware of my surroundings, of the exertion and if anything's hurting at this point – chafing, dodgy knees, a blister – this is when it announces itself. In a full marathon, this might occur at around 18 miles. Around three hours on my feet already with nearly half as much to go again, too far out to sense the finish line, fatigue and energy depletion finding easy prey in tired limbs and aching shoulders.

This is the point where experience and practice conjure up the mental tricks we play on ourselves to keep going. I focus on the distance already travelled, not on the miles still to run. I praise myself for having made it this far. I tell myself I'm the guy who... (at this point I bring to mind a past challenge or difficulty that I managed to overcome). I read the running shirts of the people around me and play images of the places they're from in my mind. I'll make use of anything I can find in my mind or my surroundings to distract myself from the thought that "this hurts!" I also draw comfort from the fact that I'm (invariably) wearing a running cap, wraparound shades and a Bournville Harriers buff around my wrist. This is curious. The reality is that I'm exposed in a simple running vest and shorts but in my mind I'm cocooned in running armour and it helps.

After 20 miles there's a change. It isn't easier, but knowing that I'm now in the 20s gives me a boost because the end will also come in the 20s. Even so, each added mile that I run now takes an age to complete. Now I stop and walk at each refreshment point and mile marker, not far – maybe 30 steps – but enough to give me enough of a reward to keep going to the next one, because I'd promised myself a brief respite. I keep my promises to myself because they give me the courage to continue on to the next drinks stop or mile marker, and the next one, until I'm at mile 24 and now I can allow myself to entertain the thought of finishing. By the time of the final mile, I'm back in the city centre. The crowd is normally out in force again, there are frequent shouts again of "Še mal" (and this time there really is only a little bit left to run by this stage) and the doubt has gone. I know I'll finish. And then it's finally over.

I've said all this to give a sense of how it feels to run the full 26.2 miles of a marathon and because of having now run the full Ljubljana marathon three times, it seems right to record that here. But on that particular morning I was only running half the distance, the physical effort required was much less than what's needed for a full marathon, and I was out for a good time in one sense only, putting myself under no pressure for a finish time. I enjoyed the occasion, the crowd, the sights, the city. By the time I crossed the line back in Congress Square I'd nudged just under the two-hour mark at 1:59:06, one of my slowest half marathons in a few years, but I wasn't worried.

Just as I crossed the line I noticed a slight commotion and heard a sudden urgency in the race announcer's voice on the powerful PA system that boomed out across the square. At first I couldn't see the reason for this new note of excitement. It certainly wasn't for my decidedly modest performance. Instead, as I looked back to one side of the finish line I saw the real focus of interest. Lemma Sisay had just crossed the line to win the men's full marathon. He immediately took an Ethiopian flag being offered to him, draped it around his shoulders and stood exposed to a firing squad of photographers' lenses and reporters' mics. He seemed slightly unsteady on his feet. No surprises. He'd just run 26.2 miles in 2:04:58, barely five minutes longer than I'd taken to manage just half the distance. I'm not stupid enough to compare myself to elite east African runners (as if...!) but it was one of those moments of perspective: whatever the personal achievement, someone will do it faster or better. Happily, I wasn't in Ljubljana to race against Lemma Sisay – or anyone. I'd had my own goal and I'd reached it.

Stage 8 was complete. I'd run the Half at the Ljubljana Marathon and been fortunate enough to be given a way in long after entries had closed. Not exactly an advert for sound project management. But I can't say I regretted the path I'd taken to get there. Once again the pleasure had been in the journey as much as the destination. I could have entered before the deadline and been assured of a place with no need to contact Valerio. I wouldn't have met Urban or Jasmina – and I've since gone on to become friendly with them both – and not recorded the interview. I would have missed the thrill of almost not getting away with it. Where would the fun have been in that?

PART 2 | THE ACTUAL RUNNING PART

STAGE 9

The Netherlands: seven hills and a dead leg

18 NOVEMBER – 131 DAYS TO GO

It was November and the weather had turned. Scarves were coming out, buffs would now feature as a standard running kit item and gloves would be essential. I'd found a race in the Netherlands, the Zevenheuvelenloop, or the seven hills run, which at least by the sound of the name, promised to defy the popular image of the Netherlands as a flat country (not for nothing was it traditionally known as the Low Countries). The Zevenheuvelenloop takes place in the Dutch city of Nijmegen. Judging by the website, it was a well-established event and I anticipated high production values with a lot of infrastructure, perhaps not on the scale of Ljubljana, but prominent nonetheless. There was a dedicated Zevenheuvelenloop app. I'd been to the Netherlands a number of times before, as a student visiting friends in Zwolle and hitchhiking around the north of the country, as a travel courier accompanying coach parties of south Londoners to the famous bulb fields at Keukenhof, as an academic assessor in Utrecht and with Liz on a short holiday to Amsterdam. However, my last Dutch trip had been more than ten years earlier and I'd never been to Nijmegen. I researched the travel and accommodation options, found hotels to be pricy and decided to take the plunge for the first time with Airbnb. A neat, terraced house about 20 minutes from the station on foot looked promising. I could fly from Birmingham to Schiphol and then take the train direct to Nijmegen. I'd fly on Saturday and return after the race. It would be a flying visit, literally.

Come the day of travel and the direct train service from Schiphol had suddenly grown an extra stage with a replacement bus which took a little effort to find. Before long though I was on my way and after leaving the bus at Amsterdam Arena, found the Nijmegen train easily enough. Less than two hours later I was in Nijmegen, said to be the Netherlands' oldest city, barely six miles from the German border and home to 170,000 people. The city stands on the Waal river, one of the wide waterways that link the Rhine to the North Sea. My Airbnb was a spotless family house with short, steep staircases. The hosts were a genial couple, slightly older than me, who welcomed me on that bitterly cold day with a shot of something warming and alcoholic. The woman was an illustrator and there was a small rack of greeting cards by the guest rooms displaying some of her work. It seemed polite to buy a few before I left, and I did. The couple showed some interest in the running challenge and inevitably conversation turned to Brexit. I explained my own opinion but, as always, was careful not to seem too forthright. Whenever this topic was raised (and I was never one to dwell on it unless the other person wanted to delve more deeply) I always tried to remember that everyone has their reasons for their own opinion on any topic. Besides, here in Nijmegen, I was a guest in their house, albeit a paying guest, I'd just arrived and none of us needed a political debate.

At the top of the house, I rested for a while, then Googled the options for dinner. The house was in a residential area. I wanted to go back to the centre to get a feel for the city but it was bitterly cold outside and I didn't want to spend too long traipsing around the streets. An Italian place in the old city near the river seemed promising. I'd try it. Back out on the street, a cold, penetrating wind cut through what turned out to be inadequate layers of insulation. I walked quickly, trying to warm up, crossed the long arc of the road back over the railway and headed into the centre. I found the restaurant, a small, modern, bustling place where space was at a premium. Happily, I found a seat at the bar where they were happy to serve and chat to me, despite being busy and constantly on the go. I ate very well and after spending an enjoyable hour in its warm interior and downing a couple of healthy measures of Chianti, felt fortified and ready to brave the cold again.

Back outside, I was struck by how dark it seemed. The old city was crisscrossed by sometimes shadowy pedestrian lanes. Despite the light from shop fronts and restaurants it was quite gloomy in places. I decided to navigate my way around the alleys to reach the river – and walked straight into a stone bollard at thigh height. I'd completely failed to see it in the gloom. The impact hurt quite a bit. The first few steps after this collision were painful and I limped. I was still determined to see the river, though, and made my way round a couple more corners until I left the high, dark warehouses and narrow lanes and emerged into a wide, open area where a couple of bridges marked the course of the river. I crossed the road to reach the river bank. The Waal was wide and dark and I felt slightly daunted by the sheer mass and volume of the fast-flowing river. I limped back through the narrow lanes and out over the railway again to the suburb and eventually the house where I was staying. My thigh hurt quite a lot. Walking into the bollard, I'd clearly given myself a dead leg. I cursed myself for such a stupid, self-inflicted injury. Once inside the house I had difficulty raising my leg and took the steep staircases warily, hauling the dead leg up a step at a time on the top staircase, which was practically a ladder. It was an unpromising condition to be in and I got ready to sleep, a little preoccupied that I might not be in tip-top shape for the next day's run. But it couldn't be helped.

Next day came and after breakfast and an easy chat with my hosts, I walked back into town. The leg was sore but it was manageable. I was relieved. Unusually, the Zevenheuvelenloop takes place in the afternoon. I couldn't remember any other major race which started so late. In any case, it was helpful for me. I had time to visit the running fair and pick up my race chip and number without any stress. I joined the throng of runners. It was a sight familiar to anyone who's ever been in a town ahead of a big race: a continuous string of pairs and groups and individuals wearing beanies, bobbles and hoodies sporting the names and colours of a hundred and more running clubs, charities or sponsors, carrying sports bags of various dimensions, from small daypacks to hefty holdalls.

The running fair was a long, thin open-air event of small marquees and exhibition stands set up along a road between the station and the city's heart. A long white frieze bearing the names in A-Z order of everyone registered for the Zevenheuvelenloop was an obvious magnet of interest. Like everyone else I was drawn to run my eyes along the long lines of type in search of my own name. Sightlines to the long board were obscured by an almost unbroken wave of bodies and backs of heads as people literally looked out for themselves and then posed for selfies once they found their own name. I waited patiently and looked for a gap. Just then an old man who looked well into his seventies spoke to me in Dutch, gesturing towards the pop-up 'wall of honour' with a smile. Irreverent Dutch humour alert: switching to English, he gestured to the wall again and said, "All the competitors…? Or all the dead people from the Second World War…? Joke! Joke!" And just as suddenly he disappeared back into the crowd.

I collected my number and Zevenheuvelenloop running top which I very much liked the look of but which I wouldn't be wearing for the race – as a Bournville Harrier, it's a token of pride and feels almost like a moral obligation to turn out in the colours of the clan; in other words, a teal vest. I lingered a little longer to browse through the running fair and then headed off to get some lunch. I wasn't going back to the Airnbnb before the race.

In the event app, the organisers had mentioned special boxes that would be placed near the start line where last-minute kit could be left. This was attractive because it felt freezing at that point even in a full set of 'civilian' clothes. Recollections can be hazy but a subsequent historical temperature check while writing this confirms that Nijmegen did indeed have its collective collar turned up comfortably against a strong breeze and a mere five degrees of sunshine at midday on 18 November 2018. I knew I would have to peel down to running shorts and vest shortly before the start. My objective was to make 'shortly' as short as possible, hence the appeal of those storage boxes. I wandered out towards the start area to have a recce. By this stage the full infrastructure of this mid-sized city race event was in place and so the start was barricaded off, with security staff also posted to make sure that no one entered anywhere before they were supposed to. At this time of heightened awareness of terrorism wherever crowds gather and with the knowledge since the bombing of the 2013 Boston Marathon that road races were not immune to the threat, the safety provisions were reassuring. But it also meant that I didn't know where I was going to leave my stuff. I'd planned for it to be as compact as possible by wearing as little as I could bear given the chilly conditions. Cold as I was, I knew that I'd be colder still once I stripped down ready to run, but that I'd soon warm up again once we got started.

The start had been organised into pens in side streets, with each pen grouping people according to their predicted finish time, an arrangement that major race runners are very familiar with. What struck me about my particular pen was that, if they'd based it purely on age instead of time, they would have been spot on. It was Sexagenarian Central. It was a reflection of our society in the early 21st century when people of my age are frequently to be found dressed in 'performance' fabrics and out running or cycling in the elements rather than taking up more sedate pursuits that prior generations would presumably have found more typical for people approaching what used to be called 'retirement' age. I often feel blessed that I have the time, health and inclination to run, and in so doing, to keep the bath chair and slippers at bay for as long as possible. Right there, though, in that residential Nijmegen side street, I was not feeling 'blessed' but cold.

As the start time approached, I realised that I couldn't put off the inevitable exposure to the icy breeze. I peeled down in the semi-crowd, trying not to attract too much attention as I quickly swapped my jeans for running shorts and exposed a Londoner's pale chest and slightly padded belly to the mid-November conditions, before quickly masking this unenticing sight with the teal of Bournville. As protection against the elements go, the vest failed comprehensively, and as I looked around, shivering in the shock of my sudden exposure to the chill, I realised that I was quite possibly the most under-dressed man in Nijmegen.

All around me, people were dressed in long-sleeved tops, running jackets, tights and all manner of other apparel that struck me at that moment as entirely reasonable and sane. I looked in vain for another soul – hapless or hardy, you decide – prepared to run the Zevenheuvelenloop in a vest and saw no one. Still, I could at least accessorise. On came the BvH buff, the beanie and the yellow gloves which are a size too small but which were a gift from my son and daughter who I always like to think of when I wear them. I packed my clothes into a tiny BvH daybag, the kind with armstraps that you can run with, although this was not my plan. I decided to skip the risk of not finding the storage box in which to leave it when the race started but to leave it in the holding pen. I'd noticed that a lot of runners had simply tied or left jackets, holdalls and various other kinds of bag on the metal barriers that separated the runners in the pen from the well-wishers on the pavements alongside. I figured that this was the Netherlands and that you could leave stuff on the street like this and no one would steal it. That's possibly a naïve national stereotype but if it is, it's a positive one. Anyway, I wasn't going to run a 15K race on an unfamiliar course with a bag strapped on my bag. Worst case: the bag and its contents would be gone when I got back. I had spare clothes back at the Airbnb and my essentials – passport, cashcard, euro banknotes, accommodation keys – I kept close, in my running belt.

I tied the bag to the barrier and hoped that I'd be able to find it at the end in the sea of bags left by others. And that was it. Adopting the penguin technique (as applied by penguins huddling to stay warm in the Antarctic), I inched my way back to the centre of the pen where the crowd was thickest, jumped up and down, clapped my arms around my midriff, performed static warm-up exercises and did everything I could to keep moving in a confined space. Soon, the pen was opened and our group walked or jogged our way around a small, leafy square. Another corner and we reached the main road and the start.

It was big, it was noisy. The approach to the start line was decked with sponsors' branded banners and panels and once again I appreciated the scale of the Zevenheuvelenloop. It has been around since 1984, virtually as old as the London Marathon, and attracts upwards of 20,000 runners. Our group moved forward, now running with more purpose. We crossed the rubber start mats which bleeped as they recognised our individual running chips, signalling our presence on the course so that our progress and importantly our time would be tracked from this point onwards. My race had started and for the first few minutes I simply took in the shouts and the clapping of supporters, the race signage, the encouragement and guidance of the race marshals and the distinctness of the roadscape – the street furniture and the characteristically neat suburban houses – which were a constant reminder that I was in the Netherlands and that this was another stage in the RUNNING: ME RUNNING EU adventure.

The first few kilometres played out along a long straight, gently inclining (runners speak for going uphill, but not steeply) road to the city's outskirts and eventually, a forested stretch. We turned out into open countryside. Ice lay around the verges, although there was no need for a visual reminder of the temperature. I'd warmed up quite quickly but from the laboured breath of the continuous stream of runners, a cloud of condensation rose. Beyond the city, the air was clear, the sunshine dappled and the semi-wooded landscape was inviting and even welcoming. I felt one of those periodic and ephemeral moments of euphoria. It felt good and right to be exactly where I was at this point. I didn't want to be anywhere else. True, the thigh I'd clattered the night before was still causing me some pain but it hadn't stopped me. I was a runner, doing what runners do. I was on an adventure. RUNNING: ME RUNNING EU was real. This latest stage had taken some planning, as each stage had so far and as each stage would, but everything so far had worked out OK. It was during this happy phase of the event that I heard what I immediately interpreted as Tibetan chanting. Improbable as it sounds, that is exactly what it was. The course passed a sign at the entrance to a Buddhist retreat whence came the incongruous (because this was the Seven Hills in Nijmegen, not the Himalayas) yet relaxing tones of the chant.

About those hills – it's true that the land rose slightly at times and we had been very gently climbing out of Nijmegen from the start. But there was nothing to trouble anyone used to running over any of the tougher terrains to be found around the Midlands. The rollercoaster of the Ashby 20 miler in rolling Leicestershire countryside, the steep climb out of

Atherstone on the Badgers 10K, and especially, the Tempo 10K Winter series up the 14% (1:7) Larkstoke incline to Warwickshire's highest point, now those are hilly runs. By comparison, the Zevenheuvelenloop is gentle and barely undulating. Not that I complained.

Before long, the trees gave way to the first signs that we were heading back into the outskirts of Nijmegen, and we were soon retracing the long road leading towards the centre, eventually crossing the finish line. I would have lingered but on this trip, exceptionally, I hadn't managed to speak to any of the other runners. I got my breath back and made my way back towards where I'd started. I found the pen and after a brief search, spotted my bag where I'd left it. Sweaty or not, this was no time to get cold again, so I performed another quick costume change in the street, this time with only the occasional returning runner and the utterly unconcerned gaze of a security guard for an audience, and headed back to the Airbnb, taking a few pictures along the way.

Stage 9 was over. I'd 'done' the Netherlands, run the Zevenheuvelenloop, and returned home intact and undamaged apart from some bruising from a dead leg, but fired up with a gathering realisation that this was becoming a bit of an adventure. Looking back, that sounds like an understatement given how much was to follow, but in those early stages there was still a sense that I was somehow 'playing' at this. I guess this was a mild variant of imposter syndrome, that sense of doubt that makes us unsure if we are really capable of doing a job or making a presentation, and that our inadequacy will be found out in full public view. Over the years I've known many people who were at times crippled by a crisis of confidence even though they undoubtedly had all the qualities they needed to do what they'd set out to do. I've also met a few who've displayed no such doubt, even though maybe they ought to have done!

I've had a long enough career and enough highlights and successful moments to know that I can do a good job, and to relish those moments when they happen. Occasionally, though, in work as elsewhere in life, events don't work out as you'd thought or hoped that they would. I've mentioned my deep-down belief that ultimately things *will* work out, although not necessarily the way I'd imagined. It's an optimism that at times defies the appearance – and occasionally the reality – of present unpromising circumstances. I've also learned from my own experience that sometimes, things have to go wrong in order for them to go right.

Ten days before the Netherlands stage of RUNNING: ME RUNNING EU, I parted company with my employer. I hadn't planned it, but it produced two immediate and very positive emotions in me. The first was relief and a sense of freedom regained – when you've built your own business or run a small professional body, both of which I'd done very happily with reasonable success and great personal satisfaction for over 20 years, it isn't easy to reinsert yourself into another organisation's hierarchy and give up your own sense of personal autonomy. As someone else's employee I increasingly felt as though I'd lost my sense of 'agency', the ability to set my own priorities, use my own professional judgement, make my own decisions and act on them. None of this is intended as a criticism of anyone else – that's not my purpose here. Instead I want to focus on the silver lining that came with this particular cloud.

It's true that I hadn't been happy at work for a while. Now, I had an immediate sense of release. I can't say that I actually heard a voice whispering "… and rel-aaax…!" but that was how it felt. The second emotion was one of excitement. Suddenly, a new path had opened, giving me a renewed mastery over my time. Unexpectedly, fate had cut me the slack I needed to focus on the challenge. I don't actually believe in fate as an unseen or divine hand dictating our lives like a puppet-master. Or maybe I just don't welcome the idea that we're all just stringed puppets performing in someone else's show! But I do believe in getting out from under, taking the positives from an unforeseen event and looking ahead. I'd set myself a challenge – a hugely enriching one – and now my time was free to complete it.

It was just as well. As shops and TV commercial breaks began increasingly to fill up with the sights and sounds of Christmas, 2018 was nearly over. Come the year's end, I would have a fraction under three months left to complete the challenge. At this point I started to tell myself that, with nine countries run but still 19 left, I would need to up the pace. I might even need a plan…

Nijmegen, Netherlands The lone Brit in a sea of local names. Below: Travelling light – Ljubljana backpack, my faithful companion.

PART 2 | THE ACTUAL RUNNING PART

STAGES 10 & 11

Denmark and Sweden: two parkruns and The Bridge

NEW YEAR'S DAY 2019 – 87 DAYS TO GO

I'd already begun to think of how I might combine a few countries for a couple of long weekends come the new year. This was partly for financial reasons – funding 19 separate trips would be extravagant and hard to achieve, even though until recently I'd had a steady income from a well-paid job. It was also a practical impossibility. As autumn set in, there were barely 19 weekends left in the calendar before the deadline and I wouldn't be able to devote every one of them to RUNNING: ME RUNNING EU. I'd begun to think about how much annual leave I could use for the challenge in the first three months of 2019 when my work circumstances changed and time was no longer an issue.

The financial challenge had just got a whole lot more significant, though. How would I fund the rest of the adventure, given that 100% of my sponsorship was going to the two charities? Seen from another angle, how was I going to stay married, given that I would probably be leaving Liz behind whenever I headed off for another stage of RUNNING: ME RUNNING EU? Liz has her own life and interests and, while her initial scepticism about the challenge had thawed and she had become ever more supportive, she wasn't about to give up her every spare weekend just to trail along. I didn't expect it and wouldn't have dreamed of asking her to sacrifice her own time just to watch me pursue my own goal.

In every sense, this is where parkrun came back into the running. It had become a tradition that on Christmas Day and New Year's Day, certain neighbouring parkruns would stagger their start times so that, exceptionally, parkrunners could chalk up two events in one day by running at one location at 9am and then hotfooting it to a neighbouring event to run again an hour or so later. At some point, the directors of the parkruns at Amager Fælled in Copenhagen and at Ribersborg in Malmö revealed that they were in talks to link up and host a New Year's

Day double (NYDD) event. The idea of the Scandi Double caught my imagination immediately. I would have been 'up' for this even if I hadn't been embarked on RUNNING: ME RUNNING EU. I could already feel the thrill of running the first event, then dashing to the station for a train to take me over the bridge across the water to Malmö. Two parkruns, two cities and two countries in one morning. Once the event directors confirmed that the NYDD would go ahead, I was already mentally crossing the bridge.

First I had to pitch the idea to Liz of spending New Year in Copenhagen. Was NYE a big deal there? I wasn't sure they even celebrated in Denmark. I looked it up. Apparently they did. Fireworks were mentioned. I also discovered that Citizen M had a hotel in central Copenhagen. Citizen M had been on my radar since reading about them in a book called *A Beautiful Constraint*, which gave several examples of organisations that had turned constraints of various kinds into advantages. The founders of Citizen M set out to create luxury hotels at affordable prices and had come up with a visually stylish and funky design that I liked the look of. I thought it would appeal to Liz, too. So when I raised the idea with Liz of spending New Year in a cold climate I had a couple of added arguments up my sleeve that I thought would appeal to her. In the end, though, if she wasn't convinced, I'd find another way to cover Denmark and Sweden. When it came to a winning argument, though, there was always a joker I could play... *The Bridge*.

People are aware of the TV phenomenon known as Scandi Noir, a genre of crime or political drama normally set in Denmark or Sweden and sometimes both together. It's been said that the storylines, scripts and settings of the likes of *Wallander*, *The Killing* and *Borgen* have encouraged British TV audiences to overcome their traditional aversion to subtitling as they (and in Liz's case and mine) became enthralled by the characters and landscapes of these dramas set in Europe's northern climes. But none more so than *The Bridge*, a dark drama with deep and captivating characters and an iconic green Porsche sports car. Liz and I had been watching these dramas for several years and a double episode on BBC4 had become a weekend highlight (what can I say? For very settled, late middle-aged married couples, connubial contentment can be made of such simple pleasures!).

Quickly established as an eerie, brooding presence in its own right, the Bridge of the title refers to the 5-mile long Øresund bridge that links the edge of Copenhagen with Malmö.

I waited for a suitable moment to broach the subject. When it came, I blurted out the question: "What do you think of the idea of going to Copenhagen for New Year's Eve?" Without missing a beat but with a discernible "hmmm…" in her tone, Liz replied: "I assume there's some running involved in this…?" I went on to describe the city's reputation for spectacular fireworks and also extolled the considerable comforts of Citizen M. There was a pause and I wasn't sure if Liz was sold on the idea. It was time to play the joker. "We can go to see the bridge, you know, The Bridge, as in the TV ser-…" "Let's do it," said Liz. And that was it.

The two parkrun directors had created a Facebook group for people interested in running the Scandi Double. It quickly became ever busier with enthusiastic comments from around the UK, tips on travel and updates on plans for the day from the two respective event teams. It was clear that I wouldn't be crossing the bridge, (I mean The Bridge!) on my own.

Liz and I flew from Birmingham on SAS on 30 December. I'd checked on the weather for the days that we would be there. Unseasonally mild temperatures and strong winds were forecast. Despite this, we dressed for what we imagined a Scandinavian winter to be like and privately I worried that, despite our preparations, we would be cold. The forecast was accurate, though. It was cool enough to feel like winter to a southern Brit like me, but not excessively so. The wind, though, was fierce and I had to think about what I would actually take with me for the NYDD runs. I'd brought more kit than I needed, just so I would have options for the unpredictable conditions on the day of the run.

I planned to run from the hotel to the first parkrun at Amager Fælled, a distance of just over two miles according to Google Maps. I'd been to Copenhagen once before but hadn't visited Amager. I had my small Bournville Harriers bag with me, small enough to strap on my back and run with, but limited in capacity. I also had a running belt for my phone, keys, money card and passport – lifeline essentials while travelling. For this particular run, carrying the passport was about more than merely caution. While both Denmark and Sweden are within the EU's 'borderless' Schengen zone which allows control-free travel between both countries and indeed all countries inside the zone, passport checks had been reintroduced in recent years since the growth in migrant numbers crossing Europe following the start of Syria's civil war, which had triggered an exodus of refugees towards north-western Europe.

I remembered our informal Bournville Harriers mini-tour to Ljubljana in 2016 when we'd travelled via train from Munich to Ljubljana and back and had seen Syrian families en route, along with the evidence of a major security operation (material, manpower, machine-guns) at the borders into and out of Austria, Germany and Slovenia. Wind forward to 2018 and while the tensions of two years earlier had eased, I could certainly expect a passport check by Swedish police during the train journey to Malmö. No passport, no NYDD. As parkrunners know, there's another four-letter acronym – #DFYB – coded into the memory of everyone who wants their parkrun time recorded in the official results: Don't Forget Your Barcode.

The originator of this succinct aide-memoire is a fellow south Birmingham-based runner, Yorkshireman Dave Johnson, who runs in the black and orange of Kings Heath Running Club, friendly local rivals of Bournville Harriers and another club with a strong community ethos. Dave does a lot for running as a volunteer, champion of the sport and as an all-round ambassador for generally being a good bloke and a responsible citizen. A lot of people know Dave – and a great many more know and adhere to the acronym he created. In the flow of Facebook chatter during December, along with #DFYB, came another repeated reminder: #DFYP. By the end of December, around 80 UK-based parkrunners were planning to head to Copenhagen for the Scandi Double, along with a smattering of parkrun 'tourists' from other countries including Poland and even Australia. To my knowledge, the messages of #DFYB and #DFYP were heeded and no one forgot their barcode or their passport.

But first there was New Year's Eve. Liz and I tend not to go large on NYE parties. It's probably that 'settled, middle-aged couple' thing again – at least partly. But in my mind there's also a belief that we've already witnessed the New Year's Eve to end all New Year's Eves. Millennium Eve, in fact, when we were in London and we did party like it was 1999 – in a thronging bar for the build-up, down at the Thames for the fireworks at midnight, then back in the bar's basement for a pulsating party all night long. Our NYEs in more recent years have been low-key – a few drinks at home with friends and neighbours, midnight with Jools. This time would be different, and we began to sense how different even as we first arrived in Copenhagen from the airport and made the short walk from the central station to our hotel. There was a buzz, a sense of expectation and, already, the sound of random fireworks. Citizen M in Copenhagen overlooks the Radhusplads, the town hall square, which was, I'd read, at the heart of the city's NYE festivities.

Citizen M has an L-shaped balcony on the seventh floor which guests can access from the bar-cum-lounge-cum-restaurant which is the hotel's social hub. I wanted to go down into the square to be immersed in the action. Liz was concerned that it might be too raucous and even dangerous in the crowd, especially as from the balcony, we could already see small figures in the dark street below who seemed to be letting off bangers and rockets at will. Liz's common sense prevailed and we decided to stay above the action. Good decision. By 10.30pm the random bangs and flashes had turned into a fusillade of rockets and explosions.

With still nearly an hour to go before midnight the skies were alight and several plumes of smoke could be seen down in the wide avenue that passed the hotel and across the Radhusplads, where large crowds had gathered. This was no official display, though. People were bringing and lighting their own fireworks, seemingly from wherever took their fancy. It looked like a dangerous, joyous, sparkling, multi-coloured anarchy – albeit one we were enjoying vicariously, seven storeys above the fray. The final minutes of 2018 were eclipsed by this epic festive combat of starbursts and explosions and the town hall's chimes at midnight went unheard as the good people of Copenhagen unleashed their inner Viking and celebrated the New Year, engulfing their city in the full cacophony of battle well into the first hour of 2019.

Back up on the seventh floor, the party continued. I don't drink much these days – I drank my life's excessive fill during my teens and early 20s – and actually now dread the thought of feeling hungover, both for the ill effects but mainly for the lost time – when you're 61, life feels too short to waste a day on a hangover. Before races I rarely drink alcohol at all (I know – parkrun's a run not a race, but still…) But this was Copenhagen, we were celebrating New Year's Eve, and the hotel bar staff were clearly keen to show off their cocktail skills… I called time on the party at 1.30am and left Liz to it.

I planned to be up at 7am and to squeeze in a breakfast before leaving the hotel at 8am. That all went to plan. I'd shortlisted my kit and accessories and made the final selection of what to wear and what else to take the night before. I'd been to the station and bought my ticket for the train to Sweden earlier that evening before the pyromania began. I felt fresh, ready to go and excited as I headed for the hotel exit. This was it. The NYDD, the Scandi Double. As the doors to the street opened I immediately felt the force of the wind. Paper, cardboard, cans, spent bangers and other nameless debris were being bowled across the wide avenue. I stepped out and was broadsided by a gust. This was going to make running interesting. I began to jog in the direction indicated by Google Maps. As I headed out towards Amager I passed a small but steady stream of recent revellers, unmistakable in last night's clothes, heads sunken into collars, battered by the wind, each one looking the worse for wear.

I felt slightly self-conscious, an incongruous figure in running tights, yomping away from the city as Copenhagen struggled with its giant collective hangover. I passed the walls of the Tivoli pleasure grounds and continued towards the bridge connecting the heart of the city to Amager, watching my step to avoid the bottles and sometimes entire cases of spent rocket-launchers lying strewn in the gutter, on the pavement and occasionally in the middle of the road. These were industrial-scale fireworks casing 24 rockets at a time. It was amazing to think that just a few hours earlier they were being let off randomly in the street. Last night had seemed like a real contradiction to the image I had of Denmark being a calm, orderly country and its people mild, restrained and less expressive than we Brits. The thought passed. I crossed the bridge onto Amager, technically an island but effectively just a continuation of Copenhagen.

The wind was really fierce here and it forced its way up the narrower streets in this part-residential, part-light-industrial area. I did a U-turn at one point as the howling gale threatened to tear off a piece of corrugated metal cladding from a building as I approached. Just then I saw three figures in running gear but walking with the same air that I had of wanting to get somewhere and improvising their route to get there. They were British. I can't remember why I knew, but I just knew. As I approached I said one word: "parkrun?" Yep. We exchanged "Where are you from?" "First time in Copenhagen?" pleasantries and I left them to their walk. I wanted to keep on jogging to the Amager Fælled parkrun meeting point. The wind made the conditions feel colder than they actually were and while I had an extra layer on, I didn't want to get chilly too early on with a run, a train and bus journey, another run then the journey back ahead of me.

My immediate destination lay in the middle of some parkland. Soon I could see a couple of other runners who looked as though they had somewhere to go. I turned a corner and there, a couple of hundred metres or so ahead, was a small crowd of people. I spotted the parkrun branding on signage that marked out the start, and then saw other people wearing the distinctive apricot-coloured parkrun running vests and shirts with the name of their home parkruns printed on the front. I stopped and stripped down to my own parkrun vest. "Cannon Hill. Where's that, then?" said a voice. Someone had clocked the name on my vest. I turned round. Birmingham, I told him. "You don't sound like a Brummie." I smiled. It's a familiar response. Despite living for over 20 years in the second city I don't seem to have picked up any trace of a Birmingham accent as far as I or seemingly anyone else can tell. Occasionally my daughter is asked if she's from Birmingham. I can't hear it in her voice but clearly others can. As the parkrun crowd gathered it became quickly apparent that this was a tourist takeover, with Brits outnumbering the Copenhageners by some margin. I exchanged comments with a few people. We spoke the language of parkrun – how long had we been parkrunning, how many runs, how many volunteering stints, preferred role as volunteers and so on. It's the small talk of parkrun but it rarely fails to start a conversation.

Of all the volunteer roles (and I've done most of them at some point) I enjoy timing on the finish line most. It's surprising how many people are reluctant to take on this role, fearful that they might get it wrong and mess up the results. I enjoy it because it's very much at the sharp end of each event. Beyond the simple arhythmic act of clicking the timer as each runner crosses the line, I love seeing the effort and exertion, particularly among the faster finishers as they strain and push themselves hard in the final metres before the line to get the max from their run and hopefully knock off a precious few seconds from their PB, their personal best, to set a new fastest personal time.

Equally, I enjoy watching and marvelling at the sheer variety of people who cross the line week by week: the kids who start small and as the months pass spring up and become taller – and faster – than their parents; those who run for fun, those of whom it's easy to imagine that parkrun has given them a lifeline to exercise and a healthier life; those who defy daunting personal challenges, those who may be challenging their own community's gender norms by running, and many more. I enjoy the differences in running styles, the contrasts in body shapes and sizes, the huge variety of running tops, club colours, charities, place names, sports brands. It would be an exaggeration to say that all of human life crosses the finish line, but there's enough variety among those who do to make it seem as if that's true. And I enjoy being part of the team that provides several hundred runners – at Cannon Hill, we've occasionally topped a thousand – with this weekly dose of fun and satisfaction.

Today, others had given up *their* time to let *us* run and enjoy the uncommon experience of a double parkrun. During the routine pre-run briefing, and distinctive in her red Smurf-style hat, run director Anne outlined the course and ran through the usual safety points, in both Danish and English. Departing from the weekly script, she noted that the numbers present would make this a record turn-out for Amager Fælled, which had been one of the first parkrun events to be set up outside the UK. She reminded everyone that this was the first part of a double parkrun and that several dozen of us would be heading off promptly to the nearby railway station en route to Malmö. There was applause for the morning's volunteers and for those of us who would be continuing the parkrun experience across the water.

I was slightly apprehensive at this point. I knew the journey plan. The local railway station, DR Byen, was just one kilometre away on the edge of the parkland. I had my ticket already so I wouldn't need to waste valuable time trying to master the foibles (because every ticket machine has its own particular foibles) of a Denmark Railways suburban station ticket machine or, just as bad, stand in a long queue growing increasingly impatient while someone else struggled with the machine. But there were other uncertainties. There would be a change of train. There would be passport control. On arrival in Malmö, timing would be tight. I would have to leave the station, find the right bus stop for the right bus and then take the short journey to the waterfront in the Malmö suburb of Ribersborg where the second parkrun would take place. I knew I wasn't alone – but what if we were held up at any of these points and were late for the second parkrun? Would they hang on for us? Lots of 'what ifs'. But now it was time to run. We were off – 150 people bunched together, most trotting slowly until space began to open up and we could run at a comfortable pace. It was a two-lap course of open parkland, mostly on tarmac paths, generally flat with a couple of barely noticeable inclines. Amager Fælled parkrun has fewer distinctive features than some other parkrun courses I've run both in the UK and elsewhere. The park is bordered by industrial premises and these came in and out of view as we made our way along the paths. The gusting wind made it slightly more challenging, although it would become even more of a factor in Malmö later that morning, as we were to discover.

I approached the finish line, hoping for some ridiculously high placing, perhaps even first man in my age group. In fact I came in 47th out of 160, the 37th of 83 male runners, and 4th in my age category V60-64. My finish time was 24:53. No personal records there, just another outing in the unremarkable middle rankings. Happily, breaking personal records isn't normally why I run, and certainly not on New Year's Day 2019. I'd just run in Denmark as part of what for me was a unique and highly fulfilling challenge. I'd met some people, had conversations with strangers. I'd been able to enjoy the maddest imaginable display of fireworks, Liz had really enjoyed the trip and I'd done what I'd set out to do. What, to use the well-worn cliché, was not to like?

I quickly changed, adding layers to fend off the fierce, gusting wind, lingered only to thank and get a selfie (or a runfie, as I'd first heard Stacey and as many others now call it) with Anne the race director, and joined the trickle of other NYDD runners making their way at a purposeful pace towards the station for the journey to Malmö. As I walked I fell into step with a woman of a similar age and made (literally) a passing comment about the trip ahead, being sure that she was also on the trail to Malmö. I mentioned #DYFP and she said that she had a man who was taking care of that for her. And she did. This was Lucille and sure enough her husband Richard was waiting at the station with her passport as we arrived. We fell into easy conversation from that point onwards and stayed together for part two of the Scandi Double.

Our train entered a tunnel, re-surfacing onto a tiny artificial island in the Øresund, the wide waterway that separates Denmark and Sweden, before rising above the water's surface to cross The Bridge. This used to be an often difficult, weather-battered sea-crossing. Now, thanks to the 10-mile-long Øresund crossing, opened in 2000, it takes just a few minutes by road or rail to cross the water between Denmark and Sweden. The bridge itself covers half the distance. For anyone who has watched the TV series, The Bridge has an eerie presence on screen and appears almost as a character in its own right. However, the railway track is suspended beneath the road bridge and the crossing by train doesn't have quite the same atmosphere, although it is still fascinating to be on a train skimming at speed just above the water of the Øresund.

This was the second time I'd crossed the bridge. While this latest crossing was part of a year-long adventure of my own creation, the previous time had been connected with a much more dramatic natural phenomenon. In April 2010 I'd flown to Copenhagen for a meeting organised by FEIEA, the same European professional body whose awards judging event had got me to Lisbon for the Portuguese stage of RUNNING: ME RUNNING EU. That previous trip to Copenhagen had been turned upside down when a barely-pronounceable Icelandic volcano called Eyjafjallajökull had erupted, spewing ash across northern Europe's airspace, grounding all flights – including my return flight and those of my colleagues in the meeting who had travelled from Austria, Slovenia, Belgium and Portugal – for several days. Across the swathe of north America known as tornado alley, flights are often disrupted by twisters. Here in Copenhagen in 2010, we'd just had all of ours cancelled by a tongue-twister!

Our meeting was abandoned as everyone sought new ways to get home. I headed for the central station to check out options to get out of Denmark at ground level, along it seemed with half of the city's tourist and business travelling population. There, a huge sea of people queued – calmly, but with a collective air of bewilderment and concern – for one of a dozen ticket desks. Eventually it was my turn at the window. "What's my best chance of getting back to London?" I asked. The Danish ticket clerk paused, then smiled: "Walk!" He could get me as far as Brussels but all Eurostar services were fully booked until Sunday. So I decided to stay put in Copenhagen until Sunday, rather than scrabble around looking for improbable alternatives: at one point my colleagues from Lisbon – António and Paula – were contemplating hitching a lift with some Portuguese military officials heading home from Norway. This bizarre scheme came to nothing and eventually they opted to hire a series of cars to get them from border to border all the way back to southern Europe.

My own escape route involved six trains, a ship and a hair-raising dash at Cologne for the vital connection to Brussels, and 21 hours of travel. By the time Liz met me at Birmingham New Street station in the early hours of Monday morning I was speechless from fatigue. But it had been an adventure. I described it at the time as 'Inter-rail for the Over 26s' and it had seemed like student days revisited, with the normal calm, colourless, processionary routine of scheduled air travel suddenly replaced by a colourful, chaotic, unpredictable and truly memorable journey in which the business traveller's customary reserve was forgotten and conversations were struck up among strangers almost from the moment the first train pulled out of Copenhagen central station just after 7am Sunday morning, bound for Hamburg. But before we'd hit upon our respective escape routes, António, Paula and I had decided that as the ash cloud had given us an unplanned free day, we'd take advantage by crossing The Bridge to visit Sweden or, as we said at the time, "When the going gets tough, the tough go to Malmö!" We stayed there a few short hours, relaxing and reflecting on the bizarre circumstances that had led us to make this particular trip, then returned to Copenhagen for our epic journeys home.

So I'd crossed The Bridge and been to Malmö before and that had been a bit of an adventure. This was another one. Once on the other side, the train stopped at the first station, where uniformed Swedish police came on board and began checking passports. Time was passing and it felt as though everyone in the parkrun NYDD tourists group – the majority of people on this particular New Year's Day train – was as conscious as I was that the clock was edging towards 11am and the official start-time of Malmö Ribersborg's NYD parkrun. Would we make it?

Finally, passport checks complete, we were under way again and eventually the train pulled into Malmö Central station. Seconds later, winterwear-clad locals on the concourse were momentarily distracted by the sight of a steady stream of more lightly dressed runners hoofing with some urgency out of the station towards the bus stops. Which stop was it for the Ribersborg bus? I decided to crowd-source the answer, go with the flow and follow the others. With just a moment's glance to check the bus number 7, I climbed aboard and was greatly reassured to see Anders, the Malmö Ribersborg run director on board. He'd come into town to the station to meet us and assured us that the event team would wait for us before starting the run.

A few minutes later we arrived at Ribersborg. The wind was fierce and we crossed the road to find other parkrunners sheltered in the lee of a café building to get some protection against a biting breeze. At 8 degrees, the ground temperature wasn't desperately cold – in fact it was unseasonally mild for NYD in Scandinavia – but here at the seaside the wind was flecked with sand and when it gusted it was almost painful to stand for too long. It was certainly powerful enough to dislodge garments from the growing pile of discarded coats, scarves and kit-bags which are a familiar sight at parkruns everywhere. The run director called everyone together with a welcome and observed that "Last week we had 12 runners. I think there are a few more here today!" There was laughter and applause. There were indeed a few more runners than Ribersborg was used to. The previous event record had been 79. Here, on this special day, I was one of 152 – a new record turnout. Just a few were local. The great majority were from around the UK, with a smattering of NYDD tourists from elsewhere.

We made our way to the start line and were quickly on our way. The course ran close to the shoreline, sheltered by a line of shrubs and trees. The wind was incredible and low hanging branches blew into runners' faces, even drawing blood in one case. The closer to the sea we went, the greater the wind's intensity and I was grateful when we turned away to follow a trail alongside a narrow stretch of water lying a few metres inland and away from the shoreline. Not that the course was sheltered at this point, but it was bearable at least. A 5K run is usually over quickly. Even so, this was one run that couldn't be completed quickly enough for me, and I was glad when finally I could see the paraphernalia of a parkrun finish: the timers, the scanners, the milling group of those who had already finished. I crossed the line, found my bag in the mound of parkrunners' kit, and quickly pulled on some warm layers including a much-needed hoodie, before heading back towards the waterfront to brave the walk across the low, narrow wooden causeway that led to Kallbadshuset, a cold-water bathing cabin and sauna that also housed a very attractive café.

After the initial confusion of wrongly queuing with the cold dip and sauna-bound citizens of Malmö, distinctive with their wrapped towels, I stepped out of the queue at the last moment. This was not the occasion to commit to a Swedish cold water naked bathing experience for which I felt entirely ill-equipped (and you can decipher that as you wish!). Instead, I joined Lucille and Richard for a warming hot chocolate and a deliciously fresh, filled roll. After two runs and the ravaging wind, these were the best of all hot chocolates, the best of all rolls.

The run director joined us. I told the tale of RUNNING: ME RUNNING EU once again and I was pleased that, just as on every previous telling, the story of the challenge struck another positive chord. In fact things had gone very well. I'd run the NYDD double, something I'd have been very happy to do anyway as a parkrunner, and I'd managed to run in two more EU countries. There was the post-run endorphin effect of feeling relaxed after exercise. I was in enjoyable company with people who clearly supported the idea of RUNNING: ME RUNNING EU. And we were in the attractive, homely, characterful cabin-like wooden interior of the 100-year-old Kallbadshuset, drinking the best hot chocolate I'd had in a long time. This was surely the essence of what's known across the Øresund in Denmark as *hyyge*, that hard-to-pin-down sense of feeling cosy and at peace with the world, chatting with friends, being in no hurry and taking the time to enjoy a moment of contentment, whatever the weather.

The Swedish have an equivalent feeling, known as *lagom*, but that's more about living with just enough of what you need, not too little, not too much, to live a life in balance. Lagom sounds a very good life recipe, but it didn't quite capture my own sensation at that moment in the Kallsbadhuset. It was a transient feeling, but it wasn't as fleeting as my seven seconds of nirvana, either, more a half hour of comforting happiness. It isn't easy to find the right words for such a rare sense of absolute wellbeing, but it's something to be savoured when it comes upon you, and I certainly recognised it when I felt it that early afternoon on New Year's Day 2019 in Malmö.

Lucille, Richard and I thanked the Ribersborg event team, made our way back over the wooden pier and braved the sandblast by the beach and the piercing funnelling wind at the bus stop before the no. 7 bus appeared for our return to Malmö Central station. We found our train, returned to Copenhagen and agreed to stay in touch in the way people do when they've spent good times together on holiday. I returned to the hotel, changed and went back out to find Liz, who'd had a leisurely start to the day, enjoying the comforts of Citizen M and exploring the city.

Meanwhile, we still had a day left to appreciate Copenhagen. Even with many places closed for the New Year's holiday and a powerful wind to brave, it was a fine place to be. I was happy. Stages 10 and 11 were now complete. I had three months left to complete the challenge and 17 countries still to run in. Now it was time to start planning properly.

As January began, I knew that I would need to start doubling and trebling up on countries within a single trip. After the Ljubljana near-miss, I also had to put some research into finding and booking scheduled races in some of the remaining countries. Given that I never needed an excuse to revisit Slovenia, I decided to look for races in the northern part of Croatia that I could reach from Slovenia. There are races in Istria and in Zagreb, the capital, but this wasn't the right time of year for them. I found a site that listed races around central Europe and discovered a half marathon in a town called Varaždin in north-east Croatia close to the Slovenian border. It wasn't far from Hungary, either. Could I reach Varaždin from

Ptuj, (pronounced p-too-ee!), a historic town, Slovenia's oldest, which I'd never previously visited? They were barely 30 miles apart and were linked by a river (not that I was planning to arrive in Varaždin by boat…). Were there connecting trains or buses? Could I combine the half in Varaždin with some running in Hungary? In the end, the travel possibilities would shape the final trip and meanwhile there was pleasure to be had from the shaping.

For me, with a love of maps and timetables, place names and travel, planning the trips, weighing up the options and settling the logistics were to become as much a part of the challenge – and the pleasure of tackling it – as the running itself. But the Ljubljana experience had taught me that the first step was to register for the race. I'd worry about how I'd get there later. By this point I'd also begun to think about a part of Europe that was as unfamiliar as it was fascinating. When I got there it would become one of the highlights of a challenge full of highlights – Baltic Week. But that comes later in the story. Meanwhile, I had to get ready for Croatia.

PART 2 | THE ACTUAL RUNNING PART

STAGE 12

Croatia: and quiet flows the Drava

SUNDAY 3RD FEBRUARY – 54 DAYS TO GO

On 23 January I wrote on Facebook:

> "You never know where running's going to take you, especially if you book races as the mood takes you. I'd never heard of Varaždin, a small town in north-east Croatia – until I discovered yesterday that there's a half marathon there in February. My name looks almost exotic as the lone GB on the list of entrants. Next challenge: how to get to Varaždin…"

And it was true. My name did stand out in the doo-bee-doo of names beginning with D in the list of registrations for the Varaždin half-marathon: Dilber, Dobsa, Doswell, Drakulic, Drzanic…

I'd quickly realised that in this part of the world it was off-season for organised running. Plenty of choice in the warmer months but my sketchy planning to date and the looming deadline had reduced my options. I'd begun to think that I might just have to pick a town (maybe by the sea…) somewhere in Croatia and run another solo run. And then I'd found Varaždin. To be precise, I pulled up a map to find Varaždin. I had some knowledge of the more prominent towns and cities of this Adriatic country, famous for its islands and coastal resorts, but not Varaždin. It's fairly small, about the same size as Banbury by population (46,000), tucked up in the northernmost part of Croatia just 10 miles from Slovenia and barely 20 miles from Hungary and it's close to the banks of the River Drava which, I would discover, runs the length of the half marathon's out-and-back course.

I was registered for the race online. Now I would work out how to get there and back in the time available. As the pace of the challenge picked up, the gap between each stage was getting tighter and increasingly I would need to keep the next-stage logistics in mind before committing to any future bookings. Options via Ptuj proved to be unrealistic. I would have to visit there another time. After checking flight-times, airfares, train and coach options, I decided that I would indeed travel via Slovenia, but by flying to Ljubljana and then taking the coach from a German-owned company I'd been hearing about called FlixBus, which seemed to operate a Megabus-type network connecting many European towns and cities. Given the choice, my preference would always be to take the train, but prospects for this were poor, with few trains and long gaps between infrequent connecting services.

A trip via Ljubljana meant another opportunity to see Stanka and Miro, who have become good friends over the years. Again, Stanka very generously gave me the use of her apartment in the city centre for my overnight stay, which meant that the next day I could walk to the bus station in barely ten minutes. It was raining hard as the FlixBus to Zagreb pulled away from the stand in front of Ljubljana's characteristic Habsburg-era but rather antiquated central railway station. There have been plans for years to modernise the station – and hopefully also to preserve what's left of its Austro-Hungarian Empire period charm. The coach was smart and comfortable, with its distinctive green FlixBus livery, and soon we were heading south from the city on the A2 motorway, skirting the small city of Novo Mesto before stopping for the border control at Bregana. Once on our way again in Croatia, we soon reached the suburbs of Zagreb and just two hours after leaving Ljubljana I was standing in the drab concrete shell of Zagreb coach station. The toilets required Croatian coins. I went into the on-site café to get some change. Ordering a "kavo z mlekom, prosim" in my best Slovene, I earned a slightly odd look from the woman at the bar as I was actually in Croatia and no doubt my English accent was impeccable, but I got my "coffee with milk, please" anyway.

Time dragged while I waited for the onward connection. Railway stations often impress with their architecture, like cathedrals to the god of travel. Coach stations rarely do. This one certainly didn't. By the time my onward coach to Varaždin was due to leave I'd begun to get itchy feet. I'd seen various buses arrive and leave, the clock was ticking and the FlixBus I needed was nowhere to be seen. I'd asked a couple of staff but no one seemed to know. Maybe the coach had been and gone and I hadn't spotted it. Unlikely. I'd been as vigilant as a train-spotter. Perhaps I was in the wrong place. It was possible, although I'd scoured the entire coach station in my quest to find the elusive vehicle. I began to run through the options, including alternative scenarios to get to Varaždin in time for the half-marathon.

With just seconds before the scheduled departure time I approached a group of drivers and said simply "FlixBus? Varaždin?" Two simply shrugged, uninterested in the concerns of a passenger of a rival company. A third casually pointed to a small, rather modest and anonymously branded minibus that had almost furtively appeared at the end of the stand. There were few markings but it bore a sticker marked FlixBus and an unobtrusive, almost apologetic sign as if merely to whisper its destination: Varaždin. This was clearly a sub-contracted local service, FlixBus in name only. Grateful, I thanked the driver who'd come to my aid, showed my ticket at the door of the minibus and calmed down, relieved at being poised for the final leg of the journey after a rare moment of anxiety.

A handful of other people arrived and finally we were on our way. There was one stop – at a remote roadside bar-café decked in the prominent red and golden yellow livery of Ožujsko, Croatia's biggest selling beer. "Ten minutes," announced the driver. We were in open countryside. Farmland. Some trees. No visible town or village. The bar appeared to be the only thing happening in these parts. I decided to let it carry on happening without my involvement and stayed outside. Once back on the road, it wasn't long before I saw the first road sign to Varaždin. Soon we began to pass the garages, workshops, out-of-town retail plots and road junctions that normally mark the approach to a town or city. And then I felt a sudden smile of recognition as we passed a football stadium and I read the name of the club that plays there. Varteks is a name that conjures up the qualifying rounds of European football competitions. This is the stage where teams from the more obscure parts of nations within the European football world battle it out for the right to play the likes of Bayern, Barcelona, Man City or Milan in the later rounds. Identifying the country of origin of the lesser-known names in the Europa League fixture lists is almost pub quiz material. Now, if it ever it came up during a quiz night at Rowheath or the Prince of Wales, I would know that Varteks (short for Varaždin Tekstil, reflecting the city's tradition of clothing manufacture) come from Croatia.

Minutes later I was taking my Ljubljanski Maraton backpack from the stack of luggage at the back of the minibus and picking my way across the bays of Varaždin coach station between pockets of exuberant teenagers enjoying their freedom at the end of the school day, many heading for buses that would take them to outlying villages and communities. I crossed a wide, open square dominated on one side by a large concrete building in a typical late Yugoslavian style. I'm no architect but I've seen a number of similar squares and buildings in countries that were formerly part of Yugoslavia until that country disintegrated in the early 1990s. The cracks had been forming below the surface as economic and political tremors began to shake Yugoslavia during the previous decade. But it wasn't until first Slovenia and then Croatia declared their independence from Yugoslavia that the country fragmented and finally fell apart. Varaždin saw its share of violence, including a brief siege of the Yugoslavian National Army's barracks by Croatian forces in the city and a few days of fighting between the opposing forces. Looking at the big ugly concrete structure, I wondered if the construction workers who built it could have imagined what was to happen to their country.

The historical clock turned back further as I walked through Varaždin's narrow streets and lanes and began to get a sense of the city's architecture, which has baroque, renaissance and even medieval features. This had been a prominent city at various times and had briefly been Croatia's capital. It certainly has a cultural legacy from the days when it formed part of the Austro-Hungarian Empire, including a renowned school of music, housed in a former palace. It sees a lot of tourists in the warmer months, with several outdoor entertainments including a rather ambiguously named Street Walking Festival, although a quick Google search revealed that this was more about jugglers and street theatre and not a celebration of the world's allegedly oldest profession.

However, there wasn't much happening on the streets of Varaždin on a cold, late February afternoon. I found the Park Boutique Hotel, my lodgings for my stay in Varaždin, and checked in. It proved to be a very pleasant, modern, small but airy place, facing the cathedral (time-keeping guaranteed thanks to the round-the-clock devotional bell-ringing) and backing onto a small park.

It was strikingly cheap given the quality and the spacious, well-appointed room and interiors generally. Once more it underlined how good quality can be found even within a limited budget if you have the freedom to travel out of season and the inclination to visit less well-known places.

It was Saturday mid-afternoon. As always I wanted to recce where I would need to collect my running number for the following day's half marathon. I'd also been sitting on buses for a few hours and needed to stretch my legs. I checked the map and followed a long looping route out from the centre of Varaždin to the Drava river, stopping at a supermarket for a sandwich and some water, and then headed through some wooded parkland until I saw the looming bulk of the Varaždin Arena. This was a large, modern sports centre on the outskirts of town. With its long, continuous façade and raised walkways, it struck me as a cross between an Olympic pool complex and London's South Bank. Among various events to have taken place within its cavernous interior, the Arena has hosted international handball tournaments (not a sport we follow so much in the UK but huge in this part of Europe) and concerts by numerous artistes, including American rappers Limp Bizkit. More to the point for my trip, there was signage on the Arena's entrance doors: TK Marathon 95 (that was the name of the running club that organised the race). Zimski Polumaraton. This was it – race HQ for tomorrow's winter half marathon.

It had taken me an hour to walk there. Now I wanted to find a shorter route back. The light was beginning to fade and I wanted to note a few landmarks along the way to use as reference points for my return in the morning for the race. It was also cooling down and I had an urge to reacquaint myself with the warm interior of the Park Boutique Hotel. I set off immediately. The route took me along a long approach road, through a rather uninviting industrial estate, across a busy highway where I had wait for a while for the lights to change, through a graffiti-spattered railway underpass and finally into a district of neat houses. Suddenly the buildings began to resemble those near the hotel, and there it was. It had taken 35 minutes to walk back. I would allow a 20-minute easy jog there in the morning.

The recce was complete. I rested, read and then headed across to the road a restaurant that had seemed OK according to my constant companion and source of travel and subsistence tips, Google. In fact the Restoran Angelus was more than OK. Again, a very good, substantial meal and a modest bill in exchange. Satisfied with the way the day had played out and feeling prepared for the next day's race, I returned to my room, laid out my kit for the half-marathon, read a little more then settled down to sleep early. On a Saturday night. It was hardly rock'n'roll but I liked it nonetheless. Maybe, for those of us of a certain age, running is the new rock'n'roll. Whatever, I had a 21K race to run in the morning. Good night!

There was no doubting that I was in the right place when I got back to the Arena the next morning. Runners everywhere, some like me arriving in track suits, hats, hoodies, performance jackets, leggings or whatever other combination of layers we'd all seen fit to don that morning. Others already there, talking in small groups of friends, family and fellow club members, a growing number exiting from the Arena building race-ready, stripped down to their chosen racewear for the day, and heading down the long straight from what would be the start line to get some warm-up motion into the legs.

I went into the registration area and joined a queue, the air full of Croatian conversation. I understood nothing. But at the same time I understood it all. This was the pre-race hubbub that every regular runner will be familiar with who has ever queued to collect a race pack on the morning of a race, that unmistakable sense of expectation, exchanges between runners, some to friends, others between strangers who find themselves together in the queue. I reached the desk and delivered my two rehearsed phrases. "Zao mi je, ne govorim hrvatski" Sorry, I don't speak Croatian. "Govorite engleski?" The guy at registration did indeed speak 'engleski': "Your name...?" And seconds later I had an envelope labelled DOSWELL, Steve. Inside, my running number, a sheet of information about the event and some promotional leaflets. I thought, "They've got my name, I've got my number!" I was practically good to go. I just had to park the warm layers somewhere and I'd be ready for the race.

I made my way to the men's changing room. At this point that sense of being in the right place drained away. I've never been one for locker room banter or overly 'blokey' environments – maybe an overhang from school days where the changing rooms in the sports pavilion were frequently a haven for intimidation. One of the other runners asked me a question, possibly to do with whether a locker was free. I repeated my entire command of Croatian. At this point there was a lull in the background chatter and a couple of the other men in the changing room tuned in. This time no one spoke English. I tried a couple of phrases in Slovene. Since the Slovenian border was barely a 10K distance away, it was likely that some Slovenians were taking part in the half marathon. Instead, there were shrugs. Slovene and Croatian are distinct but related languages, like Dutch and German, and up to a point they can be mutually intelligible, at least between native speakers, especially in a border area like Varaždin. But for this there needed to be a degree of connection and some expression of interest – or at least curiosity – about the presence of this Englishman who'd rocked up on his own in this corner of Croatia, in a race which was clearly a local event that tended not to get a great many runners from further afield. And in that changing room, just at that moment I wasn't feeling any connection. Instead, there was just a slightly awkward silence. I changed quickly, shoved my stuff into a locker and quickly headed outside for some fresh air and a change of scene.

The race would be handicapped by age group, and after a trio of hardy septuagenarian men had headed off to considerable applause, I joined the 60+ group of men and women on the start line. My positive outlook had soon been restored once I'd got back outdoors. The buzz just before a race begins is infectious and I was really looking forward to running this half marathon. Now we were off, and any thought of an age category win was quickly dispelled as one of our group moved quickly and confidently ahead. Within a couple of minutes he was already some considerable distance ahead of me. That was OK. I would run as well as I could but I wasn't 'racing' as such today.

It was mild, unseasonally so. I was quickly glad to be running in just a vest and shorts. Runners from the younger age categories began to overtake our small platoon of born-in-the-1950s veterans, although it would take them a while yet to catch our age-cat front runner who was already some way ahead. I noticed how the majority had opted for long sleeves, many including jackets and very often leggings, too. I'd seen this in other race events during the challenge. On average, runners in continental Europe tended to wear more layers than their British counterparts. Perhaps it was a fresh twist on the line that "Mad dogs and Englishmen go out in the midday sun." I've long felt that it's better to endure a few minutes of chill on the start line and then feel comfortable soon after starting, rather than to overheat and needing to look for places to jettison excess layers once a race has started. I was wearing my RUNNING: ME RUNNING EU vest, designed with my various Challenge messages included. Even if I had wanted to wear something warmer, I was happy to be promoting the adventure that had brought me here and the two charities that would benefit from it. The vest's messaging also featured parkrun branding – and that would prove to be a real conversation starter later in the Challenge.

As out-and-back courses go, the Varaždin Zimski Polumarathon's route couldn't have been simpler. We ran out along a straight asphalt road – closed to traffic – that ran alongside the River Drava until a point where the river emptied out into the Varaždin Lake, a large reservoir nearly five miles long and a mile wide. Studying the course map when I first signed up for the half marathon, I'd imagined what it would be like to run alongside such a large waterway. It sounded spectacular. Now that I was running,

I was left still wondering – a high bank separated the road from the river and the lake. Instead of the wide open watery vistas that I'd imagined, the scenery was of flat farm land with a few industrial buildings to my right and a long, straight ribbon of asphalt ahead. After about 5K we turned and headed back the way we'd come towards the Arena. Once back there, we turned again and ran a second out-and-back lap. It wasn't the most scenic of courses.

I've since learned that Varaždin Marathon95 club also hosts a half marathon in September. That one starts in the historic heart of the city, so that would appeal to runners looking for some more visual and aesthetic interest to reward their exertions.

However, let's take nothing away from the winter course, which certainly had its compensations. Being flat and straight, it was fast. With three-quarters of the race run, as I began to approach the final turn I checked my watch and realised that I might be in with a chance of ducking in under one hour 50 minutes by the finish. I picked up the pace, chose a runner ahead as a 'marker' – someone to aim for and reel in – and set about closing the gap on them. As I made the final turn, the other runner was about 50 metres ahead. I didn't want to accelerate simply to overtake them as quickly as possible because I probably wouldn't have the staying power to keep going at that pace and might run out of steam too early. Instead, I just allowed myself to nudge the pace slightly, and watched the gap between us close little by little. It may have lacked some visual variety but the course offered the advantage of a long continuous sight line that helped me to chase the marker down. I passed him with still 2K to go, I wasn't ready to go all out but I kept the parkrun pace going, as I had for the previous 4K.

The Arena grew larger and I began to hear a nearing ripple of applause from the small gathering of supporters at the finish. I increased the pace again and broke into a semi-sprint once I saw the finish line. Lungs bursting, I crossed the line, collected a medal and stopped to get my breathing back to normal. A canteen had been set up under a semi-open gallery alongside the Arena, where volunteers were dispensing cakes, hot fruit juice and a few other goodies. Just beyond the gallery a TV crew were interviewing one of the very first runners to set out. He'd been part of the 70+ trio and was possibly the oldest runner in the race. When the interview was over, chancing my luck, I approached the reporter with the mic. She spoke English: "What's your story?" I pointed to my vest with the Running: Me Running EU title and map of Europe. "I'm running in all 28 countries of the European Union before the Brexit deadline. I'm raising money for two charities. Croatia is country number 12…" She smiled: "OK, let's get an interview."

And that's how I came to be filmed for Croatian TV. I talked about the challenge, about Brexit, about my impressions of Varaždin and the half marathon. I have no idea if it was ever broadcast but at that moment I felt that here was some media interest in the Challenge. I wasn't sure if it could help in any way but it would certainly do no harm. Beyond that, despite the earlier lack of connection, someone in Varaždin now knew why I was there. I'd managed to tell my story.

I returned to the changing rooms. Once showered and dressed I made my way to the upper floors of the Arena in search of coffee before the walk back to town. The Arena café was thronging with runners and their families. Soon the race organisers appeared in the corridor outside and some of the runners began drifting out. I joined them, to find a table being laden with prizes. I stayed for the presentations, which followed the format which would be entirely familiar for anyone who takes part in races in Britain: first three women, first three men, age category winners for women and men, plus what I understood were prizes for the host club's fastest man and woman.

Finally I headed back to my hotel and summarised my own race result on Facebook:

> **February 3, 2019** Varaždin half marathon completed. Garmin teased me with sub 1:50 but official time 1:50:19 (season's best) and 49/204 finishers — ran last 6k at parkrun pace to attempt sub1:50. Flat 2-lap outback course on a closed road along the Drava river flood plain. Occasional wafts from sewage works were the only hazard. 8 degrees, light drizzle. Perfect running weather. Very well-organised. Race HQ, start and finish at city sports arena. Age cats sent out at 3-min intervals, water/squash every 5k. Bread, wafers, hot fruit juice and water for runners at the end. Decent medal. Entry fee 90 kuna, about £11! Stage 12 of RUNNING: ME RUNNING EU now complete. Many thanks to everyone who's cheering me on and especially to the fab donors who are supporting the work of RSVP and Changing Faces.

I changed and went back out to explore the city a little. It was already after 3pm and the February light would go fairly soon. The next day

I was leaving early and there wouldn't be another chance to see Varaždin in daylight. The streets were quiet. True, it was Sunday. In the summer, Varaždin sees a fair few visitors, but not in early February. I barely saw another soul as I poked around the grounds of the Stari Grad, the old castle, the white-walled, red-turreted former fortress that once housed the entire town. I walked back through well-kept lanes and took in the white, ochre, caramel and terracotta hues of this well-preserved and scrubbed-clean town in the very north of Croatia. Given an opportunity I knew that I would enjoy delving deeper and learning more about the history of Varaždin and some of its notable figures. But it would have to be some other time.

The day was grey, the light was fading and I felt tired – hardly surprising. I'd picked up favourable surface impressions of Varaždin but wasn't taking much in beyond that. There was a time when I'd consider it a missed opportunity not to spend the maximum amount of time wandering round a previously undiscovered town and genning up on its story. Right now, though, I felt a blanket of weariness drop onto me. I made my way back to my hotel room, felt warm and enclosed inside it, dropped onto the bed, closed my eyes and drifted to sleep, roused briefly only once, on the hour, by the cathedral bell.

When I awoke it was already dark. I checked for responses to the Facebook post – there were plenty – and decided to eat at the Angelus again, pack and go to bed early. I'd seen Varaždin described as Little Vienna. These characterisations often convey very little but I vaguely understood the comparison from Varaždin's former status as a capital and the shared Austro-Hungarian (in Varaždin's case, particularly the Hungarian) heritage. My last visit to Vienna ten years earlier had ended with an awards ceremony late into the night, followed by early hours spent in a salsa bar, with barely an hour back at my hotel before leaving for the airport. Not tonight here in 'Little Vienna'. With my stamina spent on the half marathon, I was going to make my excuses and spend the evening modestly (eat, read, sleep) before tomorrow's early start. And I did.

February 4 2019 After a 7am minibus from Varaždin (one passenger and a monosyllabic driver makes for two hours of silence) and a slow Monday rush-hour crawl into the Croatian capital, an hour's gap before the Ljubljana bus allows time for a quick leg-stretch and a few snaps in the city centre.

It was a chilly start as I joined the small number of people dotted along the pavements with somewhere to go in Varaždin at 6.30am. Even the bus station was virtually deserted when I arrived, although a few more travellers had appeared by the time my minibus pulled out for the journey back to Zagreb. Still half-asleep, I gazed vacantly out of the window as the Varteks stadium and city outskirts gave way to low hills and farmland. At the café stop, a woman, mid-30s, one bag, joined us for the onward leg to Zagreb. She glanced in my direction with little apparent curiosity and began what became a mostly one-sided low-toned conversation with the driver, who would very occasionally respond with a short comment, more often just a word or a mere grunt of acknowledgement. They knew each other, I assumed from previous journeys.

At this time in the morning I had no capacity for conversation, especially with the time difference. According to my body clock my phone alarm had summoned me awake at an ungodly 5am. Life's larks tend to be up, wide awake and purposefully chirping by this time. As an owl I was up and about, but only on sufferance. Happily, by the time we'd squeezed out of the traffic and into Zagreb bus station, I was alert, ready to stretch my legs and see something of the city. I had barely an hour before the FlixBus back to Ljubljana, but I wanted at least to get a snapshot impression of Zagreb city centre. I exited the bus stands out onto the street, passing the odd sight of a kiosk entirely devoted to hats, not something considered essential at British bus stations so far as I remembered. I headed under the railway lines at the approach to Zagreb's central station, pausing briefly to get a couple of pictures (I rarely forget that I'm a railwayman's son) before crossing a small park and continuing up a tree-lined avenue.

I reached a square, part-cobbled, part-lawned, with a distinct white stone-blocked and colonnaded pavilion in the middle. This looked like a commemorative structure and it has indeed had a colourful career. Built in the 1930s and variously serving as a memorial to the first king of Yugoslavia, an art gallery, mosque and museum, it's now a venue for exhibitions. The square in which it stands has also changed names several times, its identity bending to the prevailing political winds, just as people have learned to do over the years in places around the world where their survival might depend on it. Clearly Zagreb has been one of those places. Appropriate, then, that its name today is Victims of Fascism Square. I liked the feel of this part of the city and would happily have explored further. I was racking up a growing list of places to be explored at leisure on a future trip. Zagreb was now very much on that list.

By the time I'd circled the pavilion and taken in the various views from the steps in front of it, it was time to wander slowly back to catch the coach to Ljubljana. This time I had no difficulty spotting the by-now familiar FlixBus branding. There were plenty of people already on-board as the coach had begun its journey elsewhere. We were soon out of Zagreb and in no time had covered the 12 miles to the crossing at Bregana. We were decanted from the coach to show our passports at the window of a small Croatian border control office. We boarded again, the coach moved forward a few metres and then we did it all over again to enter Slovenia.

There was no stress, though. Bregana wasn't busy at that point and the whole procedure took barely 15 minutes. However, this was a Schengen external border. Although both countries are part of the EU, only Slovenia was inside the Schengen zone, which enables passport and visa-free access between the countries which have signed up to the Schengen agreement. Inside the zone there are normally no border controls and travel is as effortless as travelling between England and Wales. While it was an EU member, the UK chose not to join the Schengen zone. Meanwhile, the EU's newest member at that time, Croatia, was still four years away from joining Schengen, hence the frontier controls as we crossed back into Slovenia here at Bregana which, particularly during the summer months, can lead to lengthy delays on this busy holiday route for tourists driving to the Dalmatian coast and beyond.

Back in Ljubljana, I had time to meet Stanka again. We had a drink on the terrace of a café overlooking the Ljubljanica river – one of those relaxing must-dos when in Ljubljana – and I told her about my experiences in Varaždin. Stanka is one of a small group of Slovenians who I'd first met during the noughties through FEIEA, the European federation of professional bodies for communication professionals. We had become friends over a period of time, meeting whenever our respective associations hosted conferences, awards ceremonies or meetings of the federation's council in Slovenia or the UK. We were of a similar age and we had our work experiences in common. Stanka had introduced me to her partner, the genial, accordion-playing Miro a few years earlier, they had met Liz and we all spent time together and got on well. With a little free time in Ljubljana it was natural for me to contact Stanka.

This would be truly just a flying visit, though. I had a plane to catch that evening from Ljubljana's modern but tiny airport at Brnik, which lies 20 miles to the north of the city. There's no train link but there are a couple of reasonably-priced and reliable shuttle services offered by competing companies. There was also the bus which serves a series of villages north of Ljubljana before terminating at the airport barely an hour later. For a fare of just €4, on my no-frills budget, that was to be my mode of travel to Brnik this time. I'd see a few of the country's neat, sub-alpine villages along the way, albeit by the light of streetlamps (it was late afternoon by now and the lamps along the Ljubljanica were already lighting up). The bus would also give me a chance to tune in to the background hubbub of Slovene conversation among the other passengers. My knowledge of the language was growing but it wasn't yet broad enough to leave me exposed to a charge of eavesdropping. I'd certainly be able to pick up on the cadences, the stresses and intonations, though, and, who knows? the occasional phrase here or there. Once again, this was more than a journey from A to B (or in this case from L to B), it was another experience to be enjoyed for itself. If only in my head, it was travel and not merely transfer. And so it proved.

I arrived at Brnik early, passed quickly through security and passport control, and holed up for an hour by the self-service café with a *sendvič*, a strudel, a beer and a book. There was a small delay to the incoming service but eventually my flight was called. I boarded, got as comfortable as I could within the limited personal space of a standard seat, and read my way back to Gatwick. Garish lights, a long queue at Immigration under the large and distinctly unwelcoming sign announcing that this was the UK BORDER, the shuttle to the airport's south side, then the train to London, where I was staying overnight. It was well after 11pm when the train pulled into Victoria station. I'd been up since 5am UK time and by now I was tired, but happy. It had been another fulfilling chapter in the unfolding story of a very personal challenge and now it was complete. Stage 12 was over. In four days I would be on my way to Ireland. After that, with barely a day in between to pack again, I'd be en route to Vienna for the start of Five Countries in Five Days. The pace of RUNNING: ME RUNNING EU was ramping up.

RUNNING: ME RUNNING EU

PART 2 | THE ACTUAL RUNNING PART

STAGE 13

Ireland – the Curragh, the Curragh!

SATURDAY/SUNDAY 9-10 FEBRUARY – 47 DAYS TO GO

February 8, 2019 1725 flight to Dublin. Delayed. Aer Lingus site still says it's on time (by now it is 1750). Mr Doswell looks in vain for information. Finally the flight is called and leaves at 1900. Takes ages for the transfer to reach the terminal in Dublin. Finally get through at 2040 so miss the 2030 coach to Newbridge. Next one's at 2130. Last week's 7-stage journey to Varaždin was easier than this one to the land of Mr Varadkar. But no worries: the real fun starts tomorrow.

I posted this from Dublin airport while waiting for the next coach to Newbridge, which would be my base for Stage 13. It was to be one of the highlights of the Challenge, one that gives me a warm glow even now, as I remember it after the passage of time, because of the welcome I received in Newbridge and the kindness of the people who looked after me there, and because of the beauty of the area known as the Curragh.

The story of the Ireland stage of RUNNING: ME RUNNING EU is also part of the story of a friendship spanning a national border and the Irish Sea, between two running clubs and their members. And perhaps like RUNNING: ME RUNNING EU itself, that friendship didn't just happen but came about because of a conscious decision to create a bond between runners, regardless of nationality.

At Bournville Harriers (BvH), our club chair Stacey had had the idea in 2016 to create a twinning link between BvH and a club in another country. Based on prior links that a couple of our members had with clubs in France and Ireland, Stacey sent a couple of messages to outline the idea of a link. The approach to the club in France proved to be a non-starter but the response from Newbridge Running Club was immediate, positive and enthusiastic. The town of Newbridge lies in County Kildare, about 30 miles south-west of Dublin. One of our members had been a

Newbridge runner before coming to Birmingham, so there was already a link. By 2017, Stacey's twinning link had become a reality and over the next couple of years the two clubs each hosted a visit by members of the other club, spending long weekends in Newbridge and Bournville respectively, the dates having been chosen so that members of both clubs could participate in local races taking place at those times. I'd missed the club tour to Newbridge but I'd taken part in a hot, hilly trail 10K over the demanding terrain at Cannock Chase when we'd hosted the Newbridge visit to Birmingham. I'd been happy to drive one of the Newbridge visitors back to Bournville afterwards and we'd had a decent chat during the hour-long journey. I'd gained a good impression of the other Newbridge runners, too, and it was a common view among the BvH members who'd spent time with them that the Newbridge people were great company. So once I started to plan the Irish stage of RUNNING: ME RUNNING EU, Newbridge came quickly to mind. I wrote a message on the Facebook group created for our joint endeavours, outlined what I had embarked upon and asked about potential races.

Dates were important as the schedule tightened and the deadline neared. Although decisions I'd taken and the change of work circumstances had given me added freedom to travel and more flexibility with time, races tend to be at weekends, especially during the darker months, and the law of calendars meant that there would be fewer race weekends as 29 March loomed into view. Again, life's hard-wired forward planners will probably read this through fingers clasped in a tense grip across their face. Why hadn't I planned this months ago? For those like me for whom a coloured spreadsheet is an item of bedding in a room you probably only remembered to book this morning, and certainly not something you would use to plan an adventure, the answer would be that thinking a few weeks ahead was as 'plan-ny' as it got. If everything is planned from row 1 to column J, where's the adventure or the room for happenstance? I'm not entirely serious about this – I do realise that even a colander has fewer holes than this approach. Things can go wrong when left to chance. Suppose there had been no races on the dates available, no seats left on the plane? All I can say is that it was often those late-in-the-day decisions that led to moments of joy during the challenge. Or perhaps it was simply relief that things worked out.

I heard back from Newbridge. Peter Moran confirmed that there would be a local 10K at Athgarvan on Sunday 10 February. If I arrived in time we could also run the parkrun on Saturday at Naas racecourse, which was nearby. I remembered Peter from the Newbridge visit to Birmingham. We'd spoken briefly at Cannock Chase, where the distinct green of Newbridge shirts had been prominent among the category winners – overall, as well as age and gender – collecting prizes at the end of a tough, demanding trail 10K race on a hot, sweaty, dusty summer's day in that Staffordshire forest.

As always, I spent time checking on various ways to get to Ireland and onwards to Newbridge, always mindful of cost. Given the choice, I'd always prefer to 'slum' it on travel rather than accommodation. Within a few weeks I would be testing this tolerance by spending part of the night in an insalubrious coach station. Coach travel itself, though, was fine. A train would have been even better. And indeed both travel by train or coach plus ferry crossings via Holyhead to Dublin were options for this trip in theory. I quite liked the idea of taking the train up through north Wales and crossing Brunel's famous bridge to Anglesey and then reaching Ireland by sea. However, the length of journey time and the timetable options were problematic. I could get there comfortably enough time-wise but I couldn't risk a delay on the return.

The Athgarvan 10K would take place on Sunday morning and I would have to try to get back later that day. I had a flight booked to Vienna less than 48 hours later and I couldn't afford to miss it – my plan to run five countries in five days depended on it. I found flights on Aer Lingus from Birmingham to Dublin, out on Friday, back on Sunday, both evening flights. There was an hourly coach service between Dublin airport and Newbridge. I could pay the driver. There were trains, too, but for those I'd have to get to the station in Dublin city. More time. I'd take the coach. Last piece of jigsaw: accommodation. I checked booking.com but Newbridge didn't seem to be big on hotels or guest houses and the options suggested on the site were mostly out of town. I tried Airbnb and found a room in a home on a residential estate just a short walk away from Newbridge town centre. The host was Francis, whose warm, characterful messages while I made the booking proved to be a true reflection of his hospitality and willingness to go out of his way to make me feel welcome.

I had slight misgivings as I boarded the Aer Lingus flight, but not because of the airline or the plane, at least not directly. The wind was strong enough to buffet me as I walked across the tarmac in a gaggle of passengers, each hunched against the gusts. The turbulent conditions had led to delays across the departure board at Birmingham airport. On top of what might well be an uncomfortable journey, we took off more than 90 minutes late. I was mainly concerned about the journey onwards to Newbridge and about arriving late at the Airbnb. In fact the flight was a bit bumpy at times but I'd experienced worse turbulence. Comfort was less of a problem than time. After touch-down it seemed to take an age before we taxied to the terminal doors and could disembark. I'd just missed a coach and would have to wait until 9.30pm for the next one. The wind was fierce and bitingly cold and the airport coach stop offered little shelter. Finally, a double-decker arrived. I checked, this was my coach, and with some relief I climbed up. I'd sent Francis a message via the Airbnb app but hadn't heard back. I didn't know if he knew I'd been delayed, Clearly he *would* know that I hadn't turned up at the expected time, even without seeing my message. Hopefully there wouldn't be a problem getting into the house at such a late hour. Peter was due to meet me there first thing next morning. We had Naas parkrun to run.

Newbridge stands on the Liffey, and the town's Saint Conleth gives his name to both a large church and the main bridge that straddles the river. Having tracked the journey from the airport on Google Maps, I left the coach and followed the app's suggested route to Francis's house. It was dark and overcast and the route seemed to lead me alongside some playing fields. Where the hell was this? I'm not easily spooked but I felt uneasy. Suddenly a featureless figure emerged from the darkness and moved towards me. I really wasn't convinced that this was going to turn out well. He came closer and then spoke: "Is it Steve? Hello, I'm Francis!"

He must have heard the startled tone in my voice. "Sorry to come at you in the darkness. I thought you might need help finding the house." More than relieved, I fell into step as he led the way. Within seconds we were at the front door and in less than ten minutes I'd been offered a nightcap, which I gladly accepted, and shown my room. I'd arrived.

Saturday was a pleasure from beginning to end. I was in County Kildare, horse-racing country. I'd heard of the Curragh, as famous to racing enthusiasts as our own Epsom or Cheltenham or Paris's Longchamp. I'd heard the race results from Leopardstown and Ponchestown, but I'd never heard of Naas. Consequently, when Peter came to collect me, I hadn't realised that on that bright, breezy Saturday morning, we'd be running parkrun around a racecourse.

The usual parkrun signage and hi-viz volunteer vests, the familiar pre-run briefing, delivered with an easy-going warmth and humour, and then the run – two and a half laps around the course. The going was firm. It would be – we were runners, not horses – running on a mostly flat tarmac access path that borders the racecourse itself. It remained windy but with less intensity than the day before. I crossed the line in 23:52, 47th out of 202 runners. No records broken but it made a change to finish inside the first 25% of finishers. Peter introduced me to the run director and told her about my running challenge. I elaborated and from this she learned that I had not voted to leave the EU, a detail that she noted with apparent enthusiasm. Ireland had joined the EU in 1973 along with the UK and Denmark. The social, cultural and economic ties between Britain and Ireland are close, rich and dense, even though the historical relationship has been chequered and sometimes deeply troubled. The UK's move to leave the EU had perplexed the Irish and the uncertainty about what it will mean in future is unsettling for a country whose economy is closely linked to the UK's. Independently of Brexit, Irish citizens have the right to live, work, study and travel freely in Britain, and vice versa. This right pre-dates both countries' membership of the EU by half a century – Britain and Ireland signed their Common Travel Area agreement in 1923.

So much for the history, although I was about to learn a little more, thanks to Peter, my guide for the morning. As we drove out of Naas racecourse I assumed we'd be straight back to Newbridge. Peter runs a business and has a family. He would have other demands on his time. Happily, though, it turned out that there was time for coffee in an independent café in Naas. We chatted – about work, about family, running, Ireland. Peter mentioned the Curragh. I said I'd like to see it. Within the hour we were back on the road, heading past Newbridge and up onto wide open grassy upland plains. It was remote, imposing, beautiful – the Curragh. It occupies nearly 5,000 acres, slightly more than five Glastonburys put together (imagine the scale of that as a festival…).

Peter pointed out the grandstand of the area's famous racecourse in the distance. Soon we drove through an extensive complex of military buildings. This was the Curragh Camp, an army base and the main training centre for the Irish Defence Forces. The Curragh Camp was built by the British Imperial army in the mid-19th century as part of its preparations for the Crimean War, although the area's history as a place of assembly for armies is centuries old. Close by, the Commonwealth War Graves Commission maintains a cemetery in memory of soldiers based at the Curragh Camp who had served and died in the First World War. The graves are dotted around the Curragh's characteristically gentle, grassy undulations, watched over by lone, tall, sentinel trees.

After the impromptu tour, Peter dropped me back. I strolled around Newbridge, bought lunch en route, then headed three miles back on foot to the Curragh. I found something captivating in its wide, green vistas and spent a couple of hours there, walking, standing, gazing in all directions across the wide open landscape and appreciating the sense of being a tiny speck in a great panorama. The passing of distant horses and riders as the shadows lengthened only added to the magic of the place as I lingered a little longer. The Curragh had a brooding presence and I noted that, beyond its evident beauty on a bright day under a big sky, this would be nowhere to get caught alone without shelter in bad weather. It would soon be sunset and, much though I wanted to see how the sky would change as night fell, it would be an hour before I would reach Francis's house again – and I had plans for the evening. Peter and some of the other Newbridge runners who I hoped to remember from their visit to Bournville had invited me for a few drinks in a pub in town. With spirits high I headed back.

The evening lived up to expectations. I had slight misgivings that this would become a real 'session'. A hangover would not be the best start to a day of running and travel. Happily Saturday night in Newbridge turned into a calm but warm, friendly, funny couple of hours with lots of stories shared and laughter sparked at various points by one or another of the half dozen of us propping up the bar of a large town centre pub full of character. I recognised a couple of faces from the Newbridge club visit to Birmingham and was happy to meet one of the club members, Steven, again. He'd been the Newbridge runner I'd given a lift back to Birmingham after the Cannock Chase race which had been my introduction to the Newbridge crew. As we'd chatted on that hour's journey back, a sense of a bond between our clubs had been seeded for me. It was good to renew the acquaintance. By the end of this latest encounter, I was able to walk back to Francis's house, warmed by the evening's conviviality and fortified by the beer against the night's chill.

The chill continued overnight and found me shivering in a Bournville Harriers teal vest and shorts as we started the Athgarvan Community 10K the next morning. Peter had driven us the short distance to a local school on the edge of the Curragh which that Sunday morning served as the race HQ. Nearly 400 runners lined up, with 115 ready to run 10K, the majority opting for the 5K race. Once out and away, the starting pack quickly stretched into a long thread up and onto the Curragh. Having admired this landscape first from a car and then during the previous day's walk, I was now experiencing its contours while pushing forward in a race. I wasn't going flat out but I didn't dawdle. I saw the usual multi-coloured ribbon of running colours moving ahead of me. Among them I recognised the distinct green of the Newbridge club livery, the most well-represented club in these combined 5/10K races.

Newbridge's history as an athletics club spans the best part of a century. It has a strong performance record in all age groups and formats from juniors to veterans and from track events through the range of road race distances to cross-country. No surprise, then, that the morning's results would feature Newbridge runners among the top ten men and women at both 5K and 10K, including both the first-placed woman and man at 10K. The lone Bournville Harrier vest crossed the line in 52:30, comfortably unnoticed in the middle of the pack. A finisher's medal and technical top (a taupe body with rose-pink sleeve trim) were welcome mementos from Stage 13 of RUNNING: ME RUNNING EU. The sponsor's name on the back of the shirt – Horses Ireland – would stir strong, positive memories of my time at Newbridge and out on the Curragh long into the future.

My time in Newbridge was nearing its end. I would fly home that evening. I planned to take the train to Dublin and look around Ireland's capital before finding my way to the airport. With customary kindness, Peter insisted that he would drive me to the Red Cow transport interchange on Dublin's outskirts to make my journey easier and increase the time I would have to look around the city. In the end he drove me all the way to the city centre, dropping me within the shadow of Dublin Castle. This was way beyond the call of duty and certainly wasn't expected. I really appreciated it and thanked Peter for being so generous with his time.

Now on foot again I was keen to explore Dublin and also to find the bus stop from where I would make my onward journey to the airport. But first I had to eat. I quickly found a small Italian restaurant that looked ideal. It was lunchtime and the place was busy. I didn't have long to wait to catch the manager's attention but it wasn't as I'd planned it. Dropping my backpack from my shoulders I leaned back momentarily against a wall, which turned out to be a free-standing partition not intended to take my weight. With a crash the partition gave way and I fell to the floor with a clatter. Now I had the manager's attention. The lunchtime hubbub was stilled as dozens of diners turned to stare. There were a few smiles. Fortunately the fixture and I were equally undamaged. Bemused, the manager helped me to my feet and found me a table – clearly it would be safer all round to get me seated and fed. The restaurant quickly returned to its previous bustle. I was slightly embarrassed but mostly amused. No harm done.

There's a lot to see in Dublin, but I was content just to go with the flow and wander through narrow lanes around monuments and along the banks of the Liffey, crossing bridges, joining the throng, people-watching, just enjoying free time. It was cold, though. I found the Custom House Quay area, Dublin's docklands development of shops, bars, restaurants, with an indoor plaza and the museum of emigration. It was an inviting prospect to be back in the warmth. I hung around there for a while before heading out to find my bus. I realised that I hadn't even begun to do Dublin justice. I would return.

My flight home was on time and uneventful. Stage 13 had been rewarding. I'd run in Ireland (twice), renewed old acquaintances, made new ones, helped renew ties of friendship between Newbridge and BvH. I'd enjoyed the beauty of the Curragh and seen something of Dublin. Altogether not a bad couple of days. There would be time to savour them again in future. But not now. From a map perspective, with 13 of 28 stages complete, I was almost at the half-way stage of RUNNING: ME RUNNING EU in terms of countries. The calendar view added more than a dash of urgency. I'd started back in April 2018. Over ten months had passed. I was already almost half-way through February and the challenge deadline was waiting for me on the next page of the calendar: 29 March. 11pm to be precise, and I might need every hour of that final day. Meanwhile, the very next phase was going to be fast-moving and intense, which was just as well – I had 47 days left in which to run in 15 countries.

FB post 11 Feb Preps for RUNNING: ME RUNNING EU's week in central Europe. As well as #DFYB and #DFYP, it's also #DFYK for Czech Rep + #DFYZ for Poland. Happily Austria + Slovakia use the euro and one card covers that (I'll be shuttling in and out of Hungary so decided to forego a fistful of Forint). In case anyone thinks I'm currency trafficking, total value of the banknotes: £82.50.

PART 2 | THE ACTUAL RUNNING PART

STAGES 14-18

Five days, five countries: a short tour of the Habsburg lands in Hokas

TUESDAY 12 FEBRUARY – 45 DAYS TO GO
STAGE 14 – VIENNA; A FROSTY RECEPTION

I'm going to talk about my quick five-run medley in Mitteleuropa. But first, a few thoughts about kit and clothing... By the time I flew to Vienna, I'd learned to condense my luggage needs into a small rucksack that with a squeeze would fit under the seat beside my feet to comply with any of the European low-cost carriers' ever more restrictive baggage limits. I often booked one-way flights to take advantage of competing carriers' fare deals. Sometimes I'd fly back from a different city to the one I'd travelled out to. Either way, I had to apply a lowest denominator rule – outbound I might be offered the luxury of a bigger bag or a few more kilos. On the return, though, the limits may be tighter. Packing became a matter of careful calculation. What was the least I could get away with? In warmer months it would have been easier to wash a few things while away. But this was winter. As it was, I'd have to try to wash my running kit and hope the radiators in the modest rooms I'd booked en route were up to the job of drying things out before I had to pack them again. When setting out for 'Five countries in five days' I packed and dressed in a format that would set the pattern for the rest of the challenge.

We've all heard about people who try to take as much away on holiday hand luggage only by wearing several outfits at once on the flight. I did much the same but kept it within reasonable limits: a couple of t-shirts, then a jumper, then a zip-up hoodie. On top of those, a black Gore-Tex, North Face zip-up top with a retractable hood. This offered absolutely zero warmth (the layers beneath were meant to provide that, together with a beanie and a scarf) but it was waterproof and offered four spacious pockets into which I crammed so much that I could free up precious space in my one piece of hand luggage – my faithful small Ljubljana Marathon backpack for my Hoka One hybrid running shoes, a pair of Brooks road shoes, a couple of running tops, shorts and an old London Marathon running jacket – ultralightweight but with at least an added layer of protection against a cold continental European climate at the tail-end of winter. Some fruit. A bag of nuts and raisins. There wasn't room for much else except essential toiletries in a sealable see-through bag on top to be shown at airport security. Into the North Face jacket went a paperback, notebook, pen, Garmin watch, wallet and sundry other bits and pieces. Passport, phone, credit card and any emergency cash (euros or other local currency) all went in a running belt that I wore at all times except when in my room – and even then it was never far from my sight. By the end of the challenge and a long sequence of packing, unpacking and repacking over and over again, I knew where everything was and exactly which item went where. It felt like living in a shell. It also made life simple.

When travelling I wore a pair of walking shoes that I'd first bought for hiking in the mountains of Slovenia three years earlier. They were worn-in, well-padded and durable. They kept my feet warm and dry. Job done. I made compromises with some of the clothing I took but not with footwear. My choice of kit and clothing was practical. There were no frills. I travelled light. The focus was on the challenge, everything that I would need to complete it – and only that. I'd heard Olympic double gold medallist Steve Williams speak at a conference years beforehand about the British rowing team's highly influential coach Jürgen Gröbler. Jürgen had been single-minded. He made sure the boat had everything on board to make the team go faster but nothing that wouldn't help. Steve had brought his gold medals from the Athens and Beijing Olympics to the conference and these were passed around the room like holy relics. Athens would be a stage in my story, too, although my own challenge was hardly Olympian. But I had a purpose, too, and I was going to achieve it as efficiently as I could.

I'd got back from Dublin on Sunday night. I flew to Vienna on Tuesday evening, arriving around 10pm at Schwechat airport. I'd been to Vienna a couple of times before. I fumbled with the ticket machine for the train and paid for my journey to the industrial district of Simmering. I planned to get to my accommodation, change and run immediately. My schedule over the next two days would be very tight. The next day I hoped to meet an old colleague, Birgit, then take a train to Győr in Hungary, run again, then return to Vienna simply to change trains and head out again immediately, this time to Bratislava, the Slovak capital, and run yet again before getting a late train back to Vienna. Early the next morning I would need to be on my way by coach to Brno in the Czech Republic, and the following day onwards to Katowice in Poland before flying directly home. RUNNING: ME RUNNING EU was in full swing.

I wasn't feeling my best, though. The challenge was possibly beginning to take a physical toll. I was coughing and felt shivery, with a temperature. In my running commentary (a good title for a blog but already taken) on Facebook I joked ruefully about spreading germs across five countries. Barely a year later we would be in lockdown because of Covid and by then no one would have seen any humour in that observation. In fact the challenge itself would have been impossible. For that, and because of the political event which first sparked the need in me to embark on the challenge, RUNNING: ME RUNNING EU was a product of its time.

When I emerged from the train onto a dark, deserted platform at Simmering, I was already calculating options. Conditions were near freezing, the temperature down to two degrees and the pavements glistening with frost in places. I briefly considered postponing the run until the morning but there really was no slack in the schedule. I would simply have to run that night as planned. A 20-minute walk brought me to the Actilingua Aparthotel, an old art nouveau building whose shadowy interior vaguely recalled a setting from *The Third Man*, an atmospheric black-and-white film famously set in the dark, drab stairways, streets and ruins of early post-war Vienna. As far as I could gather, the building now served mainly as a hostel for language students. I'd found it via booking.com, my trusted source for accommodation. It was 3-star, simple, clean and perfectly serviceable for me and at £81 it was cheap for Vienna at that time.

The concierge seemed cautious about this foreigner of a certain age speaking German with a heavy accent, checking in quite late in the evening. She was 'correct' in her manner, not quite curt. It certainly wasn't the warmth of Newbridge. I half-listened to her spiel about keys, outer doors, etc., but really wanted to get changed and run. Or rather, I didn't. I felt rough and just wanted to go to bed. I gritted my teeth, though, got ready and headed out towards Vienna city centre, letting Google Maps guide me back past the station where I'd arrived barely an hour before, onwards past the Belvedere and the Albertina art galleries, to the wide open expanse of Schwarzenbergplatz and the grand, imperial architecture for which Vienna is famous. I recognised the 'House of Industry', where

I'd once attended a meeting of FEIEA as the UK representative (I doubt there's a plaque…). A couple of minutes later I crossed the Ring, the avenue that encircles the heart of Vienna and made my way to the city's pedestrianised core, to Kärntnerstrasse with its high-end stores.

Even at this hour the area was busy, the gleam of affluent shopfronts and the warm glow of street lights contrasting with the icy darkness away from the lamps and glass. The well-heeled, sumptuously wrapped denizens of Vienna matched the smart surroundings and I realised that I cut an odd, incongruous figure, running past them clad in shorts and a skimpy running jacket, clearly under-dressed for two degrees on a late midweek evening in February. There were no other runners around. Clearly this wasn't the time or place for it. Vienna has acres of parks and riverside promenades along the Danube and in other circumstances that's where I might have run. I was nearly at 6K since I'd left the language hostel. I'd reach 10K at least by the time I got back. I also had to eat. Once I reached Stephansdom, Vienna's cathedral of St Stephan, I turned round and retraced my steps, still running, until I reached the hostel. After a piping hot shower (bliss!) and a quick change I went back out, found a traditional wood-panelled weinhaus nearby still serving food (just) and gorged on wurst, sauerkraut and noodles with a dark beer from the barrel – the Austrian equivalent of good, honest grub. Once fed, I didn't linger. I'd need to be up and out early the next morning. After meeting Birgit I'd be off to Hungary.

PART 2 | THE ACTUAL RUNNING PART

STAGE 15

Györ: city of rivers

WEDNESDAY 13 FEBRUARY – 44 DAYS TO GO

Another grey, chilly morning dawned and after a brief, functional breakfast I was soon back out onto the street. I walked across a housing estate towards some striking cylindrical domed structures in the mid-distance. This was Gasometer, a district built up around some former city gasholders, now converted into shops, apartments and businesses. I found the local station and caught the U-Bahn into the centre. A few minutes later I was sitting in a traditional Viennese café, failing in my first attempt to order "einen Kaffee, bitte". Birgit smiled. "This is Vienna. You'll have to be more specific!" she said, pointing to a menu with about 40 different varieties of coffee.

I'd first met Birgit during an earlier, happy time in my career when we'd both been part of FEIEA, first representing our national organisations and later, both becoming president of the federation, as Birgit had been when I first became involved in FEIEA almost 20 years earlier. From those days I remembered Birgit's late husband Alexander as a larger-than-life character with a fine singing voice, who would break into song at the slightest pretext. His death after a long debilitating illness had brought great sadness into Birgit's life but in time she had adjusted, as people do.

Music was important to Birgit herself and I remember her impressing a few colleagues including me with an impromptu performance on a district church organ on another occasion when FEIEA's twice-yearly Council meeting had taken place in Vienna. We spoke of former colleagues and updated each other on news about those we had stayed in touch with. Inevitably the subject of Brexit came up. I made a point of never dwelling on it unless others wanted to discuss it, beyond a brief explanation of the role it played in prompting me to embark on my charity challenge. When they did, it was often to express their own confusion about why so many people had chosen to reject the EU. In such conversations I tried to explain and to give a balanced view, while making my own feelings clear. I did again here, but only briefly, because there were more interesting things to catch up on and time was short. Too short, in fact. All too quickly I had to say goodbye to Birgit and headed to the Hauptbahnhof, the central station, and bought my tickets, first for Győr and later for Bratislava.

There has always been something mysterious and romantic for me in seeing foreign destinations on railway departure boards. I feel this far less at airports. I've always found something fascinating about being aboard trains approaching frontiers, crossing them and seeing the language and signage change. It isn't necessarily about distance, though. Indeed, I'd planned the current phase of the challenge around being in Vienna precisely because I knew I could get from there to Hungary and Slovakia very easily. I'd done quite a bit of research on the borders between Austria and its two eastern neighbours. At one point I'd considered taking the train to Bratislava, then running to the Hungarian border, barely 11 miles away. However, the frontier at this point ran down the middle of a country lane and I had no idea how feasible it would be to run along it. One thing I had clear in my mind and that was not to spend any more time in Hungary than I needed to.

Of all the EU member states, Hungary stood out for its illiberal policies, politicising of the judiciary and anti-LGBT stance. Before I'd embarked on the challenge, I'd decided that I would wait for more liberal times to return before visiting Hungary. Once I'd created RUNNING: ME RUNNING EU, though, a visit to Hungary became essential. Maybe merely crossing the Slovak-Hungarian border briefly for a few hundred metres along the country lane would suffice to fulfil the terms of the challenge. In the end I decided that it wouldn't be enough, although I wouldn't linger. I would catch a train to a town in Hungary, run around it, then return. And that's how I found Győr, the city of rivers.

Take the train the 150 miles from Vienna to the Hungarian capital Budapest and almost exactly half-way there you'll reach Győr, just 35 miles beyond the Austrian border. It stands at the confluence of two rivers which then flow into the Danube nearby. It's Hungary's sixth largest city with a population of 129,000, making it only slightly larger than a town like Cheltenham. Less than an hour and a half after leaving Vienna, I was changing into my running kit on a bench outside Győr station, trying not to look too conspicuous, although this wasn't easy as men in their 60s wearing running shorts didn't seem to be a thing in Győr at that time. A couple of passers-by gave a quick, slightly quizzical glance in my direction but this was early afternoon in the middle of a working day and no doubt most people had daily concerns on their mind. After a quick check of the map I trotted a short distance down to the old town and ran a couple of circuits around Győr's pedestrianised core.

I was struck by how attractive the city's buildings were. Several had the white or yellow-ochre facades that I'd seen elsewhere in the former Habsburg lands. It reminded me slightly of Varaždin in Croatia. A large basilica stood out, not just for its imposing structure and decoration. Its Hungarian name Nagyboldogasszony-székesegyház would have given me no clues whatsoever. I later discovered that it would broadly translate as 'Our Lady of the Assumption'. The Hungarian language is mysterious, even to linguists. Nothing in common with the German, Romanian or various Slavonic tongues spoken in Hungary's neighbouring countries, the roots of modern-day Hungarian are now thought to lie much further east, in Siberia. It has some links with Finnish, apparently. As a student of languages this stuff fascinates me, but faced with this briefest of encounters with Hungarian I remained in almost total ignorance. However, I wasn't there to read street names, menus or inscriptions.

I ran onwards to the river bank and stopped to take in the panorama of the two rivers coming together to my left and some of the striking architecture behind me. I was conscious of time, though and didn't linger. From the moment I'd arrived, I would be in Győr for little more than 90 minutes before the train back to Vienna. I continued to run around the pedestrian lanes. A modern concrete structure caught my eye. It reminded me of the South Bank in London, a complex of theatres and concert halls. Indeed, this was the National Theatre of Győr. I decided that it would make a good backdrop for a photo and asked a passing student (I assumed he was and it was true) to take my picture with the Ljubljana Marathon backpack as a prop. He asked me if I was visiting Győr as a tourist. I gave him the 10-second standard introduction to RUNNING: ME RUNNING EU. I'm not sure if he understood, but he smiled amiably. I thanked him and ran on, away from the old city and back to the station.

While in Győr, I'd run for just over 7K. It wasn't much, but I'd met my own criteria for the challenge. The Vienna train arrived on time and once on board, I decided to give myself time to cool down before carrying out a discreet costume change. At first there was almost no one else on the train. Minutes later, it stopped again, the platform thronging with schoolkids. My almost empty carriage was quickly decked out in the international uniform of adolescents everywhere. This was going home from school time, a mid-afternoon scene no doubt being replicated in trains and buses across Europe and beyond. And here in Hungary, I now had an audience. Conscious of looking dishevelled and under-dressed, I decided that the rising generation of Hungarian youth had no need to see an ageing Englishman's sweaty limbs and varicose veins, quickly pulled on my tracksuit bottoms and zip-up hoody, and gazed out of the window.

The train reached Hegyeshalom, its final halt in Hungary, and crossed back into Austria. No fanfare, no passport control. No faff. Just another stage of the challenge complete. Shortly afterwards the sweeping highways, distribution depots and other paraphernalia found on the outskirts of a major city came into view. This was Vienna again.

PART 2 | THE ACTUAL RUNNING PART

STAGE 16

Don't panic, it's just the Paneláky of Petržalka

STILL WEDNESDAY 13 FEBRUARY – 44 DAYS TO GO

There are two train lines linking Vienna with Bratislava. The cities are just 35 miles apart and the journey only takes an hour. I decided to set foot in Slovakia by arriving in Bratislava's southern suburbs, then run towards the centre, cross the Danube to the Slovakian capital's historic heart and eventually return via Bratislava's main station. I was slightly apprehensive. I would be heading to Petržalka. While doing the research and travel-planning for the trip, I'd read a lot about Petržalka, this vast complex of high-rise housing estates built south of the Danube. I'd seen the photos. They seemed to confirm the worst impressions of communist-era urban planning – a continuous district of ugly *paneláky*, panel-constructed concrete tower blocks. Petržalka also had a reputation for crime. I realised that media commentators love to mythologise the 'tough' image of certain districts of big cities. But heading to Bratislava via Petržalka first made sense. That way, I would arrive on an earlier train and by the time I'd run to the banks of the Danube, crossed the bridge and run through the old town and out to the central station, I'd manage 10K. Petržalka it would be. I'd go there eyes wide open, stay street-savvy, and not give in to the paranoia.

The train partly retraced the route I'd taken back from Györ, then swung north-east, crossing rich, flat farmland. The green, rural vista stretched for mile after mile, only occasionally broken as we passed a small village. Then I saw it in the distance – one moment fields, the next, tower blocks. The change was sudden and stark. With the border nearing, Petržalka loomed large. No sooner had we crossed into Slovakia and the low-horizon countryside had become the high-rise city.

I left the train and walked down a boulevard hemmed in by tall blocks. It was dusk and the few people I could see were hunched against the cold, collars up. In normal circumstances this would have been a time to conjure some quilted, full-length coat from my Tardis-like Bournville Harriers daypack. It was a moment's wishful thinking. Instead, by a large, featureless patch of waste ground I stopped, *removed* my outer layers (nothing quilted there), stuffed them into the pack, hitched it back onto my shoulders and began to run. Again, as in Vienna, and as in Györ, there were no other runners. On Google Maps I'd seen a multi-lane highway that seemed to run parallel to the Danube. On the map, the route seemed to suggest that I'd need to climb onto a wide arc of a footbridge. It seemed a roundabout way of getting to the foot of the big bridge over the Danube, which was my next objective. Fatigued and still unwell, I clearly wasn't thinking straight at this point, because the footbridge was the *only* way across the highway.

Abandoning logic, I ignored the map and headed directly over flat ground, crossed a side road and quickly found my way blocked by a high fence separating me from several lanes of traffic travelling at high speed in both directions across my path. I cursed myself for being dense. Of course I wasn't simply going to be able to stroll or even run across a motorway, not at the heavy-lorry-hits-stupid-human level. I had to retrace my steps to that footbridge. I doubled back and found the start of the bridge, headed up and over it, crossing the rapid flow of traffic and made my way down on the far side towards a park. This was dark and not somewhere I would have normally chosen to be, least of all in an unfamiliar city after dark. However, I did spot another person dressed as I was passing at speed. This lifted my spirits. There were now two runners in Petržalka!

Ahead of me I could now see the buttress of a huge, heavy piece of civil engineering, its powerful legs planted in the park. The pillars towered over me. Perched on top was what appeared to be a flying saucer. This was the observation platform here on the Petržalka side of the snappily titled Bridge of the Slovak National Uprising; known simply as the New Bridge, although in view of the observation platform, some also call it the UFO.

I find big feats of engineering quite awe-inspiring. They can also be elegant (I'm a fan of a concrete curve on London's Westway, admittedly not everyone's idea of an objet d'art). The New Bridge is both. It's apparently the world's longest single pylon bridge with a single cable supporting the bridge deck, as I found out later. It wasn't the kind of obscure fact that came to mind as I climbed the steps on a cold February night to run across the Danube. Still, it's worth noting for any fans of bridges who might be reading this. It was the second noteworthy bridge that I'd crossed while completing the challenge, after the Øresund bridge linking Copenhagen and Malmö on New Year's Day. Final factoid which amused me when I read it: Bratislava's New Bridge is apparently "a member of the World Federation of Great Towers". There's a club or association for everything, which possibly serves as a reminder that everything and everyone needs to feel part of something bigger than themselves. Even bridges, it seems.

I knew none of these details before climbing up to the pedestrian deck and trotting onwards, high up above the dark, wide waters of the Danube. I felt tiny, a lone figure completely out of scale with the towering construction looming behind me, the bridge itself and Europe's second longest river below. Ahead, though, were the beckoning lights of Bratislava's Stare Mesto, the old city. As I passed the river's midpoint and the far riverbank got closer, I could also see the outline of Bratislava Castle on a hilltop to the left. Once on the city side and with the river behind me, I descended some steps to the riverside promenade and suddenly I was running alongside more familiar, central European architecture, back amid human-scale surroundings again. Paved pedestrian squares, cobblestones, soft, warm glowing light from traditional streetlamps and the presence of people going about their evening activities suddenly felt reassuring, almost a return to civilisation. The bars and restaurants looked very inviting and I made another mental note to return one day with time to spare and more presentable clothing than a pair of running shorts and a skimpy Bournville Harriers top.

I made my way through the old city, circling back a couple of times to find one of Bratislava's curiosities, Čumil (The Watcher) – a bronze statue of a helmeted sewer-worker peering cheerily out from a manhole cover. The old city has a few statues and sculptures but, as with Čumil, they would be best visited during daylight and at leisure. At this point I had neither. Pleasingly, the old city's subdued lighting brings a gentle, comforting, enclosing atmosphere to the small squares and narrow, interconnecting lanes. In some urban environments heading up into the shadows might seem forbidding. Here, the soft glow of the lamps on a crisp February evening offered a safer, much more welcoming contrast with the harsher cityscape that I'd run through on the other side of the river and the almost overpowering scale of the bridge.

Conscious of time, I stopped only briefly to check my directions, before beginning a gentle ascent away from the historic heart of the city towards the central station. At the entrance to the station building I quickly pulled out my track suit bottoms, running club hoody and London Marathon jacket. The jacket had been a consolation prize that I'd received after being unsuccessful in the ballot for places for the big running event in my home city, and one of the biggest in the world where demand outstrips capacity by around seven to one. I'd donated my entry fee to charity and received the jacket in return. Feeling warmer and more suitably clad for the journey, I entered Bratislava Central station with just a few minutes to wait before the train back to Vienna.

In my mind I'd imagined that a rather grand Trans Europe Express type train would be required to cross an international frontier and connect two capital cities. In fact within 15 minutes a more modest but perfectly clean, modern regional train pulled in, run by the Austrian railway company ÖBB, which is the big player in the region. I was hungry and had hoped to buy something to eat before boarding but at that hour there was little to be found at the station's rather underwhelming facilities, a small kiosk which wouldn't accept a card payment, while my current holding of euros amounted to just enough to buy a bottle of water and a small packet of peanuts. Better than nothing, though, and I wasn't worried. I would be eating in Vienna before long. Much more importantly, I'd now run for the third time in just under 24 hours, and in three countries. The latest run from Petržalka across the bridge and through the historic heart of Bratislava to the station had been for just over five miles. Not far, but it had added to my growing scrapbook of experiences, sights and impressions – quality rather than quantity. And now Stage 16 was done.

The return journey took just over an hour, a little longer than scheduled as the train seemed to wait for some time on the approach to Vienna's gleaming showcase of a central station. I was impatient to be off the train and onwards to my next rendezvous. Doris was another former colleague from the FEIEA days. Sharp-witted, playful and amusing, and with a great sense of personal style, Doris had always been entertaining company during the long meetings with European colleagues and the dinners and receptions that had offered a sometimes incongruous mix of formality and folk entertainment. I'd contacted her shortly before arriving in Vienna and we'd arranged to meet, albeit briefly.

I'd warned her that I would be dressed very casually and would be 'fresh' from the day's running, so no elegant Viennese venues, please. By the time I reached the bistro-style restaurant Doris had suggested, it was later than planned and the kitchen was shortly to close. I ordered swiftly: Wiener

Schnitzel. No prizes for originality but I didn't regret the choice. Ditto the Grűner Veltliner wine. We caught up on our news. I told her about Running: Me Running EU. Again, like Birgit that morning and others before, Doris was keen to understand what had led to Brexit. We discussed it a little but soon returned to other, more entertaining topics. And in that way 90 very relaxing minutes passed quickly. All too soon it was time to say goodbye.

I headed to the U-Bahn, made my way back to Gasometer station, took the slightly daunting walk across the dark, lonely housing estate – no loitering, eyes alert – and returned to the hostel. It was midnight. I set my phone alarm for 7am. I was due on a coach to the Czech Republic at 9am.

RUNNING: ME RUNNING EU

STAGE 17

Brno – Checking out Czechia's second city

THURSDAY 14 FEBRUARY – 43 DAYS TO GO

I could have checked out without seeing the rather frosty concierge again. The room was pre-paid, I'd consumed nothing at the hostel, there was no need for any kind of inter-action. But still… It seemed wrong to leave without some sort of acknowledgement that all was well and now I was going. I saw her just as I was about to drop the key in the box. I said I was off. "Did you go out at night to run?" she asked. I was surprised. I hadn't realised that she'd noticed. I said that I had and in a brief moment where the next word could simply have been "Auf Wiedersehen," I added a short explanation of my purpose in Vienna, about five countries in five days, about Running: Me Running EU. Suddenly it was as though someone had turned the heating up several notches. Immediately her manner warmed. She smiled and told me that what I was doing was really good. With that endorsement, a hearty farewell (such a contrast to the icy greeting on arrival) and "Good luck!" to spur me on, I headed out for the short, 20-minute walk to where the next stage would begin.

Vienna International Bus Terminal (VIB). The first two words convey a sense of grandeur and prestige. The second pair, less so. Nonetheless I was expecting something smarter than the reality of VIB. Certainly not the grimmest transport interchange of its type that I visited during the challenge (for that, see Stage 20, and the location may surprise you – unless you've also been there, in which case it's probably already on your lips). Another benefit: VIB wasn't far from the hostel. In fact I'd chosen my accommodation partly for that reason. Increasingly, as I approached the business end of the challenge, I was beginning to think more like a project planner, connecting the 'dependencies' of one stage of the journey with the next and considering my use of time carefully.

Time. I was six weeks out from 29 March with 12 countries still to get to and run in. There's nothing like knowing a precious asset is in short supply to make you start using it carefully. That's a generalisation. Maybe other people do pay more heed to time. I tended not to, although I'd already passed that point in my middle years when a sense of the future being endless began to change. Time isn't limitless. In fact, as Mark Twain once said about land, they're not making it any more (there may be another view about time but theoretical physics is way beyond the scope of this tale).

What is worth noting is that by this point in my life I now had a vague sense of personal mortality that may have also played a part in spurring me on to take on this challenge. However, no such thoughts of life's finite span were in my mind as I checked out of the hostel with the concierge's warm, friendly well-wishing and "Gute Fahrt!" adding to my sense of wellbeing on that cold grey morning. I walked the easy mile to Erdberg and the VIB. In place of grandeur and prestige I found a very basic collection of bus stands below a flyover. I'd booked the next leg of the journey with FlixBus, the German-owned fast-growing, 'EasyJet' of coach travel which in early 2019 hadn't yet extended its network to the UK (it has now). And fairly promptly soon after 9am I was comfortably on board the distinctive lime green-liveried FlixBus service to Brno as it climbed onto the A23 motorway, crossed the long, narrow island which divides the two branches of the Danube flowing through Vienna and headed almost directly north towards the Czech border.

From Vienna to Brno is just over 80 miles, comparable to the journey from Manchester to Birmingham or London to Dover. Unlike those familiar places, I had no mental picture of Brno and had never visited the Czech Republic, or Czechia as it is now coming to be known. I knew something of its journey from communism to democracy, of the role of Vaclav Havel, the playwright who became a president, in the dissident movement that led to the so-called Velvet Revolution in 1989, that amazing year of change in Europe, and the velvet divorce that quickly followed, when Czechoslovakia's two nations had separated peacefully into two independent republics. I'd even studied that episode of recent history ten years earlier during my 'midlife (no) crisis' return to university. I'd written an essay about why the Czechs and Slovaks had agreed to go their separate ways so peacefully, while Yugoslavia had disintegrated with such violence. Different countries, different circumstances, different personalities and personal agendas.

Flixbus dropped me at Brno's transport hub, a railway station, bus terminal, a spaghetti of tramlines and a small swarm of taxis. I didn't need any of those, though. There in front of me, with its wide 19th century façade, was Brno's four-star Grand Hotel. In case anyone infers that I'd thrown the budget out, I should say that I'd paid just £63 for the pleasure of staying here. As with other better-value bookings I made during the challenge, not staying in prime tourist destinations brought decent accommodation within my budget. Prague is practically the European capital of weekend breaks but far fewer people visit Brno, although it's certainly worthy of visitors' time, as I found. And because I was in town midweek in mid-February and the Grand Hotel was far from busy, I discovered that my £63 outlay had given me a mini-suite with a separate bedroom and sitting room. I struggled to get *The Grand Hotel Budapest* film out of my mind and while Brno's hotel of a similar name didn't match that screen creation for its lavish cream and pastel interiors, it still had an air of faded, old-empire grandeur about it.

It was lunchtime. I was hungry. But I knew the light would fade from mid-afternoon. I decide to run first, shower, eat, then explore the city a little. I unpacked my running kit, still damp from the inadequate time I'd had to rinse and dry it on the hostel radiator back in Vienna (the 'grand' in the Brno hotel's name certainly didn't reflect this newly arrived member of its clientele). Once togged up ready for a cool blast of a stiff mid-February breeze in Brno, I headed out, ignoring the faintest of quizzical glances from the staff on the reception desk as I passed. Once outside I decided to make the spiral climb that would take me to Špilberk Castle, Brno's most noteworthy landmark which stands on a rock above the old city. This is a well-preserved medieval fortress, its off-white walls and red tiles typifying the defensive architecture of central Europe. I skirted the base of the hill and reached a small, well laid-out park, which provided a perfect visual setting for a prominent, elegant 1960s building that clearly served some cultural purpose. I learned that this was the Janaćek Theatre, part of the Czech National Theatre, Brno's opera house, which also stages ballet and other artistic performances.

I found the entrance to the grounds which surround the castle and began to climb the hill. It was reasonably steep and challenging enough. Half-way up I stopped to take in the view across the city and out to the countryside in the semi-distance. From my Facebook post later that day:

> "Stephen at Špilberk. Just run to the top of this bloody hill. Near-death experience as lungs are still wheezing like a perforated bellows, but what a view."

A young couple saw me lining up to take a selfie and obliged me by taking the picture. They seemed shy but friendly as we spoke briefly in English. Was I a tourist? I explained my reason for being in Brno. I had the sense that with this new information they reappraised the unexpected, slightly sweaty, under-dressed figure in front of them. They seemed to like the story and with a final round of courtesies we parted company as they returned towards the city below while I continued my steady ascent to the castle. On another day, had I been a tourist, I would have paid the entrance fee and visited the castle, taking my time. Instead, I circled the fortress, gathered a quick sense of its dimensions, layout, look and feel, and then spiralled slowly back down the hill, continuing into the old town to a large, cobbled central square, noting a couple of places where I might return to eat a little later.

The sense that this wasn't a tourist town was heightened by the general demeanour of the people I saw. There were shoppers with baskets and bags, office workers a little more formally dressed, a couple of groups of workmen (no women) literally in blue-collar workwear carrying out streetworks, a few lone individuals selling periodicals and lottery tickets from kiosks, one or two beggars. There were no gaggles of tourists led by guides holding umbrellas, no young couples strolling languidly through the streets of Brno's old city, no late middle-aged travellers clutching guide-books or listening through headphones while gazing at historic facades. There were certainly no other runners. I pushed on, climbed a few flights of steps and looked back on the scene where tram lines curved sharply into view and converged at some distance below me. Every few seconds another tram would appear and negotiate the curve, a locomotive would head through the station to the left, carriages would slowly come to a halt at a platform. Seen from this position, central Brno was a giant model railway layout.

I ran back down to the lower level and paused the run at the entrance to the Grand Hotel. My first thought was to get some water, then carry on with the run. But I was hungry and tired, not from running itself but from the accumulation of fatigue – interrupted sleep, early starts, travelling, plus the lingering effects of the bug that had made me feel under the weather when I'd arrived in Vienna. That was just two days ago but already it felt as if I was having to make an effort to delve back into the memory vaults to recall arriving at Vienna airport. Since then I'd run in Vienna, then Györ, then Bratislava and now Brno – four countries in not much more than 48 hours. No wonder I was tired. But I still had six more weeks of the challenge to go. I had to stay healthy. I decided to give myself a break and to heed the wisdom of Barrie Roberts, the elder statesman of Bournville Harriers and one of its original members, who was still running and competing for his native Wales in his late 70s (now in his 80s, he still is). Barrie maintains that rest and recovery are essential parts of running, and so is eating well. Here in Brno, I'd run just over 8K. For RUNNING: ME RUNNING EU, that was enough. Stage 17 was complete. I'd give myself a break, refuel, rest, recover and stay fit for the next stages of the challenge. Once showered and changed, I returned to the square, found a simple restaurant and ate.

This was one of the lonelier days of the challenge. Even when I was in previously unvisited towns and countries, I was usually able to enjoy passing conversations at some point during the day. At times, chance encounters turned into some of the highlights of the entire experience and the people I met while running or travelling remain rooted in my memory. I'd been fortunate that my long day in Vienna had been bookended in the morning by coffee with Birgit and in the evening by the meal with Doris. Here in Brno, I knew and met no one apart from the couple on the way up to the castle. It wasn't a problem – as an only child, I'd long since learned to get by on my own company. I also enjoy moments of solitude, but I'm not a natural loner and wouldn't want to go for too long away from company and conversation. Happily I knew that the next stage would give me a real opportunity to meet and speak to other people. I'd planned it that way. On Saturday morning I would be back among the parkrun community, this time in Poland. Meanwhile, the meal was restorative and I decided to visit another of Brno's notable buildings, the Villa Tugendhat.

The German-born architect Mies van de Rohe designed this 1930s modernist house before he became the last director of the famous Bauhaus art school. The Bauhaus finally closed under pressure from the Nazis in 1933 and van de Rohe left for America. As concrete houses go, this one has style. Split-level, spacious, bathed in natural light and with a commanding view from its high-slope position overlooking the city, the Villa Tugendhat is a UNESCO-listed site. Another reason for wanting to see it stemmed from my studies in politics: the agreement to formalise the Czech-Slovak 'velvet divorce' was signed here in 1992. I wondered if that event was commemorated inside, perhaps a copy of the signed act of separation, but I didn't get a chance to find out, arriving just minutes after it closed for the afternoon. No matter, I'd seen the house and now took the chance to explore the well-heeled neighbourhood of substantial houses in which it resides. I ambled slowly away from the Villa Tugendhat and wound my way down the hillside back to the centre until I reached the Grand Hotel once again.

I caught up on some messages, including those posted by people who'd kindly donated to RSVP and Changing Faces via the BTMyDonate page. It was a thrill to think of all this support for RUNNING: ME RUNNING EU. It was also satisfying to be reminded in this very concrete way that me running my way across Europe was encouraging people to contribute to the work of the two charities. There were very few occasions when I'd ever felt less than utterly convinced about the challenge. My morale was routinely high – but even when it slipped a little, the reminder that the challenge was generating valuable funds for charity was usually all it took to get my thoughts back to a good place. And on this day in particular, the latest tally from BTMyDonate had given me reason to feel very satisfied. There had been a flurry of new donations and the fundraising had just topped £1,000.

Among other things, the Czechs are famous for their beers. That evening, I decided to keep it simple on the food front and find a bar where I could eat while judging Brno's brewing prowess. After a brief search I turned a corner and did a double-take as the unmistakable cockerel insignia of Tottenham Hotspur came suddenly into view. This turned out to be the Spurs Sports & Coffee Bar. I'm not sure why Brno would be a bastion of Lilywhite support and I'm sure the bar would have been absolutely fine but I walked past anyway in favour of finding somewhere more… Czech. The bar I chose would have won no awards for the warmth of the welcome. I tried to order in both English and Czech (armed with a phrase-book app on my phone plus the vaguest knowledge of how Czech is pronounced). Either way, the rather surly barman was unimpressed. Still, the beer arrived and the food was surprisingly good. There was a buzz about the place. I stayed on and by the end of a third beer, any memory of the brusque reception had been replaced by the warming glow of alcohol. I slept well that night.

The next morning I was reminded that I was in the land of Kafka, that great literary chronicler of absurd, random, arbitrary experiences, especially of individuals in their encounters with officialdom. Happily, I wasn't put on trial for no reason, nor did I metamorphose into a fly. Instead, I had a brief exchange at the bus station information desk which I captured on

Facebook later that day:
> "Lessons in ambiguity while travelling. Today's example. Conversation at the FlixBus kiosk...
>
> Me: Dobre den. Good morning. Which bus stop for the FlixBus at 10.00 to Katowice?"
>
> Mr FlixBus: It's not here yet. It will be from anywhere on the bus station. It will not be a FlixBus."
>
> Me: In that case, will it have a number?
>
> Mr FlixBus: It will be silver..."

The coach duly arrived. It was indeed silver. I'd booked it via FlixBus but the service was provided by a local partner operator. A group of Czech and Polish students on board quickly struck up a conversation in English and somehow I became involved: who was travelling where and why. I briefly outlined RUNNING: ME RUNNING EU. The students were less interested in the challenge than in the idea that an Englishman in his early 60s should be travelling around continental Europe on a coach just to run. For an instant the thought crossed my mind that the Czechs clearly had no monopoly on absurdity. I dismissed it and returned to the chat.

Time passed quickly. Before long, we were leaving the highway and passing through the outskirts of a substantial town towards the centre. This was Omolouc. Just as when passing the Varteks football stadium before the Varaždin half marathon in Croatia, I suddenly began to think of the early rounds of European football competition. The names of Omolouc and the next stop, Ostrava, would typically appear among the fixtures of the qualifying rounds of UEFA's tournaments. It was probably pub quiz territory (again) to be able to name the countries where such clubs played their football. At a push, people could probably place the clubs representing capital cities but it might be a stretch to identify Omolouc with its 99,000 inhabitants as Czech. I like to think I have a decent knowledge of European cities and countries and where they lie in relation to each other but that knowledge tends to dry up east of Vienna. Now I knew where Omolouc was.

At the small, humdrum coach station the driver announced that we would be back on the road in 15 minutes. Cue an exodus of smokers, leg-stretchers and – in my case – people in quest of caffeine. I found a simple café after walking the circuit around the perimeter of the very modest terminal building. A very pleasant woman asked me what I wanted. English was no use. Apart from "Dobrý den" (Hello) and "Děkuji" (Thank you) I had no Czech. I tried German. There were willing but helpless smiles. Some might wonder how much language is actually needed to buy a takeaway coffee and a bag of crisps. Clearly not much, though apparently more than we could readily muster between us at that moment, is the honest answer. But you can get a long way with smiles, pointing and a desire to get what you want. A couple of minutes later I was the happy owner of a bag of Bohemia-branded paprika crisps and a white Americano in a Styrofoam cup.

Things often taste just that bit better when you've had to work for them. I got back on the coach. By now, conversations had tailed off as people focused on their phones and headsets. Recaffeinated, I sat back as we continued before another short stop at Ostrava in the region of Silesia, which straddles the Czech-Polish border and is one of Europe's great coal and steel producing regions, the size of four Yorkshires. Barely ten miles further up the road, we crossed into Poland.

PART 2 | THE ACTUAL RUNNING PART

STAGE 18

Poland, parkrun and pointed hats

SATURDAY 16 FEBRUARY – 41 DAYS TO GO

Merely evoking the name of Katowice made my stomach tighten a little. Being born into a family which had lived through the Second World War and a society that had been shaken, scarred and re-shaped by it, I grew up with the names of significant figures, titles, places and episodes of war branded into my memory. The Nazi occupiers had treated Katowice and its citizens appallingly. Many people were massacred indiscriminately. Beyond this grim history and the region's heavy industry, I knew little about Katowice, except one small fact of which even most people who live there would have been completely unaware. The next day was Saturday and at 9am in Koszciuszki Park in the south of the city just beyond the A4 motorway, there would be parkrun.

The coach pulled in to a very workaday terminal – just a couple of bays on a run-down side street – and I exited into Katowice. It was icy and the cold was a sudden contrast to the coach's fuggy warmth. I shivered. My trusty Google Maps led me across a wide square through which tram lines criss-crossed and clanging trams curved their way across the open space, depositing shoppers, students and sundry city-dwellers into this spacious hub from where they headed off in all directions to go about their business. There was movement, energy and purpose – something I'd sensed was oddly missing from Brno's atmosphere. My hotel stood just metres from the entrance to the main station, an impressive modern gateway confidently announcing the city of Katowice for those arriving by train, in contrast to the more mundane and modest side entrance of a coach terminal through which we'd almost apologetically slipped in without fanfare. I checked in.

Plan A was to recce the location for tomorrow's parkrun, check out the shuttle service to the airport and my flight home later on Saturday and also to remedy a source of embarrassment, but more on that shortly.

Meanwhile I became acquainted with Katowice. It struck me as a city that both matched my preconceptions and defied them at the same time. Walking up the main road heading south from the centre, I noted the coal-blackened brick and stone facades of a succession of buildings. I could even taste a faint 'coalness' in the air, although that might just have been my imagination. This and the city of trams and monumental open squares was the Katowice I'd imagined – a relic of the eastern bloc, a city that bore the scars of heavy industry. The bold, contemporary swagger of the station, though, was another Katowice, a modern, prosperous city in a successful Poland that had joined the European Union a decade and a half earlier and had made the most of its economic benefits. The bustle, the city of people with places to go – this matched my general impression of Polish people: industrious, purposeful, with a firm sense of who they are. Of course these are an outsider's subjective impressions and I had no doubt that a few conversations in bars would have revealed divisions – social, cultural, political – that can be found in many societies, and certainly in Britain. This was my second visit to Poland following a work trip to Krakow the previous autumn. A third – to Poznań – would follow later in 2019, also for work, with another parkrun, but that's not part of this story.

After half an hour on foot I found myself on the outskirts and crossed the busy motorway that skirts the city's southern edge. Just beyond the motorway bridge, here was the gated entrance to Koszciuszki Park, a large expanse of trees intersected by loose-chipped paths. At its heart was a plaque commemorating a certain Tadeusz Kościuszko. A little online browsing later revealed that Tadeusz was a Polish war hero and military engineer who'd fought the Prussians and Russians. Interestingly, he clearly had form against the Brits, too, having fought under George Washington in the American War of Independence. He also designed West Point, the US's famous military academy, and it's said that he left the proceeds of his will to the education and freedom of slaves in the US.

With those credentials, his reputation is certainly unlikely to suffer the fate of slave trader Edward Colston, whose statue was hauled from its plinth daubed in blood-red paint, dragged down the street and dumped in Bristol Harbour. This cathartic act of protest-as-performance would take place a year later – at the time of my visit to Katowice, Colston's statue was still on its plinth. By positive contrast Kościuszko's place in both American and Polish history continues to stand the test of time and his memory is venerated in the form of parks named after him in Chicago and Milwaukee, and here in Katowice.

Tadeusz may have battled against my compatriots but the Kościuszko Park in which I stood felt somehow familiar and naturalistic. It turns out that it was indeed laid out in a deliberately 'English' style in contrast to the ultra-neat ornamental parks found in some countries. Several sculptures were dotted around the park, along with war memorials. At the heart of the park was a circular grass clearing bordered by a broad, cobbled path. This would be the start and finish point for tomorrow's run, according to the course map on the Katowice parkrun page. At least, I hoped so. There was ice everywhere, certainly enough to guarantee cancellation at my local run in Birmingham. However, there was nothing to suggest that the event team in Katowice had any intention to scupper my plans for Saturday morning.

I headed away from the peace of Kościuszko Park and back down towards the centre. Approaching the coal-blackened facades once again and with the wan afternoon light already beginning to fade, my eyes were drawn to a very seductively lit café that seemed to offer a couple of dozen ways to savour coffee and cake. Cold and weary from the trudge out and then back into town, and both thirsty and hungry (I'd had almost nothing since leaving Brno), I was drawn to the door like a moth to a flame, took a seat, and rehearsed how I would attempt to make my order in Polish. I didn't have to. "Hello, what would you like today?" said the young woman from behind the counter in clear, confident almost accent-less English. I'm sometimes slightly disappointed to be addressed in English when I've steeled myself for an exchange in a foreign language, however brief, but this time I was glad simply to respond in my own mother tongue. The next half-hour was welcome. Fed, watered, caffeinated and warm again, I overcame a strong urge to settle deep down in my very comfy armchair and sleep on the spot. Reluctantly, I reacquainted myself with the chill out on the street and went to recce where the airport shuttle would leave from the following day.

Planning my 'escape' route after each stage became a familiar part of the routine during the latter stages of the challenge. As I neared the 'business end' of everything I'd set out to achieve, I focused more and more on scheduling and left little to the vagaries of chance. Beyond the obvious priorities of coach and flight departure times, I had to know when I would run, how much time I would have to stay and chat, the time needed to return to hotels, shower, change, pack and check out, how long it would take to walk (always the default option) to the point where I would catch a bus, tram or train to the airport, transfer time, etc. I'm not naturally so careful. Perhaps I was turning into my father.

At moments when I caught myself in planning mode I thought "Stacey would approve!" remembering her unspoken but evident surprise at how much I was making the challenge up on the hoof. But by this stage there was no slack in the schedule. I could rarely afford to miss a plane or a coach and have to wait another day or more to get back home. The added cost was one thing but the loss of time could put a major dent in the whole challenge. Travel can be uncertain – after all, that's part of the thrill – and a cancelled service wasn't something I could control. But by now I was very disciplined about staying on track with every stage that was within my control. Not very rock'n'roll, admittedly, but the lure of the prize, completing RUNNING: ME RUNNING EU, had become an almost all-consuming mission.

I felt a growing notion that this challenge was 'why I was here'. I don't want to over-state what this feeling represented. It certainly wasn't anything like a religious calling. I hadn't been visited by angels with a map of Europe, a journey planner and a timetable. It was more a sense of the 'rightness' of what I was doing, that I was somehow destined to pursue the challenge. Put like that, it does sound almost spiritual. I suppose I do have a vague, woolly idea of karma, a sense of somehow 'knowing' if I'm doing the right thing, of being rewarded in some way when I do, and of suffering the consequences when I don't. Cosmic musings aside, at this point on a Friday afternoon in mid-February 2019, I certainly felt that life had brought me to this cold city street in southern Poland for a reason.

But being vaguely aware of my place in the higher scheme of things did not prevent me from feeling acutely self-conscious about something altogether more mundane. Running around Brno and particularly in Vienna and Györ, I'd noticed a few glances. Nothing surprising there – I accepted that in locations and in icy conditions where runners were rarely to be seen, an under-dressed man of a certain age hoofing around the city would be likely to attract attention. However, I'd become aware that many of such glances were more specifically directed towards my right knee, which bore a rather unsightly coil of varicose veins. Increasingly when out running back in Birmingham, I'd noticed that people would glance at my leg. I'd even taken to referring to the bulbous protuberance as 'Elephant Man's right knee'.

The next morning in Katowice was forecast to be cold but bright. At parkrun I wanted to talk to people – but I didn't welcome the thought that my unsightly knee would invite attention. I thought about wearing a buff over my knee cap but decided instead to find somewhere to buy some leggings. Should have brought some with me? Ah, the beauty of hindsight... I found a branch of Decathlon, asked tentatively in English and was immediately directed to a very friendly assistant whose approach to service made me feel as though she had really been waiting all day to find me exactly what I was looking for. One happily purchased pair of black New Balance (Men's, Large) running leggings later and I was equipped to make a maiden appearance at Katowice parkrun with my varicosed knee safely out of sight.

I headed back to the hotel via the central station for no other reason than to indulge a passion for railways. This has never left me since my earliest memories as a boy in shorts (the recurrent leg-wear theme is unintended) visiting old pre-electronic, pre-computerised signal boxes that relied on telephones, bells and hefty levers, to watch the trains from on high and see my father go about his daily work as a British Railways signalman. For me, there's a thrill to studying the names of distant destinations on the large displays that dominate a station concourse. Growing up in south London, nowhere was that far away and the destinations at the end of the line – Dover, Brighton, Bognor – seemed run-of-the-mill. Cross the river, though, and the railway termini to the north – Euston, Kings Cross – offered a glimpse of more distant places – Manchester, York, Edinburgh.

Growing up in a railway family, trains were almost a religion and major stations were cathedrals to the god of travel. That's a bold claim: to visit a great Gothic cathedral is to leave the everyday outside and to enter another realm. By contrast it's a struggle to be transported anywhere – literally or otherwise – when it's rush hour on a crowded concourse and the trains are late. On a good day and in the right conditions, though, there isn't much to beat the imposing interior of some great terminus, when the light filters in from high windows and the departure board holds the promise of elsewhere, of travel to distant destinations with evocative names – Prague, Vienna, Berlin, Warsaw, Minsk.

You could certainly reach most of these from Katowice. But I was just a window-shopper, merely passing through. I headed back to the Hotel Diament, caught up on some messages and rested for a while. Later I found a simple eatery that seemed popular with young couples but suited me. The staff were chatty and easy-going, the service swift, the food filling (steaks and burgers with a local twist) and the beer highly quaffable. I could have lingered but I felt slightly sleep-deprived and wanted to be on form for the following morning. I called it a night.

Saturday morning offered a crisp chill and an overcast sky as I made my way back to Kościuszko Park, arriving at the parkrun rendezvous to find… nothing. No one. The patches of snow and ice remained, though, and I wondered if it had been called off after all. Before leaving the hotel I'd checked the parkrun Facebook page and seen no notice of cancellation. Still, I fretted slightly. It wouldn't affect the challenge, of course. I could still run. But after five days of travelling and running solo I was ready for some company again and a return to the welcome familiarity of parkrun. It was 8.30am. I waited. Then they came. First a family clutching parkrun signage, then other volunteers. Runners appeared through the trees from several directions, converging on the circular cobbled clearing at the heart of the park that would become parkrun central for next couple of hours.

I introduced myself to the first group. The father was the run director. He'd seen my Facebook message. The whole family greeted me warmly, the teenage children self-consciously practising their English. I explained RUNNING: ME RUNNING EU. They listened politely. I wasn't sure if it struck any kind of chord with them but it didn't matter. Over the next few minutes the weekly pop-up community that's familiar to parkrun regulars everywhere began to be recreated here in Katowice. The signage was set up around the course. Friends arrived and gave each other hearty greetings. Some runners' outer layers began to be discarded and left strewn around the nearby benches (others were clearly going to run in everything they were wearing and in these low temperatures I could see their point). I peeled down to my own chosen running garb, the white RUNNING: ME RUNNING EU vest overlaying a long-sleeved top and now enhanced by the new leggings. The run director welcomed everyone and gave the ritual parkrun briefing.

Although it was in Polish, which I don't understand, it was also language about parkrun – and I'm fluent in that. The gestures and cadences made it clear when he was referring to the course (two laps), the barcode scanners (no barcode, no time) the finish tokens (don't take them home), and the volunteers (applause). Then I heard a reference to 'Anglik' (Englishman) and 'Steve' and eyes turned towards me. I gathered that he had referred to the challenge because there was another round of applause, this time in my honour. I nodded and beamed a smile back in acknowledgement. Just as we all began to walk towards the start, a voice said, "Hello Steve. I'm also a tourist from England." And so began my introduction to Dariusz, who had studied in Katowice and later moved to the UK, put down roots in the north-west of England, and who was back in town for a visit – and a parkrun.

After the run, we would talk some more and Dariusz really made me feel welcome. Meanwhile, there was some hoofing to be done. Under the watchful but unseeing gaze of Tadeusz Kościuszko, whose stern stone features looked out from the monument to his memory here at the heart of the park, we headed out from the cobbled circle and along tree-lined paths through which a little weak, warmth-deficient sunlight was finally filtering down through the canopy. The course looped round one side of the park, still under the cover of trees, briefly re-emerging into the open centre circle before continuing back beneath the trees on a different loop, forming a distinctly lop-sided figure of eight. I crossed the line in 22nd place and a time of 25:37, a few seconds off my average time for all parkruns (not fast but consistent). There was cake and what appeared to be hot apple juice being freely offered in plastic cups from a small samovar-style urn. If this was a local custom I was all for it but hesitated and held back, feeling slightly like an interloper. With perfect timing, Dariuz reappeared and gestured towards the post-run refreshments. "Help yourself, Steve!" So I did.

For reasons I never fully established – a birthday? an anniversary? – several of the runners were now wearing short, pointed hats with an elasticated band. "Here, Steve – join the party!" Dariusz was now wearing one of the mini dunce's hats and held one out to me. I decided to observe the 'When in Rome...' principle and put it on. After all, I might never have another chance to drink hot apple juice and wear a pointed hat in Poland! Time stopped for a moment, people lingered and I savoured the scene, now sharpened as the clouds receded further, leaving the centre circle and the post-parkrun party bright at last in the hazy sunlight.

But I had to go. The schedule was tight and clock-time reasserted itself. It would take me 30 minutes to get back to the hotel. If I walked briskly, I could get back in time for a quick shower and maybe even the tail-end of the breakfast service before checking out and making my way to the far side of Katowice station to pick up the minibus to the airport, which was 25 miles away with unpredictable traffic in between. The Ryanair flight to Stansted was at 2.35pm. I wasn't going to miss it.

After a quick round of thank yous and goodbyes I headed back to the city centre. I kept to the schedule and managed to hoover up a quick breakfast before checking out. By this stage of the challenge, packing and checking out of hotels had virtually become an automated process. Hand luggage only and every item in its pocket, place or compartment. Everything pre-paid, no extras, nothing to settle. Just get the hell out and move on to the next stage.

The minibus shuttle pick-up point wasn't marked but within minutes of my arrival, people with luggage began to gather. The minibus was late, inducing a twinge of concern about how long it would take to reach the airport, but there was no need to worry. The roads were clear and we were at the airport in good time. The rest of the journey was uneventful. Clearing Stansted was easy and by the evening I was back home in Birmingham. Five countries in five days… one of the great logistical challenges had been completed. The whistlestop tour through countries of the former Habsburg empire hadn't always been easy but each stage had given me new and often unexpected experiences. And with Katowice parkrun, the week had ended on a very high note. One more country to go and then the remaining stages would be down to single figures. Plus I wouldn't be alone for country number 19. Liz was coming with me. We were both looking forward to it. We'd never been to Malta. For me, after the weeks of travelling through the winter chill of central and northern Europe, running in Mediterranean conditions would be a novelty. Bring it on.

Final weeks, seeing the whole jigsaw at last

It was at this time that I put the final pieces of the Running: Me Running EU jigsaw together, if not yet in the form of bookings then at least in my mind. For a long time I'd bracketed Cyprus and Greece together and assumed that I would travel from the divided island first and then move on to the cradle of western civilisation, possibly running on one of Greece's own myriad islands. Certainly it seemed to make sense financially and logistically to do it that way rather than make two return trips from the UK. However, I also had to factor Romania and Bulgaria into the plan for the remaining days. Maybe I could build in a Balkan sequence, running my way through a succession of countries that had formerly been part of the once mighty Ottoman Empire. While that plan had a certain logic on paper – well, on a map, certainly – it didn't take me much modelling of a possible itinerary to realise that it wouldn't work in practice.

At one point I considered the idea of travelling through mainland Turkey to northern Cyprus, the Turkish-controlled part of the divided island that isn't recognised internationally, and then across the so-called Green Line, the United Nations administered buffer zone, to the part of Cyprus that is internationally recognised as a sovereign state and is part of the EU. The Greek and Turkish Cypriot communities have been separated since 1974. From time to time there have been glimmers of hope that politics and public sentiment on both sides could align to make a reconciliation possible. In 2004 a referendum to that effect was held in both communities. In a very high turn-out, Turkish Cypriots voted in favour of reunification, Greek Cypriots to reject it. And that's how things stood 15 years later as I contemplated travelling from one side of the island to the other.

To say there are sensitivities in making that journey is an understatement, but while it's possible to take that route, it can be unpredictable: crossing the Green Line can be suspended for periods of time without warning.

The authorities in the Republic of Cyprus (the Greek part of the island which is in the EU) frown on travellers who enter the island via the Turkish-controlled north and can officially disbar non-EU passport holders who first arrive from the north. While ease and convenience were not my main criteria while planning each stage of the challenge, I did need my remaining journey times to be reasonably predictable. And once I'd registered for the Logicom Cyprus Half Marathon and knew that I had to be in Paphos ready to run on 17 March, I gave up any remaining thoughts of following an Ottoman trail.

In any case, my dates for Romania were now also fixed. I would be working on behalf of my client euRobotics at the European Robotics Forum in Bucharest on 20–22 March. Lavinia was my main client contact at euRobotics and is now a good friend. She knew of my passion for running and was also very supportive of the idea of RUNNING: ME RUNNING EU. I'd seen the Forum dates a few months earlier, realised that this would also help me set up the Romanian stage of the challenge, and pitched her a work proposal. She'd agreed and in return had also asked me to play a part in organising a charity run for Forum delegates while the Forum was taking place. Not only that, I could run in the event as well. The stars were clearly aligning for RUNNING: ME RUNNING EU. And now another plan was forming. Bucharest is quite close to the Bulgarian border. Maybe I could combine Romania and Bulgaria… That still left Luxembourg. I would squeeze it in somehow. It was also at this mid-late February point that I decided exactly how I wanted to spend my final day of the challenge and where I would go to start the final run. It would be fitting, epic – and Greek.

PART 2 | THE ACTUAL RUNNING PART

STAGE 19

The Maltese mishap

SUNDAY 24 FEBRUARY – 33 DAYS TO GO

Malta Marathon Cancelled as Gale Force Winds Batter Island
(23 Feb, 7.34pm, headline from the LovinMalta website)

I was glad that Liz would be sharing this next, most holiday-like part of the adventure with me. We'd been anticipating the warmth of an island that basks comfortably between Sicily and the coast of Tunisia for some time. Even so, we were pleasantly surprised by the warm, spring-like breeze on our faces as we came down the steps from our Air Malta flight from Heathrow on that late-February Friday afternoon. A bus took us from the airport to Sliema and the Waterfront Hotel from where we had a fine view across the extensive harbour towards Valletta, the capital. Seen from the vantage point of the ninth-floor balcony overlooking the water and harbour craft of a renowned tourist resort in the Mediterranean and judging by these first impressions, this was probably going to be the most relaxing stage of the entire challenge. Or so it seemed.

It's possible to take a bus, drive or walk from Sliema around the contours of the harbour to Valletta. The simplest route, though, is via the small ferry that takes just five minutes to cross the waterway. We set out for a day's leisurely sightseeing by walking the short distance from the door of the Waterfront Hotel, whose name tells you everything about its location, and along the harbour promenade. Today was a day for relaxing before the following morning's half marathon, which would finish right here on the waterfront. At least that was the plan. We soon saw the first sign that events would take another course: "Ferry suspended due to unsafe weather conditions." Really? True, there was now a bit of a strong breeze but was that really all it took to stop the ferry crossing? We decided to walk instead. It would be a couple of miles but we could take our time. I knew that I had until much later that evening to go and pick up my race pack from the Nike Store in Sliema. Normally I would have done that first but there was no pressure on time and I wanted Liz to enjoy the day.

An hour later, we were in the historic heart of Valletta, once a strategic stronghold for the Royal Navy and headquarters of the Mediterranean Station, Britain's most prestigious fleet, which existed even into my own lifetime until it was finally disbanded in 1967, three years after Malta gained independence. I remembered three things about Malta. First chronologically, its connection with the Order of the Knights of St John and the Crusades in the Holy Land, a connection that remains visible today through the cross of St John, also known as the Maltese Cross, one of the two crosses which symbolise Malta. Wind forward to the Second World War and Malta's famous 'finest hour' in 1940 when its starving population withstood siege and constant bombardment by the Luftwaffe and the Italian air force. For its fortitude and successful resistance, Malta was collectively awarded the George Cross, Britain's highest civil award for gallantry, an image of which now forms part of the official flag of Malta. Thirdly, I remember the name Dom Mintoff featuring prominently in news headlines from the 1960s. As I recall the Maltese prime minister of the time was portrayed as a defiant figure. He was clearly no pushover in his negotiations with the departing British authorities, although the nuances of the story and its place as another footnote to the end of Britain's imperial presence in the Mediterranean were beyond the range of a primary school-age south London boy.

The wind was picking up as we wandered around Valletta's baroque Italianate streets but we still had no inkling yet of what was to come. We found ourselves at Fort St Elmo near the tip of the peninsula on which the old city stands and visited the museum. Occasionally I would spot a running top – unsurprising as the Malta Marathon and Half Marathon bring in a sizeable international field of runners, with several hundred tackling the full 26.2 mile event, while a couple of thousand like me would be expected for the half. No doubt we were a welcome economic presence on the island at this time of year outside the normal tourist season. Liz and I made our way back to the City Gates, past the strikingly modern concrete and limestone Parliament Building designed by Renzo Piano, also notable for London's sky-piercing Shard tower by London Bridge. The Shard stands barely metres in distance but an architectural world away from the signal box where my father had worked for so many years.

In 2018, Valletta had been the European Capital City of Culture, a title and status which the city continued to proclaim via banners and signage with evident pride. Another focus for identity comes through Malta's membership since 2004 of the European Union. The EU symbol can be seen everywhere. Academic research suggests that being part of the EU has brought a variety of benefits to Malta, not least by helping it to weather the financial crisis of the late noughties far more successfully than if it had had to face it alone. Certainly the signs of substantial investment are plain to see, just as I'd noticed in Poland and would see again in the Baltic states. There's a whole lot more confidence and security to be had by being part of a major economic and trading alliance than by going it alone, it seemed. In each country I'd visited, there was a sense of a shared European identity but this in no way diluted a much stronger local sense of national identity. Malta was still Malta, EU or not, Poland the same. Lithuania retained its own distinct identity – as I would see – and possibly cherished it all the more for having only gained its independence in 1991. That was certainly true of Slovenia, which had made a conscious decision to leave Yugoslavia and seek independence and yet had still voted overwhelmingly to join the EU.

It would be tempting to dwell on this and think about how well Britain would now fare in the face of future challenges and how well-equipped it would be to function alone in an increasingly unpredictable world. After all, Britain had signed up to join what later became the EU back in the early 1970s because it feared being left behind as France and West Germany notably made great advances economically as part of the European Economic Community. Who knew what kind of storms lay ahead, economic or otherwise, and how well any of us would weather them, whether inside the EU or not? By now, though, such weighty thoughts had been replaced by a more worldly and immediate concern. We were hungry.

Chief Executives like to talk about economic 'headwinds' to describe adverse conditions and headwinds – real ones – were exactly what we experienced as we sat down at a terrace table. Inevitably there would soon be a reference by one or the other of us to Postman Pat's windy day episode – a stock family reference since our children were young enough to be enthralled by Pat, Jess the cat, Rosie and Jim and other TV characters whose adventures had formed part of the backdrop to family life – and Liz got there first: "It's a very windy day in Greendale…" It was indeed. By now hats were at considerable risk while parasols and awnings were being given a vigorous workout, so much so that we quickly gave up on the idea of an al fresco lunch and moved inside.

Later, back at the hotel, we watched the skyline darken as rain clouds moved in fast. Below, even within the harbour's shelter, moored boats were moving from side to side. I decided to head down to the Nike store to pick up my race pack. It looked like a half-hour walk and the later I left it the more chance I had of getting wet.

It was early evening. On arrival at Nike there was no need to ask where to go. A longish queue had formed from the back of the store. I then heard the people in front of me talking about the chances that the race would be cancelled. The rumour was clearly passing down the queue. The mood quickly changed, a sense of expectation becoming one of uncertainty. A voice was raised above the hubbub. Someone – a race official? – was giving an update further up the queue. He came towards the back of the queue and repeated his message. It was likely that the marathon (and therefore the half marathon) would be cancelled. The race began in open countryside. Buses were due to ferry us early the next morning from the promenade to the interior. From the start, the course descended on open roads past fields until it reached the suburbs, continuing down to Sliema and following the promenade alongside the harbour for the final two kilometres to the finish arch, which I'd passed on the way here. Except that now this was increasingly unlikely to happen.

The weather forecast was bad. Conditions were likely to become unsafe for runners and marshals alike. In those circumstances the Malta Marathon organisers would make a 'safety first' decision and call it off. I asked if this was now definite. With a clear tone of regret, he said it was probable but that we should check the website later for confirmation. We should still collect our race packs, though.

The mood in the queue was now an uneven mix of disappointment, resignation and for some, frustration – "it's only rain!" Fifteen minutes later I had my race pack: a branded Malta Marathon bag, blue and yellow running top, a brochure outlining what Malta had to offer, and a running number – now almost certainly destined never to be used. A lot of runners, partners, families and friends had come to Malta for the half and full marathons. As a message on the event website confirmed by 8pm, we were all going to be disappointed.

I walked back to the hotel in persistent squally rain. The wind had picked up considerably and the inflatable finish arch was lurching around with each successive gust. Back at the hotel I gave Liz the news. "I have to run, though," I told her. "I won't get back to Malta before the end of the challenge. I'll just do what I've been doing in other places and run independently. It's still running. The rules allow it!" That wasn't in dispute. It was my challenge and I'd set the rules at the outset. Liz was uncomfortable about it, though: "'What if it isn't safe?" The squally conditions had worsened and it was now an unrelenting downpour. I left the question unanswered. Instead, I Googled nearby restaurants and found a likely looking place just a few streets away. By the time we were back down at street level, the rain had become relentless and a large and growing slick of water had gathered around the hotel entrance. Water had begun to spread across the road outside. Hunched against the rain and wind, we dashed between doorways and covered arcades until we reached the restaurant, which lived up to the reviews. The highlight was a very attentive, characterful and entertaining waiter who brought real personality to the meal. For a while I put the race cancellation out of my mind. Glowing with wine, well-fed and entertained, we braved the monsoon again and made it back to the hotel.

I posted on Facebook that evening and told people the bad news that the event had been cancelled and the reasons why:

> Pity, but clearly the right decision as tonight's conditions are likely to continue, with force 9 forecast for the morning and weather being described as a cyclone. First cancellation in 39 years since it began. The finish comes along the Strand at Sliema (past our hotel), which is a river at the moment. I'll find a way to get out and run, though.

Comments of support and commiseration came quickly as friends read my post about the race being cancelled. Looking back through the Facebook archive, two stand out. One, from Laura, a fellow runner with a sense of adventure probably came closest to capturing my own feelings about it:

> "Take care, but I'm sure you'll find a way!"

And this from the ever-kind-hearted Rachel:

> "So sorry the race was cancelled. Hope you are enjoying a relaxing morning and a nice breakfast."

I still laugh when reading that. If only she could have known how the next morning would turn out!

The scene the next day was startling. The wind was absolutely howling, the road below was full of water and the harbour, supposedly a shelter from the open sea, was alive with white-capped waves. It looked ominous – and this was from nine floors up. Liz told me she really didn't think I should go out. Part of me agreed with her. The other part said that running was the reason I'd come to Malta, that I had a challenge to complete and people were sponsoring me to do so. The reality was that if any of the sponsors could see what we could see, they'd probably be begging me not to do it.

What can I say? It's true that I had misgivings. But I imagined myself living with a future regret if I did the sensible thing. I didn't want that. I decided that I would dress with as many protective layers as I could – long sleeved top, jacket, gloves, shorts, leggings on top, long BvH socks over the leggings, neck buff, beanie hat – and just get it done. I made sure I had my phone with me. The scene in the harbour might be worth capturing.

Down in the hotel reception, guests were staring at the scene outside while the staff were taking steps to keep the water out. I headed past them, out of the door into a ferocious wind. The road was still full of water, although some had drained away. I managed to tiptoe across some shallow patches, although wet feet were the least of my concerns at this point. Full of tiny particles, the wind felt like sandpaper on my face, so much so that I tried to angle my head away to avoid taking the full blast head-on. As exfoliation techniques go it was crude, brutal and not to be recommended. My main concern was now to avoid getting grit in my eyes. I began to run with eyes screwed up to reduce the risk. Immediately there was another hazard. When running trail or cross-country in clinging mud which threatens to separate foot from footwear I sometimes say that the mud wants my shoes. Here in the full force of the storm on the promenade at Sliema it was clear to me that the wind wanted my hat. Even though it was a tight-fitting beanie, the strength of the wind simply tore at the edges, so that in one awkward protective manoeuvre my hand was simultaneously holding my jacket collar up to protect a cheek while gripping the hat to keep it in place and at the same time peering out from between eye-lids reduced to slits. And yet I was running. The challenge would be fulfilled.

The water in the harbour was monstrous. A small yacht had sunk. Several others had broken their moorings. On the promenade itself a kiosk was being battered; a section of its wooden fascia had been blown loose and was swinging wildly with every gust. But it was the sight of the water in the harbour that drew my attention back with a mix of awe and fascination.

It was alive with a fearsome power like some wild creature that rocked and crested in waves of immense energy. I continued further, managing to keep moving, almost power-assisted while running in the direction of the wind. Just go with the flow, I thought, as I approached a curve in the promenade. I looked ahead and stopped. As the harbour water hit the centre or angle of the curve, propelled by the extreme force of the wind, it was being forced against and over the retaining wall and onto the promenade. With no sense of approaching danger, I pulled out my phone and clicked on the camera to capture the scene. It was a picture I was destined never to take. Instead, this happened…

> **Facebook post 24 Feb** Well, given the horrendous conditions, Stage 19 was always going to be dramatic. But I wasn't expecting this. With small boats starting to capsize even here in the harbour opposite the hotel, I knew the wind would be strong as I ventured onto the promenade. What caught me out was the water coming over the promenade wall. As the swell spewed water onto the tiled waterfront, I'd just thought to myself, this reminds me of the power of the water flowing towards Niagara Falls when suddenly a wave came crashing over the wall in front of me, taking my legs away and washing me completely helplessly into the road before the sea sucked the water back into the harbour. Utterly drenched, I quickly staggered to my feet before a bus passed where the wave had dumped me. Slightly shocked, I went into autopilot and started running in the other direction. I looked down and saw blood from my knees and on one of my BvH socks. Two runners came past. "God, you're soaked!" said the woman. "And you've got a war wound! Get a photo!" Sadly my phone is also drenched and not working. Anyway, that, ladies and gentlemen, concludes my running in Malta. Stage 19 was short but eventful. If you'd like to support the work of RSVP and Changing Faces, here's the link: https://mydonate.bt.com/fundraisers/runningmerunningeu

I wrote that post a couple of hours after the wave had hit me. By then, I was safely back in the hotel, Liz had cleaned up my bloodied knees. The protective layers had mostly done their job but the leggings that I'd only recently bought in Katowice had ripped as I scraped to a halt, knees-first on the road where the wave had thrown me.

I had been out for a little more than half an hour. After the incident and the encounter with the couple on the promenade I'd continued the run for a few more minutes in punishing conditions – the facial shotblasting effect in the ferocious headwind was quite painful – until I'd collected my thoughts sufficiently to realise that there was nothing more to be gained by persisting with this reckless run. I stopped, left the promenade and returned to the hotel. I felt as if I'd had a narrow escape. And I had. I looked back at the tumult of the water in the harbour with its sheer raw power. The moment felt cinematic. If this was a movie scene the soundtrack would have to be suitably elemental. Something classical. Mussorgsky's *Night on the Bare Mountain* would do it. Certainly not Handel's *Water Music*. It seemed surreal and I had a sense of looking at myself, a hapless bedraggled figure trudging back to the shelter of the hotel. I knew Liz would be appalled when she saw me and heard the story. I'd encountered the water. Now it was time to face the music.

Only one picture exists from that episode, which Liz reluctantly took at my request. Standing on our hotel room balcony (I was drenched and still dripping. Liz did not want stormwater on our room's carpet, reasonably enough) and with a facial expression – dazed, vacant, slightly in shock – that reflected the drama of the moment.

Gingerly, I showered and changed. With my knees now covered in plasters, we spent the next couple of hours peering out through the glass of the balcony window – now firmly shut – at the striking panorama. Upturned hulls, semi-submerged yachts, the mast of another poking out from the water's surface, the deck beneath it visible but fully underwater – and all of this *inside* the harbour. We watched as a group of men on a small cutter attempted to secure a large old double-masted yacht which was threatening to break its mooring. Meanwhile, further away to our left where the mouth of the harbour narrowed before opening out to the sea, waves of white water rose angrily before crashing down.

That afternoon, my 'Maltese mishap' and its aftermath gave rise to several exchanges with friends on Facebook, mostly fellow runners from Bournville Harriers.

> (David): "My goodness. I hope you're OK. That must have been pretty alarming when it happened."

> (Me): "Slightly stunned, I must admit. I do remember a strong sense of concern about not colliding with a wall or other debris and then a powerful urge to get off the road sharpish because I'd seen the bus before the wave hit me. I took a chance by going out in those conditions and came unstuck – but clearly it could have been much worse. A karmic lesson."

(Suz): "What an adventure you're having. You really should have TV crews following you."

(Me): "Or paramedics."

We had one more night in Malta, which was just as well as no flights were possible that day. By the evening the wind had died down but it was the next morning that we would see the extent of the storm's damaging effects. A keen breeze still blew as we walked along the promenade towards the curve where my unscheduled trial by immersion had occurred. Street furniture had been blown from its fixings. The kiosks offering bus and boat tours had suffered considerably under the previous day's sustained battering. Reminiscent of a lesson from the tale of the three little pigs, flimsy structures had fared badly. A couple of the less robust cabins had disintegrated completely. All showed some signs of damage.

STAGE 19

The Maltese mishap
"What caught me out was the water coming over the promenade wall. As the swell spewed water onto the tiled waterfront a wave came crashing over the wall in front of me, taking my legs away and washing me completely helplessly into the road before the sea sucked the water back into the harbour. I looked down and saw blood from my knees and on one of my BvH socks." This is the only photo, taken back at the hotel after Liz had washed the blood away.

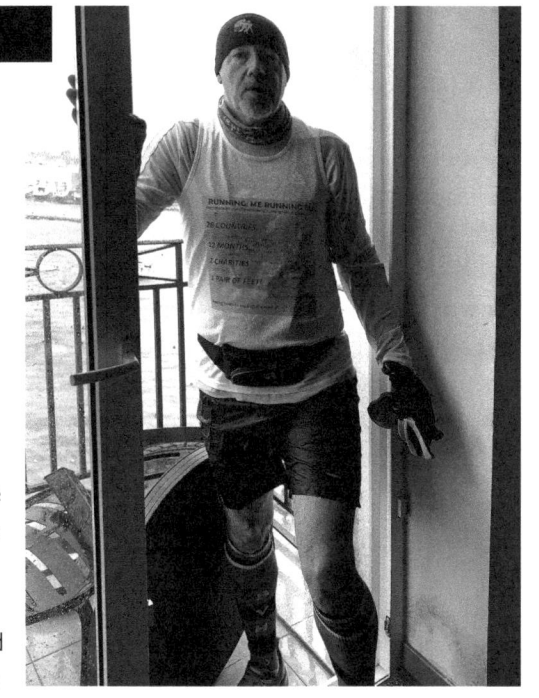

We had some hours to kill before our flight and took an open-top bus tour of the island. From the upper deck we could see more evidence of the damage. Some trees had been uprooted and we had to duck a couple of times as the canopies of twisted trees brushed over the top of the bus. In one narrow cove the water's surface was covered with the debris of splintered wood, shattered moorings, uprooted vegetation and a tide of detritus from blown-over rubbish bins.

There was a silver lining. Beyond the storm's effects, Malta looked inviting, particularly around the waterfronts, and we resolved to return one day.

Later I checked several news sites for information, both about the storm itself and about climatic conditions in Malta generally. Clearly this had been no ordinary storm. I learned that the wind was a *gregalata*, a north-easterly that regularly buffets the Maltese islands. But this one was exceptional, blowing itself to such an intensity that it produced the worst storm to hit Malta in 34 years. As I'd discovered spontaneously from first-hand experience earlier, weather events of this magnitude can be measured in expletives. I also knew from bookworming my way through my early teens – before the partying began... – that there's a more widely accepted gauge to measure the strength of winds: the Beaufort scale. A moderate breeze – the kind that runners would describe as "quite a bit of headwind" – gets a 4 on the Beaufort scale. We talk about a 'force 8 gale' and that's taken straight from the Beaufort scale. The top of the scale is 12 – that's a hurricane. Go out in one of those and you're likely to be blown, Dorothy-like, all the way to Kansas. Actually, that only happens in Hollywood. In reality, being caught outdoors in a hurricane will almost certainly result in death or at least serious injury. The cyclonic storm that hit Malta that day was officially recorded as a 10 bordering 11, between a storm and a violent storm in Beaufort terms.

The Times of Malta reported on what we'd witnessed...

> **Destruction across Malta as gale-force winds batter islands**
> Record gusts of up to 101km/h leave trees uprooted, walls toppled and seafronts flooded
>
> **People advised to stay indoors**
> Authorities advised people to stay indoors unless they needed to travel. According to Wind Finder, in the early hours of the morning, Malta experienced gusts of winds that are described as a "high threat to life

and property". The Maltese Islands Weather site said on Sunday morning that the northeast wind was at its strongest in many years. The 101 km/h (Force 10, almost Force 11) gusts measured by the site's weather station in Għarb were an all-time record.

For this moment of jeopardy to happen at such a late stage in the story of Running: Me Running EU echoed one of the classic storytelling conventions. Among the many reactions from friends following my Maltese 'mishap', my friend Stacey had spotted it and put it wryly into words:

> "The lengths you will go to for a bit of light and shade in the story of your epic journey… the hero of the tale must come through hardship on the way to victorious completion of the challenge. Well done on another stage complete and the battle scars to remember it by. Hope the knees and phone make a very speedy recovery!"
>
> (Me) "To be honest my main regret is that I wasn't able to get some pictures, but taking a selfie while simultaneously being swept off the promenade would have been beyond my photographic skills. I remember momentarily thinking, here comes a wave but if I step into the road (which was already awash), I'm going to get wet. Next second I was flotsam and heading into the road anyway. Anyway, another unexpected twist in the challenge. No project completely follows an MSProject plan. This stage has certainly thrown some curved balls. Let's see what Stage 20 brings!"

Always conscious that the continuing story of my progress around Europe needed pictures, losing the use of my phone had deprived me of an opportunity to capture this particular moment in images. It was likely that pictures would be available from media sites so if (as I planned) I found a future audience willing to hear the tale of my experiences (especially this one) I would still be able to illustrate it with some striking images. Nonetheless I didn't want to be without a phone for long. A few days after getting back home I would be heading out again for what had already crystallised in my mind as 'Baltic Week'. I would need a phone – and not just for photos. February was clicking into March, the final month of the challenge. Eight countries left to run. This really was now the business end of Running: Me Running EU.

PART 2 | THE ACTUAL RUNNING PART

STAGES 20-23

Lithuania, Latvia, Estonia, Finland (Baltic Week): snow, ice and a yoga warmdown

TUESDAY 5 – SATURDAY 9 MARCH – 20 DAYS TO GO
STAGE 20 – KAUNAS: ANOTHER SECOND CITY

I knew very little about the three Baltic states of Lithuania, Latvia and Estonia apart from a few random facts. Improbably, given its tiny size, Lithuania had once been part of an empire with Poland. Latvia's capital, Riga, had once been a German-speaking city. Estonians spoke a language close to Finnish. Once independent countries, all three had been swallowed up by the Soviet Union and had regained their freedom when the Iron Curtain fell at the turn of the 1990s. Both Latvia and Estonia had sizeable Russian minorities. Estonia had a reputation as a high-tech country. I began to check out running and travel options. I drew a blank on races. The Baltic states are cold at that time of year and there were no obvious events to sign up for so early in the new year. I didn't have time to wait until spring when the race calendar would start to pick up again.

However, I knew that Finland was now part of the international parkrun family. I checked out the Finland parkrun website. There were three weekly events, including one in the Finnish capital, Helsinki, itself. I browsed a map of the Baltic region. Estonia's capital Tallinn looked north across the Gulf of Finland towards Helsinki. Saint Petersburg (another parkrun city at that time) wasn't far away from either. I was briefly tempted to include an excursion to Russia in my itinerary but I quickly discounted this as a diversion too far. I could spare neither the time nor the added cost of visiting Russia. Plus, I would need a visa.

Tantalisingly close though Saint Petersburg would be once I was up in the Baltic states, it was a distraction. And yet… didn't it make sense to visit a city I'd always wanted to see when I would be so close? Would I ever be back in this part of the world? Tempting. I checked distances and train timetables. Tallinn to St Petersburg would take over seven hours by train. The border crossing might also be lengthy. I wasn't sure how welcome the sight of a British passport would be at the Russian border. Would there be added rigmarole? Travelling between EU countries, I'd got used to hassle-free transfers, especially between the countries within the EU's borderless Schengen zone. That thought was a reminder of my purpose. This was RUNNING: ME RUNNING EU, not some follow-your-nose tour of the eastern Baltic. I resolved to stick to the original plan. I would find a flight from the UK to Vilnius, the Lithuanian capital, hopefully travel onwards by train to Riga, and then onwards again to Tallinn.

As I zoomed in on my map a line of dashes appeared across the sea between Tallinn and Helsinki. A ferry! Reaching Helsinki by ship, now that was certainly appealing. I did some more Googling and found three shipping lines that made the crossing. This was a well-established route. So I would progress through the Baltic states, finish in Finland and fly home from there. I would run 'free' in the three Baltic states and then take part in the Tokoinranta (Helsinki) parkrun. Since parkruns routinely take place on Saturday mornings, I would need to reach Helsinki at the latest by Friday, the earlier the better, to give me time to check out the location for parkrun the following morning. From that point onward, I planned from Helsinki backwards. I would travel to Lithuania to Latvia to Estonia and then take the ferry to Finland. However, my original plan A did not survive the flight search. I couldn't find a flight from any airport I could easily reach at a price I was willing to pay to get me to Vilnius at the start of the week. I'd need to find another route into Lithuania. And that was when I learned that Wizzair flew from Luton to a place called Kaunas. I'd never heard of Kaunas and knew nothing about it except that it was in Lithuania and that the flight would get me there on a Tuesday for £24.99. For now, that was all I needed. The rest of the week would pan out.

I booked it. With one stake in the ground for Baltic Week, I checked out flights back from Helsinki at the weekend and found one with Scandinavian carrier Norwegian that flew on Saturday evening. That would give me a few hours to clean up, relax and see something of Helsinki after parkrun. At just under £50 it was more expensive than the outward flight but the combined return fare was acceptable. So far so good. Now for the trains... here I drew a blank. There were barely any, none were direct, and those few that I could find involved lengthy changes. The Baltic stage would be a whistlestop tour and I didn't have the slack in my schedule to waste time hanging around waiting for connections.

However, further Googling revealed that a good express coach service connected Kaunas with Riga and then Riga with Tallinn. While, as a railwayman's son and another's grandson, I'd always opt to travel by rail than by road if possible, the coach service was fast (four hours for each leg), direct, timely and cheap. The travellers' websites and blogs also seemed to agree that the coaches on these routes were modern, air-conditioned and comfortable. It was a deal. I booked Kaunas-Riga (€18, about £15.50 at the time) and Riga-Tallinn (€14.40, around £12.50) online, and printed out the tickets at home. Now I just needed to find places to stay. Someone reading this might be concerned that I'd committed myself to flights, coaches and a ferry crossing without having any idea where I would actually sleep in any of these Baltic cities, but I'd already checked out accommodation and prices and knew that in the cold, early weeks of a new year, the hotels on Booking.com had plenty of availability all well within my budget. So I put the final jigsaw pieces in place and booked hotels in Kaunas, Riga, Tallinn and Helsinki. The trip was set up. I was ready for Baltic Week.

If the New Year trip to Copenhagen had been at the luxurious end of the challenge, the first stage of the trip to Kaunas was at the bucket-shop end of travel. And that's no reflection on Kaunas, which proved to be a fascinating pleasure. No, if the bucket was the need to travel via Luton, which I've found to be the most underwhelming of all the 'London' airports, then the hole in the bucket was the timing. Over the years, I've quite often flown at ungodly hours. For this trip, I would have to be at Luton before 4am for a flight at 5.45. National Express coaches could get me direct to Luton from Birmingham's Digbeth coach station but too early or too late for my flight. I was prepared to wait for a few hours if necessary and find somewhere at the airport to get my head down, but unusually Luton Airport closes its terminal after the last flight of the day and doesn't allow travellers to doss down in the terminal. I wasn't flying back to Luton, so driving and leaving my car wasn't an option, either. I would just have to travel the long way round, taking the coach to London and then another one on to Luton. There would be a few hours' gap between arrival and departure again from Victoria, where London's ageing, entirely uninviting coach station remains, despite many projects to vacate its prime Belgravia location in favour of a modern, comfortable new terminal with better links to the capital's motorway network.

Many experiences in life are worth having, even if they don't seem so at the time. Spending night hours at Victoria Coach Station in London was not one of those experiences. After a three-hour journey down from Birmingham I arrived at Victoria shortly before 1am. It was drab, cold and smelt of vomit fused with diesel fumes. The plastic 1980s seating was full of people, most waiting for their own onward journeys, some just there to doss down for the night, even Victoria Coach Station being more appealing than a night in a doorway. Happily, a branch of Subway was open and I lingered there with a hot chocolate and a filled roll for as long as I could without loitering, which was actively discouraged. For the next hour and a bit I walked up and down, occasionally crouching on my trusted Ljubljanski Maraton backpack as a cushion, and watched as the occasional coach arrived, emptied, filled up with a new load of sleepless passengers and departed.

Time dragged. Too tired to read, but with nowhere to sleep and, frankly, being unwilling to do so in the presence of some decidedly dodgy looking people, I just sat it out (except there wasn't really anywhere to sit) and willed the time to pass. Slowly, it did. Eventually, the Luton service details appeared on the screen. Finally, the Luton coach arrived. I boarded, as did half a coach-load of other travellers and on time at 2am, the coach pulled out into the sodium glare of streetlights. It took just over an hour to reach Luton airport. At least there was no more waiting around. My flight's gate was already showing on the departure board. I went straight to it and joined an already lengthy queue waiting for the gate to open. I'd wondered who else would be flying to Kaunas at this inhospitable hour on a late winter Tuesday and what kind of fellow passengers I'd meet. They turned out to be mainly young people – singles, couples, families with babies and toddlers. There was little conversation, and what little I heard was subdued. It really wasn't the hour for eager discussion. I had the distinct impression that I would be the oldest person on the flight and one of very few Brits, possibly the only one, judging by the unfamiliar language I heard when people did speak.

Once on board, conversation briefly rallied as people stowed their bags, found their seats and exchanged comments before settling down for the flight. Sometimes on flights abroad carrying mostly Brits, there's a sense of only finally leaving the UK once the plane touches down at the destination. This felt different. We hadn't started taxiing to the runway and yet I had a sense that I was already in Lithuania. After the safety briefing, the engine note picked up and we began to move. Baltic Week had begun.

The flight took nearly three hours. I dozed a little but as I well remembered from the days when Gemma and Luke were infants, the day for young families tends to start early and so there was plenty of chatter, feeding and some audible admonishments for the more fractious of the younger passengers. Before this trip, I'd checked out transfers from airports to city centres. Plan A would always be a train or a metro or, failing those, a bus. Taxis were not an option. As Liz will confirm, I have an aversion to taxis if any kind of collective public transport is available and if not, frankly I'd sooner walk, although I recognise that often that simply isn't practical.

Happily, there seemed to be a bus service into the city from the airport. I had no preconceptions about Kaunas. I'd read a little about it and knew it was Lithuania's second largest city, an important economic and cultural centre that had briefly been the country's capital. One former citizen of Kaunas moved to Britain in 1900, changed his name to Montague Burton and founded the Burton menswear chain. Kaunas was once home to a large Jewish population. Their fate, in common with those of so many Jewish communities in this part of Europe, was a history of pogroms and persecution, especially by Soviet or Nazi occupiers, as well as episodes of local hostility, too. This was a dark stain in the history of the wider region.

One uplifting story caught my eye, though. In 1940, with Kaunas in Soviet hands, the city's Dutch consul quietly arranged for a couple of thousand Jewish people to be given transit visas to reach Curaçao, a Dutch Caribbean territory. Kaunas's Japanese consul acted in a similar way. Between them, acting on their own initiative, they enabled thousands of Jewish people to escape both the present persecution and the coming Holocaust. The world has no shortage of suffering and distress (I'm thankful that my own life has been easy) and it's easy to feel that on our own we can have no impact. But the story of the choices made by these two relatively minor officials and the action that they took was a positive reminder that individuals can find the power and the means to transform the lives of others for good.

Kaunas International Airport was small, modern, with a light, airy terminal. Within minutes of landing, I'd breezed through passport control and was outside, checking which bus stop to wait at. A bus arrived. I headed to it: "Kaunas?" The driver nodded and I bought a ticket. The journey to the city was short and very quickly we reached the bus station which, it seemed to me, was exactly how the arrival point in a city should be. Smart, stylish, spacious, clean and welcoming, it gave me a very positive first impression of Kaunas, as if it was rewarding my decision to come here to run. I reflected that whoever was responsible for replacing London's drab and dreary coach station could take some useful notes here.

I headed out to find my hotel. My route took me past a strikingly large shopping mall, as bright and airy as the airport and the bus station (this was becoming a theme in Kaunas). It was called Akropolis, a name that resonated because of where I was now planning to end this year-long challenge. On a whim, I walked through it, found a pharmacy, and bought some large plasters to ensure that, whatever else I experienced while out running later, nipple rash would not be part of it. There were cafes, a cinema, a bowling alley, brand name clothing outlets. Whatever I was expecting – a lower level of affluence than in the UK, perhaps – was confounded by the Akropolis, which could have graced any city I'd previously visited. The far end of this large glass retail temple opened out to the river, which I'd made a note to run alongside later.

I pushed on towards my hotel and five minutes later, Google Maps suggested I was standing in front of it. If true, this was slightly unsettling. I stood at the entrance to a construction site, or rather, at this stage in the project, a destruction site, where a wrecking ball was bringing down the remains of a building. I skirted round the other side and after a couple of false turns, found the hotel entrance through an archway and off a small parking area. A small, characterful, clean and comfortable place a stone's throw (or in this case a tossed piece of building rubble) from where I shortly planned to run.

The young guy on reception welcomed me in English, explained the essentials – breakfast, check-out time – and apologised for the noise from the building work opposite. I wasn't bothered about it. I had other plans. It was early afternoon, it was winter, daylight would begin to fade before too long here in the eastern Baltic and I had some running to do. I hadn't eaten but wasn't very hungry. I decided to skip lunch in order to get going. I found my room on the first floor, changed into my running gear and headed out – but not before catching the attention of the young receptionist, who looked slightly startled to see this Englishman visibly well beyond the first flush of youth and inadequately dressed for a Lithuanian winter, who had just arrived and was already heading out. I smiled and briefly explained my purpose in being in Kaunas. The receptionist seemed genuinely interested and wished me well.

Buoyed by the support I stepped out and began to trot back through the archway and down the central avenue that serves as a spine for the centre of Kaunas. It was bitterly cold with a sharp, gusting wind, but at least it was dry. I planned to run for about an hour, maybe 8-10K, depending on what I encountered and saw along the way. The centrepiece of the old city is a wide, open cobbled square surrounded by historic buildings in a variety of styles, notably Baroque and Gothic. I seemed to be the only person running anywhere in the centre of this understated but rather lovely city but it didn't matter. There were statues and spires and within just a few minutes I lost my self-consciousness and sense of being an odd one out and began to enjoy the surroundings. This was Lithuania, Stage 20 of RUNNING: ME RUNNING EU was under way and I was very happy to be in Kaunas.

Beyond the old city, the buildings backed on to the River Nemunas, one of two which meet at Kaunas and among the largest rivers in eastern Europe, although it isn't notably wide at this point. I ran around the point where the two waterways flow together and planned to follow the Nemunas to a footbridge onto a low-lying island. I came alongside a busy embankment road and immediately wanted to drop down the high bank to the river path below. It was very steep, though and a continuous safety barrier ran the length of this embankment. The only break in the barrier opened onto a staircase that was so steep that it was virtually a concrete ladder. A text advised "Draudziama". This meant nothing to me. However, there was a large, unambiguous No entry sign, a white horizontal bar on a red circular sign that says "Stay away" in the international language of signs. I was tempted to ignore it in order to get the fairly fast, intrusive road traffic alongside me out of sight and earshot and continue the run at water level. At the same time, there was no value in taking a tumble and spraining an ankle, least of all at the start of Baltic Week, with three more countries to run over the next four days. That would really scupper RUNNING: ME RUNNING EU. So I decided not to turn a Draudziama into a crisis but continued on until the embankment dropped down naturally towards river level.

Finally I crossed onto the island, which was little more than a long, fairly narrow sandbank topped with watermeadows and a few stands of trees. I ran round the island perimeter in about 15 minutes, cut through what seemed to be an abandoned factory at the tip, then made my way back across the river to the city side. I headed back to the old city with a photo opportunity now in mind. I reached the large cobbled square and approached a statue of a former mayor captured striding purposefully across the square. There were few people around at this point, although a trickle of teenagers with assorted backpacks suggested it was going home time from a nearby secondary school.

A boy of 13 or 14 passed nearby. I asked him if he spoke English. His name was Petrus. He answered "Yes" in the way that younger continental Europeans so often do, with an accompanying tone that said "Doesn't everyone...?" I pointed to the statue, asked him to take a picture with my phone and stood alongside the mayor, adopting his striding pose. He took the picture. I checked and asked him to try again. The picture was just a silly throw-away idea but it might as well be a good shot. I wasn't going to be back in Kaunas any time soon. Take two. Happy with the second attempt, I thanked Petrus and told him why I was in Kaunas, about running in every country of the EU. "Cool", he said, and went on his way. Now there were two other people in Lithuania who knew why I was there! I continued the run for a few more minutes before deciding that Stage 20 was complete.

I found my way back up the central avenue and trotted through the archway to the hotel. The young receptionist asked me about where I'd run and explained a few points of interest. When I think back to my short stay in Kaunas, I realise that it was that sense of interest that he showed in me and my reason for being there that left such a positive impression. That night I decided to treat myself to a decent dinner and took up the receptionist's recommendation of a nearby restaurant. The meal was excellent, the wine similar and the bill ridiculously low. As I was to find again during the later stages of the challenge, in several of the formerly communist countries in central and eastern Europe that joined the EU in the great wave of expansion in the mid-noughties, the cost of living can be startlingly cheap for a western European traveller.

With few exceptions during the challenge, I dined, stayed and travelled modestly but chose hotels carefully, balancing location, price and quality and was more often than not pleasantly surprised by how good a hotel was considering how little I was paying to stay there. It was true in Kaunas, it had been true in Croatia, and would be emphatically so again in Bulgaria. On this first night of Baltic Week I went to bed early and very satisfied.

STAGE 21

Latvia: the sudden pleasure of a crowd

My coach to Riga was at 12.30pm. I had a couple of hours to look around Kaunas again so after a leisurely breakfast I partly retraced my steps from the previous day's run and became a tourist for a while, taking pictures and enjoying the architecture of the old town. Back at the hotel as I checked out I heard the familiar whirr of a printer behind the desk as the friendly receptionist completed the formalities. He then turned back to me holding a small package, a small towel and soaps tied with ribbon with a pre-printed message under the hotel's name, wishing safe travels to the recipient. He gave a shy smile: "I give you this to wish you comfortable feet and happy running in Riga and in other cities." It was a pleasing gesture and once again it gave me the warm feeling that here in Kaunas I wasn't alone with my challenge.

It had been a simple exchange but it sent me off in an upbeat mood as I walked back to the bus station. I had time to buy a sandwich and chocolate for what would be a four-hour road trip to Riga, the Latvian capital. Again, I was struck by how shiny, clean and modern the bus station was and how much of a positive final impression it would surely give other travellers as they left Kaunas. My coach arrived. I joined the short queue and as I reached the door, the driver took my home-printed ticket and passport. "Ste-phan. Rrrobert," he said, with a rolled 'r', confirming that the first and middle names on his manifest matched my travel documents. If he'd seen my surname too he didn't seem to think it necessary to say so. He did spend a couple more seconds on my passport, though and had just one more thing to say: "Brr-rexit!" He glanced at me with a rueful, bemused expression, as if I was in some way the embodiment of this unfathomable referendum decision – and perhaps for him, I was. There were no other British travellers that morning – and he waved me aboard. 'Stephen Robert' was good to go.

Online travel site research before the trip had suggested that inter-city coach travel was the fastest and most comfortable way to move between principal points in the Baltic states. The Lux Express coach that would take me to Riga lived up to expectations. It was clean, warm and comfortable and I was immediately happy with my choice. Once beyond the suburbs, the road soon began to pass through the flat, birch-forested landscape that would accompany me for much of the rest of the journey to Riga and the next one to Tallinn, too.

The endless forest and hamlets of tiny wooden dwellings closely matched the vision I had of these lands around the eastern Baltic region as a whole, most notably traditional rural Russia. It was a reminder that barely 50 miles away lay a small exclave of Russia – a piece of Russian territory separated from the rest of Russia itself, wedged between Lithuania, Poland and the Baltic Sea, called Kaliningrad. It's no backwater, though. Kaliningrad is home to the Russian Navy's Baltic fleet and it's far enough south for its waters to be free of winter ice. On this trip, though, it was as near as I would get to Russia. I looked at the map. Russia is vast. I tried to estimate how much of Britain this 'small' piece of Russia would cover. I was surprised. It's roughly the area of London and the Home Counties combined and certainly bigger than Yorkshire, the largest English county. Satisfied that I now had a sense of scale, I put the map reading on pause. It was an enjoyable digression, one that helped fill the four-hour journey to Riga. I switched back to the simple pleasure of gazing out of the window, enjoying the landscape. I dozed, a passenger's privilege.

The border passed almost without notice. Once across, I checked how far was left to go. Still another 50 miles. I was happy with that. There's something about being on a coach or a train that's almost cocoon-like, a feeling of being off the grid and free of responsibility for the duration of the journey. I'll never travel to space but I figure that this is my version of an astronaut's feeling of weightlessness. Maybe not wanting a journey to end is another form of procrastination, something I've experienced throughout my life. I prefer to think of it as unplugging from who the world wants and needs me to be and simply enjoying the moment, literally taking time out.

Eventually the continuous countryside vista of trees and occasional rural dwellings came to an end. More urban features began to appear. Road signs to Riga became more frequent and the industry, railway lines and road junctions that are part of the landscape of the approach to a large city increasingly came into view. I noticed another change. Masked at first by the fresh dazzle of city lights, the day's light was beginning to fade. Finally, the coach pulled in to a drab, old-fashioned terminus that was much more in keeping with the image I might have had of Soviet-era public infrastructure and very different from the smart, modern terminus I'd left at the start of this journey in Kaunas a few hours earlier. But here and now, I had no more thoughts of the previous city. I left the coach's warm, cosy cocoon and stepped down onto the cold, concrete pavement. It was getting dark and the cold wind was piercing as I hauled my trusty Ljubljanski Maraton backpack onto my shoulders.

The arched canopy of Riga's main railway station loomed close by, separated from the bus and coach station by a narrow canal which was iced up, not that I needed a further illustration of just how cold it was. I stood freezing to check the map and confirm my route to the hotel. I'd checked earlier but wanted to be sure. The map took a while to load. If time had been suspended on the coach ride from Kaunas, now I felt every second as I willed the map to appear on my phone screen while I shivered. At last it did and I followed the route, although it took me a couple of attempts at navigating the narrow lanes, returning to where I'd started, before finally realising that an unassuming and dimly marked door in a side street was the entrance to my hotel for the night.

I wondered what I would find inside. The answer was immediate. Warmth! I closed the large, heavy wooden door behind me and was immediately greeted cheerily by three young receptionists, one of them welcoming me almost as if I was a family friend who'd just got back from a trip. She asked me what I was doing in Riga. I told her. The surprise showed on her face. "You are… running here in Riga? You are… strong!" I smiled, accepted the compliment and glowed a little, and not just because it was wonderfully warm inside.

The Rixwell Old Riga Palace Hotel interior was full of dark-beamed wooden panelling. I had a sudden sense of how coming home might have felt to a Baltic seafarer from the days of yore. I was quickly checked in, given my key and directed to my room, which was small, wood-panelled again but otherwise quite plain, and perfect for my one-night stay. So much so that I had to remind myself that I was in Riga to run and that I had to go and do it now. I quickly changed into my full-fat running outfit – merino base layer, long-sleeved running top, a rather worn pair of Karrimor tights that I really needed to replace, London Marathon running jacket, Bournville Harriers neck buff, hat and gloves and, of course, my Hoka Ones which had become my running shoes of choice for the challenge since autumn had started. Blue, with yellow laces, the Hokas had always looked Swedish to me and it seemed fitting to be wearing them here in the Baltic region.

I checked the route I wanted to follow, alongside a stream bordered by what seemed to be a narrow strip of park that formed a semi-circle around Riga's historic city centre, and then out along the waterfront of the Daugavas river. I planned to run for about an hour, covering 10K. I headed downstairs, out through the reception, opened the heavy wooden door, exchanged the hotel's enveloping warmth and light for the cold, dark streets of Riga and began to run. I saw the bus station, heard trains leaving the large terminus as they headed for the bridge over the Daugavas and began to follow some tram tracks as they curved to where the park began. I saw the stream and began to follow it. There were a few people about, one or two glancing in my direction as I passed them – there were no other runners – but otherwise I was alone.

After the initial shock of cold and the strangeness of being newly arrived in an unfamiliar city, I quickly warmed to the endeavour. This was RUNNING: ME RUNNING EU and I was in Riga, creating my adventure with every step. I kept going but quickly realised that my run would be punctuated as the park was intersected with road crossings. I followed the park's curve, nipping across quiet roads when I could but observing the protocol of pedestrian crossings when I encountered people waiting patiently to cross the wider, busier roads. I'm a believer of 'When in Rome...' while travelling and tend to toe the line in a foreign country. On this cold winter night in Riga, though, toeing the line came at a cost as I willed the long seconds to pass and the lights to change so I could keep running and fend off the chill blast being funnelled from the north by Riga's wide river.

By the time I reached the Daugava itself I'd warmed up a little, although even staying in constant motion did little to keep the wind from penetrating the few millimetres of thin fibres that separated my skin from the Baltic chill. The river was wide, dark and vaguely menacing. I looked back to the city side, which seemed much more inviting. I ran along the river embankment, separated from the wide expanse of water by a low wall. There was no one else around. On the far shore, lights twinkled but the night sky and a quarter of a mile of wide, dark flowing river combined to make me feel something I rarely felt during the whole of the challenge – lonely.

I kept going, past the old city, under the striking, multi-arched railway bridge over the Daugava where trains frequently rumbled to and from destinations beyond the far shore. I ran further still. Ahead, I could make out the dark form of another bridge. It seemed a long way away. Did I want to go that far? Maybe not, but I kept going anyway for just over a mile until I eventually reached the bridge. It turned out to be a motorway crossing, all concrete and hazy lights way above me, which increased the sense of sombre darkness as I passed into the tunnel-like space beneath it. For a few paces all was black and I could barely see my feet. I felt uneasy and alone.

My sixth sense was telling me to be careful. I continued to head along the river briefly but I'd been running for an hour by this point and I decided to turn back. As I approached the underside of the motorway bridge again I looked into the gloom and steeled myself to run back through it. I almost jumped when I then noticed movement. Someone was under that bridge. No, not someone but several people. I realised that they were moving together, towards me.... Runners! And there then appeared one of the most welcome sights I could ever have imagined. As many as 30 runners out together for a night run. I'd almost prayed for company. Here was the answer.

"Do you speak English?" I shouted. The front runner pointed back into the pack. "Yes, I do!" came a disembodied voice. "Can I run with you?" "Yes, join us!" I turned round, edged into the middle of the pack and fell into step with Alise, the friendly owner of the voice I'd heard. And that's how I came to run with the Riga Marathon training group. They ran every Wednesday evening and I'd had the sheer good luck to catch them as they headed along the river before tacking left away from the waterfront along the edge of a park and back towards the city centre. Alise spoke good English and I was delighted that she was so willing to spend the time talking to me as we ran. We talked the talk of runners – races, distances, conditions, motivation, the pleasure of running.

The time passed quickly, although by the time we eventually stopped, I'd been running for nearly two hours. We were outside a fitness studio in a side street. Alise said that this was their base and that they finished their midweek session here with a yoga warmdown inside and I was welcome to join them. By this time it was well into the evening, I was hungry and I had to find my way back to my hotel. I didn't have a clue where I was but I had my phone so I would find it. I quickly decided that karma had given me the chance to run with the Riga Marathon group, so I would just go with it. I accepted the invitation and went inside the studio. Alise found me a yoga mat and for the next 30 minutes of triangles, boats, chairs, downward dogs and countless other yoga contortions I discovered how unsupple and unexercised so many of my muscles were. It was an ordeal, a struggle and I loved it.

Too soon (yet not soon enough) it was over. There was just time for a couple of group pictures backlit against a giant Riga Marathon photographic backdrop that filled a wall of the studio, some heartfelt thanks and goodbyes from me and I was back out into Riga's frosty January air and trotting back in the direction of the railway station from where I would find my hotel. The shower was bliss. Changed and back in warm clothes I went out to find somewhere to eat. By this time restaurants were starting to close. There were plenty of burger and pizza places but I wanted a meal to reflect that I was in Latvia. Eventually I found what I was looking for. I've forgotten what I had but it was a simple, warming meal that didn't make me feel as though I could have eaten it in every other city in Europe. Instead, it seemed like the perfect way to round off what had begun as a lonely experience but had ended in the warming company of fellow runners. Looking back as I write this, I see it as a Maya Angelou meal – I don't remember what I ate but I'll never forget how it made me feel. After the run, the encounter with the Riga Marathon group, the yoga and the dinner, the Riga stage of RUNNING: ME RUNNING EU had been a very happy and satisfying experience.

And it wasn't yet over. Not quite. As the day before in Kaunas (was it really only a day? It felt much longer) I had time to look around Riga the next morning before moving on. I left my bag at the hotel to pick up en route to the coach station and now, briefly unencumbered, I looked round Riga's historic core. The city has many fine buildings and I enjoyed a couple of hours of casual wandering. It's certainly an attractive place for a stroll, with many cobbled streets and lots of easy-on-the-eye cityscapes full of varied architecture on a low-rise, human scale, less monumental than cities like London, Brussels or Paris. I skirted the edge of the stream and park that I'd worked my way round at the start of the run the night before, wandering up lanes and down side streets, generally following my nose.

At one point I was struck by the unexpected sight of a British flag on what proved to be the back of the Latvian National Theatre. I peered through the locked gates. There on a small, isolated outbuilding enclosed behind a high wall was a Union flag and a sign that said "Brexit: Open for Business".

I wanted to know why it was there but there was no time and I never did find out. Perhaps it was just an ironic theatrical comment on how Latvia saw Britain's decision to leave the EU. Like the other two Baltic states, Latvia had made joining the EU one of its priorities after gaining independence from the Soviet Union, part of the wider 'return to Europe' that so many countries in central and eastern Europe desired once the iron curtain had been lifted. Perhaps Latvia saw it as a paradox that a country could declare itself to be 'Open for Business' while putting up barriers to trade with its neighbours. I would like to have found out more but it was locked up and there was no one around to ask. Instead, I only had time to take a couple of pictures, get a coffee nearby and then head back to pick up my bag. It was time to leave Riga. I had another coach to catch.

RUNNING: ME RUNNING EU

STAGE 22

Estonia: the beauty of Tallinn

The route from Riga heads directly north to Tallinn and for much of its length it skirts the Gulf of Riga, part of the Baltic Sea. Much of the landward scenery was forested, so I had the choice of sea or trees for much of the four-hour journey to Tallinn. A third of Latvians live in Riga itself and the population seems sparse along this coastline. The coach passed what seemed like a continuation of the previous day's landscape: long stretches of birch forest, occasionally broken up by small groups of wooden huts and houses which to this native-born Londoner looked like dwellings in a fairy tale. We crossed the border into Estonia. More sea, more trees, only now the evergreens became more prominent. So did the snow. We were heading ever further northwards. Just over 100 miles after leaving Riga, the coach reached Pärnu, a spa and seaside town. From here, the coach was drawn away from the coastline, sticking unerringly to the N on the compass for the remainder of the journey.

Estonia feels Nordic and looks rather like Scandinavia, although definitions of both normally wouldn't include Estonia. Nonetheless Estonia has close and long-standing ties with Scandinavia. Estonians speak a language that's close to Finnish. Not least, its capital, Tallinn is linked by a short sea-crossing to Finland's capital, Helsinki, which is definitely Nordic, although sticklers would claim that strictly speaking, even Finland isn't quite part of Scandinavia. I'll get to Helsinki at the next stage. Now, it's time to tell the Tallinn part of the story. Like the other Baltic states, Estonia became independent from the former Soviet Union in 1991 following four years of what became known as the Singing Revolution. Since singing its way to statehood without bloodshed (why fight when you can sing?), Estonia has joined both the EU and NATO. Russia has never been happy with having NATO forces on its doorstep, which explains some of the modern-day tension between Russia and the countries of the west. I reflected on this once or twice during Baltic Week but did not dwell further. As we know now, those tensions would escalate violently in Ukraine, but I had no inkling on that cold, snowy day in February 2019. I was here to run.

I had no expectations of Tallinn. I'd seen no pictures, except of the handful of hotels I'd checked out on Booking.com before opting for the Imperial on the basis that it was right in the city centre but close to the ferry terminal for the sailing to Helsinki, looked OK and was within my budget. So I had no preconceptions. Even so, the immediate environs of the suburban terminus where the coach finally stopped were slightly underwhelming. But I knew that this wasn't the city centre and that the vicinities of coach stations were rarely exciting. More pressing was the need to get out of the snow, which was coming down in a dense, moist white blanket, and to find my way to the old city, the historic centre which would be my base for what was left of the day and for my brief stay in Tallinn. I was already on a fairly short time-frame and the weather conditions weren't ideal for running. I found my way to the busy tram stop, asked fellow would-be passengers for 'Vannalinn' (old town) and was directed to catch the next tram which was just arriving. I clambered on through a middle door and joined the throng of people huddled in the steamed-up carriage, unable to avoid breathing in the fuggy aroma of wet garments but suddenly happy at no longer being snowed on.

The only problem was, I hadn't paid my fare. I couldn't see a ticket machine. I realised that most people had passes but a handful were boarding at the front and paying the driver. The carriage was crammed with people and bags. I weighed in my mind the effort required to inch my way to the door, climb down from the tram and then to re-board at the front, against just taking a chance that no inspector would come aboard to discover my crime against Tallinn Transport in the short time I would be on the tram. 'When in Rome' came to mind again and I decided to do the right thing, feeling relieved when I'd finally done so and paid the driver.

I finally left the tram at Balti Jaam, which sounds vaguely like a uniquely Brummie culinary fusion but was in fact a railway station and the nearest stop to the old town which, as I discovered, stands on a rock above the rest of the city. The snow was falling thick and heavy, just as it lay on the ground. So thick that it had carpeted everything in a continuous white padding, levelling off the sharp angles of walls and edges of paths so that it wasn't at all clear where to go. Google Maps gave me the direction I needed but I couldn't pick out the path to take me there. Ankle-deep in snow I walked backwards and forwards across what turned out to be gardens below the old city walls, wasting what I felt was precious time. The conditions were decidedly poor for running and the snow was getting thicker all the time. Finally I found the road that took me to my hotel and trudged into a lovely, fresh, attractively-decorated pine interior. I was caked in snow and the reception carpet was already more than damp from what had no doubt been a steady trail of guests bringing the clinging, wet, white weather in with them.

Another hotel and another friendly receptionist's welcome. Despite its name, the Hotel Imperial exuded no haughty grandeur. Instead, it was intimate and inviting. I was rapidly registered as the hotel's latest resident. Once in my room I quickly unpacked my running gear and changed, ready to run. I was a bit uncertain about the snow and ice. I'd slipped a couple of times on the walk to the hotel entrance. I was wary of taking a tumble. Uppermost in my mind was a fear of a fracture that would scupper the rest of the challenge. I was conscious that I was now making good progress and was on track but that there was little slack in the schedule and certainly none for recovery from a broken ankle. I would have to take it carefully.

I headed out. I had no fixed plan for this run. Possibly I would make this a short one, in view of the conditions. It had stopped snowing but the snow cover was thick and the going was slow. I ran down to the park area I'd seen at the foot of the city walls. At first I thought of stepping onto a long wide band of snow that I took to be a broad path, but something made me stop. Was it really a path, or maybe lawns? It was impossible to tell. Everything was white and now night had fallen the light of the lamps spaced wide apart threw shadows that made shapes and angles difficult to decode. However, I could just about make out the snow-smudged outline of a path that seemed to zig-zag its way across these gardens. Now I realised that the lamps followed a similar contour. That must be the main path. I decided to follow it and a few hundred yards further on I was glad I had. That previous wide band that I thought might be lawns turned out to be a long meandering waterway, the remains of the moat that once surrounded the old city and now a continuous pond that had been entirely covered in snow – the perfect camouflage to catch out and drench an unwary runner. Happily I had been wary and I was glad I hadn't set foot in it.

After a few minutes around the park I began to climb up to the old city and here Tallinn really came into its own. If the area around the bus station had been nondescript and rather drab, Tallinn old city proved to be jaw-droppingly beautiful. A local guide describes it as the best-preserved medieval city in northern Europe and I can absolutely believe it. It's all pastel pinks and creams and yellows, red-ochre tiles, Gothic spires, cobbled lanes, wealthy merchants' former townhouses, medieval churches all laid out on the city's original 13th century grid. Many of those homes and churches would each have been a jewel in their own right. Here up high in Tallinn's old city they could be found by the streetful, one after the other.

As I turned each corner I was simply amazed by what I saw. And then through a gap I glimpsed the most controversial jewel of them all, the Alexander Nevsky Cathedral, built in 1900 and a symbol of Czarist domination, a piece of pure onion-domed Russia in the heart of medieval Tallinn. Now I'd seen the cake, the icing and the cherry on top. I ran around the old city, pausing at moments to capture impressions of the beauty all around me. I have the pictures and they show the forms, the angles and the hues but they do not capture the atmosphere. That night, running on a white carpet, lit by lamplight, with the endorphin effect only adding to my sense of pleasure in the detail, the overall spectacle and the thrill of experiencing such unexpected beauty, I was now on a high that would never be topped during the whole of the rest of the challenge. In the weeks that remained there would be many unforgettable moments, just as there had been during the previous months. But there was nothing quite like running in the snow that night in Tallinn old city. Continuing the run, I returned to a look-out point that offered a fine panoramic sweep across the rest of the city with several buildings glowing with illumination. I was cold, my feet and ankles sodden, but I was barely aware of it. I couldn't drag myself away. Instead, I retraced my steps back up and around the old city and doused myself again in its splendour.

Eventually I decided it really was time to return to Earth. I followed the steps down the side of the old city hill, ran back through the park, skirting what I could now clearly see was a moat, albeit one that remained hidden under a thick blanket of snow, and made my way back to the hotel. I'd been out for over an hour and run just under five miles. Not much mileage – but enough…

That night's shower was among the best so far. Not that the bathroom was extra special – it was fine – but the shower's high pressure massaged the chill from my skin and left me tingling and refreshed. The 300m walk to the restaurant I chose ('Choice' is over-stating it. Many restaurants had stopped serving already, leaving just a few touristy joints around the main square) was perilous. The cobblestones were glazed with ice, I saw three people separately fall, while several others narrowly avoided a similar fate. There was no grit. I slipped and skidded every few yards and eventually had to take pigeon steps to try to stay on my feet. I wondered if it was often like this in Tallinn in winter. After a forgettable meal (at least I think it was forgettable. I've forgotten it...) I took the icy peril challenge once again but made it back unscathed.

I updated Facebook, made my plans for the next day and settled down to sleep.

STAGE 23

Helsinki, Finland "Language differences aside, it was parkrun very much as we know it. The welcome, the briefing, the marshals, the course signage, the timing, the finish tokens (including the plea to hand them back and not to take them home afterwards), the barcodes, the scanning. Most of all, that distinct pleasure of being part of it, a feeling of being connected to a wider community of people who share the simple, positive, mutually supporting, inclusive values of parkrun. And not forgetting the coffee!"

PART 2 | THE ACTUAL RUNNING PART

STAGE 23

Finland: a ship, more ice and parkrun

It was Friday 8 March. Just 21 days remained before the RUNNING: ME RUNNING EU deadline and I was now on a ship heading to Finland for the next stage of the Challenge. My destination was Helsinki. When researching travel options for Baltic Week, I'd found three ferry lines operating the Tallinn to Helsinki route. Trawling through sailing times and ticket types, I was pleasantly surprised to find a no-frills fare for just €10 on the Eckero Line's noon sailing. No guaranteed seat at that price but I figured that, if necessary, I could do a lot worse than walk the decks and gaze at the sea and shorelines for a couple of hours. Happily it was much better than that. The MV Finlandia proved to be a very comfortable, modern and spacious ship with plenty of seating to choose from for those of us making that particular crossing. It was quite busy but far from crowded. After a gentle one-mile walk from the hotel to the ferry terminal that would have been easier but less picturesque without the ice and snow, I'd joined a small, growing line of foot passengers waiting to board the Finlandia. Once the gate opened, boarding was straightforward, calm and uneventful.

Most of my fellow foot passengers were travelling light and seemed to be either Finns returning home for the weekend or Estonians heading for the attractions of Helsinki. It was off-season and there were few tourists from elsewhere, at least on foot. Once on board, numbers grew as we joined those emerging from the vehicle decks. The sense of purpose as many made straight for the Finlandia's restaurants and cafes confirmed my feeling that this was a familiar journey for many of those on board. We sailed at noon, and that meant lunch. I located the self-service restaurant and joined what was already a sizeable queue. By the time I was served the Finlandia had already nudged away from its mooring and was slowly gliding past Tallinn's ferry terminal quays. All conversations around me were in Finnish or Estonian and, much though I like to have a few words of greeting, request or appreciation in the language of wherever I go, to my regret I knew nothing of either of these languages. In fact they are quite closely related and to a certain extent Finns and Estonians can understand each other. But I couldn't, so, here at the lunch counter I might have to rely on pointing, nods and facial expressions, or go hungry. Happily, my tentative request in English for the dish of the day, coffee and some water was immediately met with a warm, assured: "Of course, sir. Now, would you like hot or cold milk in your coffee?" This had been my experience almost throughout the entire challenge.

In a world where some English language competence is usually found in people wherever I might be, it may often not be *essential* to speak the other person's language, but to do so helps to make a powerful connection. The mere fact of showing your willingness to connect by offering a greeting, a request in a shop, a "please", a "how much?", a "where can I find…?" or a "thank you", in a language that isn't your own, can disarm and bring out the best in otherwise naturally cautious strangers, and socially even a very limited survival-grade smattering can open many doors. Here on the Finlandia I didn't need it, which was just as well.

Fortified by my lunch, I went on deck for fresh air. I wasn't disappointed. It was definitely fresh, meaning icy. Tallinn had receded, Estonia was low on the skyline though still clearly visible, while open water lay ahead. I took in the sky, the sea, the breeze, the cold. A few minutes were enough. I returned to the warm interior, read for a while, had another coffee and then went back outside. By now an archipelago of rocks and islands had come into view as we approached Helsinki.

We docked. By this time I was already below decks with the other foot passengers until the large panel-like door slid back and we left the Finlandia. Helsinki port lay ahead and there at a small rail-head was the tram stop. I'd researched the travel options and weighed up the merits of an hour's walk on icy pavements against a much shorter tram ride to the central station with my hotel close by and the chance to check in, change and get out running before the light began to fade. I took the tram.

I'd chosen Hotel Arthur because it was close to the start of the Tokoinranta parkrun, which takes its name from the inner harbour area where the weekly 5K run takes place. While still in Estonia I'd contacted the Tokoinranta parkrun team via the event's Facebook page to let them know I was coming, explained what I was doing and how I'd decided to make their parkrun part of my challenge. It was what had become by now a succinct, standard message:

> "Hi Tokoinranta parkrun! I'm coming to run with you this week. I'm running in all 28 countries of the European Union by 29.3.19. It's my own personal challenge for 2 UK charities. I call it RUNNING: ME RUNNING EU. Last night I ran in Riga, tonight in Tallinn. Finland is country number 23/28. Looking forward to seeing you on Saturday!"

The response was also short but enthusiastic and its warm, welcoming tone left me with a small glow of anticipation:

> "Hi Steve. This sounds like a wonderful challenge, we are honoured you've chosen our little parkrun as your run in Finland. I look forward to meeting you on Saturday? Cheers, Karlina [this week's RD (*Run director*)]"

The response was as positive and welcoming as I'd hoped. Now I knew they'd be expecting me. It might also make it easier to meet people and talk to them about the challenge once I was there. First things first, though. I was making my way to my chosen base for Stage 23.

In contrast to the rather quiet, characterful hotels I'd enjoyed in Kaunas, Riga and Tallinn, Hotel Arthur was bustling and basic. Heading into one of several doors into reception I found a sea of cases, backpacks, bags, dogs and several extended family groups, seemingly from everywhere (and now that I had joined them, from the UK, too). I queued to check in and waited. Eventually my booking was processed by an overworked receptionist who clearly had no time or inclination for charm. But the transaction was swift and within five minutes I was in the rather spartan room that would be my base for this next stage of the Challenge.

I quickly changed. Vest, long-sleeved top. Tights, long BvH running socks over the tights. Hoka Ones, London Marathon running jacket. Neck buff. Running beanie. Padded gloves. Sound like a lot of clothes to run in? Wrong! I'd seen the heavy, warmth-retaining clothes people were wearing on the street. It was barely above zero outside, heavy with snow clouds and an icy breeze. This afternoon was about acclimatisation, doing a recce of where tomorrow's parkrun would be, and getting to know Helsinki a bit. I was there for little more than 24 hours so I wanted to make the most of it while there was still light. I wanted to run. I didn't intend to freeze.

I headed out. I was going to follow my nose, vaguely tracking the contour of the large, sprawling harbourside to which every street seems to lead in the heart of Helsinki, but with no other plan than to explore this side of the city, to see what I found along the way, and run. First, though, I would recce tomorrow's parkrun rendezvous.

As chance and treacherous conditions would have it, the event team had temporarily had to move the start of the course to an alternative location to reduce the risk of runners becoming victims of Helsinki on Ice and take a tumble, so tomorrow's start would be closer still – just across the Kaisaniemi Botanical Garden, a small park which began at the end of the road behind my hotel. I trotted gingerly to the make-shift meeting point. Conditions were truly dicey. The paths were ice rinks, some so smooth and slick that running was impossible and walking extremely hazardous. In the UK I would have expected to see local authority signage and barriers to keep people away but here, as in Tallinn the previous night, it was simply open season for slips, trips and falls. I guessed that people in the Nordic states just accept it as a feature of their climate and get on with it. Certainly I felt sure that, had this been Cannon Hill parkrun, the next day's event would have been called off already. Here, there was no chance that an early on-the-day inspection would find these conditions improved and any safer, so I was concerned at first that the event wouldn't go ahead. However, with the course adjustment made, the event director had assured me that there was no risk of the next day's event being cancelled.

I skirted around the slickest part of the iced-up patch, eventually found firmer ground with a better grip and began to trot cautiously along the side of a waterway, following its course until it soon opened out into Helsinki harbour. The scene here was of boats and masts, the water's surface capped with ice floes, like a thick, shattered pane of opaque white glass. Occasionally working boats of different sizes would push their way through the heavy floes. So far as I could tell, they were all service vessels; these were surely no conditions for pleasure boating. I continued the run, occasionally stopping to capture the scene with photos. It began to snow and the air filled up quickly, the flakes swirling all around on a keen, icy breeze.

I noted how thoroughly the occasional passers-by had insulated themselves from the conditions. Heavy, full-length, padded coats, faces enclosed within deep fur hoods (or maybe faux-fur – who could tell in this thickening flurry?), thick gauntlets, boots and scarves. As my immediate baptism of ice coolly demonstrated, conditions in 'Hesa' (the local nickname for Helsinki, like Brum for Birmingham) could be less than hospitable and the Hesalainen themselves dressed appropriately.

At this point I laughed at myself for being so lightly clad in contrast. I allowed myself a fleeting moment of self-satisfaction that, while the locals were trudging past, clad (I imagined) as heavily as reindeer-herders in Finland's northern Arctic fringe, I was toughing it out in the thinnest of 'performance' running layers. I imagine we all have momentary musings that rarely survive ten seconds of reflection before we discard them just as quickly. And as throwaway thoughts go, this one barely made it to the next corner. As I approached, preparing to turn left and follow the waterfront around a jetty, I saw a door open in what looked like a windowless metal cabin. From it emerged an old man, tall, stooped, wearing only Speedos. You read that correctly. This sight was so unexpected that I stopped. Focused on his task and untroubled at my presence he crossed my path to the water's edge, descended some brick steps cut into the quayside, and lowered himself into a small patch of deeply uninviting water that had been freed from the surrounding harbour ice.

Baffled, I simply stared as, after a few seconds in the water, the old man, who looked well into his seventies and was possible older still, emerged from his icy plunge and slowly re-climbed the steps. In awe and still slightly disbelieving, I felt compelled to hail this feat of endurance: "You're a very brave man!" I pointed to the water, then to him and gave a thumbs-up. He didn't speak English but seemed to pick up the note of admiration from my voice and gesture. He shrugged in return, half in acknowledgement but also as if to say, "There it is. I'm Finnish. What else would we do?" Impressed and chastened by this hardy nonchalance, I resumed my run. Finland 1 England 0.

It was late afternoon in very early March and the light was beginning to fade. I'd passed boats, jetties, pontoons, quayside huts, cabins and an array of Helsinki's distinctive maritime buildings. I'd heard harbour sounds, occasional toots from passing vessels, the cry of gulls and a muted background of road traffic from the city behind me. Here, though, was calm. There were no other runners. In fact there were fewer passers-by now. The weather was closing in as the light drained away. I'd been out for an hour. It would take me a while to reach the hotel again. And I'd need to dry my kit. The radiator in my room looked up to the task but still, it would need a few hours. I decided to turn back and call it a day. I'd gathered an impression of Helsinki as a port city, I'd now run in Finland, although the 'formal' run for the Challenge would follow tomorrow. It was now time to rediscover the modest comforts of Hotel Arthur. I retraced my steps, running gently but with no photo-stops this time, pausing only when the lights were against me at several crossings and to check my route a couple of times. By the time I re-entered the hotel's bustle it was nearly dark outside.

Being close to the central station there were eateries aplenty of the kind to be found near central stations in major cities right across Europe. At this late stage in RUNNING: ME RUNNING EU, that was a claim to knowledge that I could make from direct experience. So it may have been convenient just around the corner to have a few dozen ways to eat Italian or in burger chains or other fast food options, but that wasn't what I wanted. What did real Helsinki people eat when they went out on a Friday evening and where did they eat it? I decided to look on Google and found a smallish and seemingly authentic Finnish restaurant just a 10-minute walk from the hotel in the opposite direction from the central station. The Kolme Kruunua was in a residential street close to another stretch of Helsinki's harbour, although that's almost to state the obvious: in central Helsinki you're never more than a few minutes from the waterfront.

It was bitingly cold to walk there and the warm, cosy conviviality once I'd entered the Kolme Kruunua and closed the door behind me washed over me like a balmy breeze. They were full, but no problem. I was on my own, I could sit at the corner of the long, highly polished wooden bar and they would serve me there. I sat down and looked around. Finns often see themselves as reserved but that hasn't been any barrier to friendly encounters I've had with the Finns I've met who, while calm and not given to loud guffaws of joviality, have been warm and open. Certainly here at the Kolme Kruunua on a Friday night in early March, people were calm but visibly enjoying themselves. The atmosphere, animated but not boisterous, soon enveloped me so that, although alone, I felt that I belonged here, too.

I looked on the menu for something that sounded hearty and warming and would unmistakably place me in Nordic climes. Sautéed reindeer (please don't judge me, Rachel and other fans of Christmas – it wasn't Rudolph!) with mashed potato and lingonberries. That would do it. The barman who had also become my personal waiter recommended a blueberry pie. No sooner suggested than accepted and served. And devoured... Perhaps I could have lingered over it for longer... Suffice to say that the hunger from an afternoon's icy running was soon satisfied and I left feeling full and happy.

My Facebook posts during March 2019 were almost entirely devoted to the latter stages of Running: Me Running EU. Almost. The Helsinki stage coincided with International Women's Day, and I chose to mark it by posting about my aunt Doris, a woman whose independence of mind and taste for adventure had long earned my admiration, so that it was an easy decision to dedicate this telling of my own adventure to her, hence the dedication at the beginning of the story.

The Facebook post was succinct but heartfelt:

> "My Aunt Doris drove army trucks during the Second World War. She was in Brussels on the day it was liberated from the Nazis. She was just 21. During the British occupation of western Germany she drove army officers on the sometimes hazardous Helmstedt corridor through the Soviet sector to Berlin. At a checkpoint, she once had to fend off a Red Guard's sexual advances while the British officer in the car did nothing. She rose through the ranks and became an officer in her own right. After the army she became the bursar of a well-known Catholic college. A keen sailor, she crewed a sailing yacht over the North Sea in her 70s. She's now 95 and mentally as sharp as ever. I am immensely proud that she's my aunt and I wanted to share her story on International Women's Day."

My aunt lived for a further three years. During that time I was able to tell her about my own adventure and it was heartwarming to know that she approved.

I was up early the next morning. Both my phone's alarm and my body clock told me so. 7am is early enough for an owl like me, especially when it's 7am EST, which is two hours earlier than UK time. I wanted to get down for a light breakfast a good hour before the morning's running began. I'd eaten well the night before. I also had every intention of sampling for myself Tokoinranta's post-parkrun cake and coffee culture. But running 'fasted' wasn't part of my challenge today. In keeping with the overall hotel experience, breakfast was functional – and quickly over.

Soon after 8am I was out and heading into the Botanical Gardens for a warm-up run (in every sense) before hooking up with the other parkrunners on the harbour side of the gardens. The meltwater had frozen again overnight but it had also snowed just enough to provide some surface grip and, while conditions still offered opportunities for impromptu skating, the paths were more manageable. I spotted another runner, then a pair of runners and sure enough a small group was beginning to gather. I joined them. There were smiles, greetings. I recognised the run director, Karlina, from her picture on the event's Facebook page. "Hi, I'm Steve. I'm running a charity challenge. I wrote to you–" I didn't need to elaborate. "Steve! Yes, well, hello, and welcome to Tokoinranta. We're delighted that you've chosen to run with us here today." Others offered their own greetings and joined the conversation. I couldn't have been made to feel more welcome. It was another moment of absolute validation for the challenge, filling me again with a fleeting but genuine sensation of not wanting to do anything or be anywhere else other than being there at Tokoinranta with Karlina, her event team and other parkrunners on that cold, bright March morning in Helsinki.

I noted the familiar parkrun signage – the logo, livery and typeface – and the to-me unfamiliar language on the Start and Finish (Finnish!) signs and on the volunteers' high-viz jackets. The words from Mr Spock of the USS Enterprise came to mind, adapted for the occasion: "It's parkrun, Steve, but not as we know it…" Actually, language differences aside, it was parkrun very much as we know it. The welcome, the briefing, the marshals, the course signage design, the timing, the finish tokens (including the plea to hand them back and not to take them home afterwards), the barcodes, the scanning. Most of all, that distinct pleasure of being part of it, a feeling of being connected to a wider community of people who share the simple, positive, mutually supporting, inclusive values of parkrun. And not forgetting the coffee!

We were just 25 runners – far fewer than those of us who'd taken part in both events in the New Year's Day Double in Copenhagen and Malmö and a mere fraction of the hundreds I'd expect to see on a typical Saturday in Birmingham. Watching our feet carefully – snow and ice carpeted many of the paths and it was still decidedly iffy in places – we started and made our way alongside the swathe of railway lines emerging from the central station. We climbed as the path rose below some trees and crossed a footbridge over the tracks, dropping down the other side until we began to follow the edge of a large lake. The course tracked this all the way round, past banks of reeds, and waterfowl of various types. I was impressed by the sense of calm (that word again) of this wide open vista so close to the centre, and the value to the wellbeing of people in Helsinki to have such a large place of light and water and haven of nature in their midst.

There were plenty of people around, too, even at that time, especially dog-walkers and parents with young families, plus a few more elderly people. It took a while to skirt round the lake. Eventually we were climbing back up a short, fairly steep incline to the level of the footbridge, returning to the other side and finally to the edge of the botanic garden where we'd started. My Tokoinranta parkrun was over, at least the running part of it. One of the runners was vlogging the event, running with a selfie stick as he recorded the experience. He asked me if I would say a few words about Running: Me Running EU on camera. I obliged. The easy conversations continued for several more minutes, as they do at parkruns everywhere I've been.

Eventually the ever-friendly Karlina (from Latvia, via Manchester) and the other volunteers began to gather up the signage and equipment and invited everyone to join them for the next and final stage of the Saturday morning parkrun experience at a nearby café called La Torrefazione. Occupying three tables, nearly a dozen of us had made the 10-minute walk from the icy finish of the course to the warmth of this light, bright, relaxed, modern café, which was worth a visit on its own merits and was certainly the icing on the ice as far as the chilly morning's parkrun pleasures were concerned, and not only because the Torrefazione offered a discount for parkrunners (another reason for #DFYB). The sense of bonhomie was palpable as stories were swapped, family details shared and further weekend plans revealed. I stayed for half an hour, wished it could be longer but had to get back to the hotel, shower, change, pack and check out before noon. I said my goodbyes and left, glowing with the warmth of being in the parkrun bubble and particularly this one, with these people.

My flight back to Gatwick wasn't until late. I had time to explore Helsinki a little more. The look and feel of each country I'd passed had become notably more Nordic as my Baltic Week journey went on. Some of the old buildings in both Kaunas and Riga had hinted at their historical links with the once-extensive north German trading community of the Hanseatic League. By contrast, Tallinn looked and felt discernibly Scandinavian, even if its imposing Alexander Nevsky Cathedral looked as though it had been transplanted straight from Red Square. This thought reminded me of another example much closer to home in Birmingham. Get a feel for the distinctive artisan style of worker's cottages as you stroll around the leafy avenues of the enlightened Cadbury family's model village of Bournville, and then you'll be more than surprised to turn a corner and discover a 14th century Byzantine-style place of worship.

This is the Orthodox Church of Holy Prince Lazar, a piece of Serbia in the Birmingham suburbs, built for political refugees from the former Yugoslavia after the Second World War. Incongruous to my eyes, it must have seemed like an oasis of home in an unfamiliar city for those refugees. Once across the Baltic to Helsinki, though and this really did look and feel like true Scandinavia, even if that's not a term the Finns themselves use about their own country.

After the thoroughly satisfying morning I'd enjoyed, I thought about how easy it had been to find myself in the community with a common purpose: runners, parkrunners, fellow Europeans who simply wanted to live their lives within the orbit and embrace of other considerate, like-minded people. I'm no stranger to quoting authors, historians, songwriters (if someone else has captured a thought or a feeling so memorably or aptly, why not share their words and give them the credit?). When I do, though, it's rarely Wordsworth. And yet this was absolutely one of those "Bliss was it in that dawn to be alive but to be young was very heaven" moments. I wasn't young, but I was healthy, fit, where I wanted to be, excited to be there and free to do what I was doing. Isn't that a reasonable working definition of heaven and worth every bit as much as being young? Well, it is when you're over 60! I remember my childhood teens and twenties with great fondness. But I also remember the doubts, insecurities and lack of confidence of those earlier years, too. Happily the confidence has grown immeasurably over the years – another reason why I'd been able to set out on this adventure that had brought me to Helsinki. At that moment on that Saturday afternoon in March 2019, I could say that there was nowhere else I'd rather have been.

I spent the afternoon walking, simply enjoying the sights and spaces that I found along the way. Connecting several was the Baana, the cutting that once saw trains heading out between the city's freight port and the central station. It had fallen into disuse and there were plans to redevelop it. In fact this may yet happen. For now, though, the Baana has a new life as a pedestrian walkway, trail and cycle path with planted areas and recreational features along the way. As a rather narrow brick and stone canyon below street level, it's neither New York's High line not Derbyshire's Tissington Trail, but like them both, the Baana is a testament to some creative thinking and a desire to preserve a part of railway heritage and give people a new outdoor amenity and a space to relax.

I followed the Baana for a couple of kilometres west of the centre, before exiting to a wide, fairly busy road which took a while to cross. On the far side I had another glimpse of water, an inlet within a semi-secluded green haven away from the hubbub, although as big cities go, it isn't hard to leave the traffic behind in Helsinki. This calm, green place turned out to be a district of cemeteries. It was very cold and there were few people around. Occasionally a lone individual would pass, almost always a woman, with flowers and an expression of contemplation, en route to visit a grave and remember the dead. I skirted the water for a while but felt hungry and in need of warmth and a change of scenery.

It really was bitterly cold and not even the constant motion of walking could do much to offset the air's jagged chill. I retraced the Baana, stopping when I reached the steps to the street that would take me to HAM, Helsinki Art Museum. I made a pitstop to eat in the museum café and then visited the HAM's current headline exhibition, a showcase for the work of Tove Jansson, creator of the Moomins, rather odd, bulbous cartoon creatures once unkindly dismissed but perhaps accurately captured by a Times critic as 'a family of hippopotami with scrotal noses'. I knew the Moomins from childhood, although at that time I'd found them curious rather than engaging.

Fed, warmed and further fortified by images of Moomins and details of their creator's life, I left the HAM to brave the icy chill again and pick up the trail back up the Baana. I walked long enough to decide that, stimulating though it was to see Helsinki and refreshing though it felt to be out in the open, the compromises I'd made with my clothing in order to travel light hadn't given me a lot of insulation for these cold conditions. Even so, I didn't want to sit out the remaining few hours in a café. I'd liked very much what I'd seen and done in Helsinki and wanted to get as much from my time here as I reasonably could. I walked on and entered a wide open area of snow-covered lawns and paths, dominated by a huge, imposing modern structure that seemed to serve partly as a building, partly as a giant public sculpture. I had no idea what it was but it seemed to attract of steady stream of people, mostly of student age. Was this a university? A concert hall? I approached to find out. In fact it was Oodi, Helsinki's new public library and meeting space, all curves and planes with a sweeping spruce-timbered façade and a lot of glass.

Opened for the first time just weeks earlier, Oodi defied my expectation of such large buildings, which often make statements about power and prestige but which just as often exceed a human scale. Drawn to join the numerous people I could see who were already inside, I followed the ant trail of new arrivals and found my way in. First impressions: it was warm inside! Primary goal achieved, I read the signage and headed to an upper floor. Here was a large open stepped area, a wooden terrace where people were sprawled singly, or in groups, some with headphones listening to… music? lectures? podcasts? who knew? It's true there was a student feel to the majority of those making use of Oodi's interior and electricity – quite a few were charging mobiles via the many sockets freely distributed along the terraced steps.

But I didn't feel out of place – I'd been a student second time around not that long ago so it felt familiar – and there were other people of varying ages who were also making use of Oodi's space to meet, mix and mingle. That was the uplifting conclusion about the place. Although it was a library and while there were lecture halls, rooms for workshops and other locations for specific purposes, a large part of Oodi was just a public realm, a space for people to be themselves. It seemed to chime with my sense of Scandinavian societies creating assets for public good rather than turning every plot of de-industrialised land into another opportunity for private development. Good for Helsinki, I thought.

Back outside, night had fallen. I made my way to the central station, found the service to the airport and arrived with plenty of time to check in, pass security and grab a snack. I boarded the Norwegian Air flight. As I reached the aircraft doorway I noticed that the plane was a Boeing 737 Max. I knew there had been questions about the craft after a crash in Indonesia but I figured that Norwegian was a grown-up airline that knew what it was doing. I didn't give air safety another thought during a smooth and comfortable journey. It was Saturday 9 March 2019. We landed shortly after 11pm UK time, I caught the train and stayed overnight in London, a very successful trip complete. Six hours after my plane touched down, another 737 Max took off in Ethiopia and crashed immediately, killing all on board. The 737 Max was grounded worldwide with immediate effect.

PART 2 | THE ACTUAL RUNNING PART

STAGE 24

Cyprus: at last, some warmth

SUNDAY 17 MARCH – 12 DAYS TO GO

Facebook 16 March "As race swagbags go, this one's pretty good. A hefty bar of (don't call it Turkish) Delight that may exceed my carry-on weight limit, a bright purple technical top, the usual gels, leaflets and a free 2-day bus pass for anywhere in the Paphos area. Had a pleasant lunch (chicken souvlaki, yoghurt and honey and two coffees, thanks for asking) so will now check out the marathon expo. Oh, and it's 18 degrees and the sun is shining."

My first impressions of Cyprus were positive and I was upbeat for the half marathon. There's something about the early spring warmth and light of a Mediterranean island that can really lift the spirits after the long cold, dark months in Europe's more northerly climes. It was true that I'd felt much the same on arrival in Malta before the 'mishap', but I'd checked the forecast for Paphos and this almost balmy weather was going to hold. Yet another airline, TUI, had brought me here. I knew of TUI mainly as a package holiday operator, but it offered a return flight from Gatwick that could get me directly to Paphos and back over the half marathon weekend, so I snapped it up to avoid missing out and being forced to make a lengthier, more expensive and uncertain journey via Larnaca. I also knew that package travel was susceptible to delay and flights at an ungodly hour. TUI had indeed contacted me three days before departure to announce that my flight out had been put back and was now scheduled to arrive at 10pm. That was no disaster but I hoped that this wouldn't affect the onward journey to Paphos itself. I'd now be looking for my accommodation – Seaside Luxury Flat: Natalia House 102 – in darkness and would have to locate a key-box to let myself in. I'd booked it for two nights, with a day to acclimatise, collect my race number, recce where the race would start and generally check out Paphos.

Meanwhile, I wondered if the flight would be mostly filled with families with young children or groups of mates ready to large it in Paphos, now perhaps with a few hours of extra 'fuelling' to top up their holiday spirits.

A hint of what might be in store came in the confirming email when I booked the accommodation: "Important information – This property will not accommodate hen, stag or similar parties." If other properties in Paphos were more accommodating for the hen-and-stag crowd, the flight could turn out to be raucous. In fact it wasn't. The mood was upbeat but relaxed and it was apparent that Paphos was popular with a wide span of age groups including a large contingent of people of my age and older. Judging by snippets of conversation, a number of people on board were familiar with Paphos and were coming back for a second or third time. At the gate at Gatwick I'd looked around to see if there were other possible marathoners or – as in my case – half-marathoners taking this flight. There were a few likely candidates but no obvious runners. It didn't matter. I would see plenty when I reached Paphos.

The next step would be to reach the town from the airport. Plan A had been to take a bus. But after TUI's message that the flight would not arrive until 10pm, Plan A was no longer viable as the last bus of the day would have left long before the plane touched down. Given my aversion to taxis on the grounds of cost except as an extreme last resort, I consulted Professor Google once again and found a shuttle coach that did the rounds of the main hotels in Paphos and which according to the map could drop me close to Seaside Luxury Flat – Natalia House 102 (no pets, no hen parties) for €12.24, or £10.60. I booked it.

My apartment stood in a low-rise block behind the main drag into central Paphos, at the back of a large courtyard-cum-car-park. In the dark it took a couple of rounds of retraced steps to find the right staircase and the key-box but without too much faff I was in. The apartment was simple but spacious. I wondered if the owner had left a welcome pack in the fridge – cheese and cold cuts, some bread, maybe even a beer (well, I could hope) but there was nothing. I was hungry and could have eaten something fairly substantial but by now it was late, nearly midnight and I decided to make do with the remainder of snacks accumulated during a day of travel, much of it spent hanging around for trains and a plane. There would be time to eat properly tomorrow.

Paphos is renowned as a centre of antiquity and its archaeological park which covers the ancient Greek and Roman city is a UNESCO World Heritage Site. Paphos is also the legendary landing place of Aphrodite, pagan goddess of fertility, after she emerged from the sea. The story may simply have emerged from a fertile imagination but Paphos does very well from its divine connections. Her name is everywhere, from Aphrodite Jewellery ("Life is not perfect. But your jewellery can be!") and Aphrodite's Secret Nut Shop (honey-roasted cashews a speciality), to the New Kings of Aphrodite restaurant (3.5 on TripAdvisor). And indeed the star attraction in my race bag was a 300g box of a brand of sweets called 'Aphrodite Delights' (local name is loukoumi geroskipou. We'd call it Turkish Delight – but probably not while we're in Cyprus). On a much larger scale, just down the coast lies the Aphrodite Hills resort and tennis academy. Aphrodite and Paphos; they go together.

A less obvious connection was Milton Keynes. Known for its grid layout and roundabouts and sometimes derided for its concrete cow sculptures, the Buckinghamshire new town, now a city, would not have figured high on a list of likely associations with Paphos. But members of one of MK's running clubs, Redway Runners (named after the city's extensive red-paved network of foot- and cycle-paths), had clearly adopted the Paphos Marathon as a club tour event of choice. There were dozens of Redway Runners in town. I saw them on the street, in bars and cafes, at the running expo and, later, at the eve-of-event pasta party. It's a large club, with well over 3,000 members at the time of the 2019 Paphos Marathon and it was clear that a fair chunk of the membership and their assorted family, partners and friends had decided to turn the opportunity to run in Paphos into a spring break.

The morning was bright and sunny, flags fluttered and the sea sparkled. As I strolled down past a succession of restaurant terraces, cafes, mini-markets and souvenir shops I felt the sun on my face and arms and was filled with a sense of wellbeing. The road dropped down to skirt the beach and a familiar scene of palm trees and parasols now accompanied my steps around the edge of the bay towards the harbour and the castle. Here the race would start and finish and today I would collect my race pack from the marathon expo at 'En Plo', the event HQ close by. It wasn't hard to find. An expectant tide of running kit-clad people flowed towards the harbour, following the ample signage. The marathon and half marathon were clearly the biggest event in town over this weekend. For out-of-season Paphos, the influx of guests and visitors that the race had brought to this south-west corner of Cyprus must have been an economic godsend.

En Plo turned out to be a small exhibition hall in a single-storey stone building that had once served some maritime purpose for the port authorities. For much of the year, people would drop in to visit one of the art exhibitions that formed its standard offering. This weekend, though, En Plo had become Marathon Central and its sparsely furnished interior and modest 'expo' of sportswear retailers, energy gel providers and promoters of other race events shared one end of the space with members of the event team who were handing out Logicom Cyprus Marathon 2019 race bags and running numbers, to the people who would be gathering close by next morning to run either the 21K race (my chosen distance) or the full 42K marathon.

I collected my race pack and number – 1670 – made a brief circuit of the expo stands and headed back out into the sunshine. Several of the next day's runners were having their picture taken next to a branded backdrop (Logicom Cyprus Marathon – 21st Edition, with a logo illustration of a silhouetted laurel-leaf capped runner bursting through a red finish tape next to Paphos Castle). A couple of Redway Runners asked me if I would take their picture. I did and they returned the favour. We spoke briefly about the race, their club and Milton Keynes, where I'd worked for more than five years, following those Redway paths a few times every week. We wished each other well for the next day's racing. I now had time to kill. I would explore but first it was time to eat.

This corner of Cyprus lives from its tourism and the farming that helps to feed it. Beyond the beach attractions and tavernas in this prominently English-accented holiday town (there's also a notable German presence, Russian, too) there are quad bike tours, boat excursions and the Paphos Aphrodite (of course) waterpark.

One amenity that tourist towns generally don't lack is a choice of everyday cafes and restaurants. There may well be places in Paphos that cater for gourmet palates too but I wasn't out for fine cuisine. It was the day before a race and I simply needed a Cypriot version of 'good, honest grub'. I chose a busy café-taverna – almost every place was taken – and sat at a terrace table with a view towards the sea. I would have enjoyed some company. There were a couple of other lone diners but both were women and I really didn't want to encroach on them. No one needs some random bloke invading their privacy and space, however well-intentioned. I looked on the menu and found something suitably fuelling and filling – grilled chicken, some vegetables, salad, pitta, a mint yoghurt sauce. Standard fare all along the seafront strip. The simplicity would be welcome. It just needed to be fresh and tasty. And it was.

Full again and re-energised, I spent a couple of hours in the afternoon simply walking from the seafront up to the traditional heart of Paphos. Although this was the 'old town' it all looked freshly renovated, as indeed it had been to coincide with Paphos's designation as European City of Culture in 2017. Laid out in front of the mock-classical town hall and other municipal buildings was a large, open plan square smartly paved with flagstones in several contrasting shades of grey (but fewer than 50...). The square was dotted with sculptures, art installations and neo-classical columns. For wedding photographers it would offer a wealth of angles and vistas to capture images of their newly-married clients and guests emerging from the town hall. In these spring conditions in the late afternoon sunshine it was a pleasure just to stroll around the square in a gentle breeze. In hotter months the setting would have offered little shade, although well-tended tree-lined gardens lay to one side. It was just under 3K from the seafront, much of it uphill, and it had been worth the walk. I was glad I'd made the effort to leave the touristy strip to see a little of 'real' Paphos. Now it was time to head back and rest for a while before the day's next highlight – the Cyprus Marathon pasta party.

Marathon regulars will know that pasta parties are 'a thing'. The complex carbohydrates in pasta provide a very effective store of slow-release energy for sustained exertion like long-distance running. Other foods (rice, quinoa, sweet potato, to name three) are also rich in the nutrients needed to help keep marathoners going – but when marathon organisers lay on a prepared meal on the eve of a race it invariably involves pasta. At least, I haven't yet found a coupon in my marathon pack inviting me to a pre-race rice rave or a sweet potato party! Around 7pm I dropped by the pasta party venue – the Almyra Hotel, where the shuttle bus had deposited me the night before. Although 'pasta party' conjures up some kind of convivial experience typically it's a no-frills affair in a large hall where frequently bored looking serving staff continuously ladle helpings of pasta onto plates with a serving of Bolognese or an alternative sauce, which runners then take to long unadorned trestle tables to eat in groups or alone. It's pasta, but not really a party. Consequently, my expectations were low.

Happily, the Almyra's setting was smarter than some I'd seen – there were linen tablecloths and large round banquet-style tables. Armed with my plate, I spotted a group at a table with one empty place and decided to start a conversation. After the initial round of 'where are you from?' and 'which distance are you running?' I discovered that they were Russian and members of a running club in Moscow. Seemingly in common with almost everyone under 50 during my challenge, regardless of nationality, they spoke clear, American-accented English to a high standard. I told them about RUNNING: ME RUNNING EU. They seemed slightly intrigued to encounter this Englishman of their fathers' age (I know because they asked me mine and then told me) travelling solo on a running adventure around Europe. They were curious, open and willing to talk. It was refreshing. They reminded me of the 20-somethings I'd encountered while studying for the Master's. I enjoyed the chat. Equally, I did not want to impose unduly on their time. As soon as our plates were empty I thanked them for their company and left. Time to check out Paphos seafront by night before heading back to Seaside Luxury Flat – Natalia House 102 to read and rest before Sunday's race.

The next morning there was a keen breeze as I walked the mile to Paphos Castle and the race start area. Conditions were warm – temperature already in the high teens and destined to reach 20C – and dry. It would be a morning for running caps and shades. I had both, giving a debut race appearance to a Cyprus-branded cap I'd bought the day before. After the weeks of running in cold climes, clad in long sleeves, gloves and leggings, it was a pleasure to be down on the start line simply in shorts and a vest, the RUNNING: ME RUNNING EU vest I'd painstakingly art-worked and had printed as a one-off. Always conscious of the need to keep the story fresh for the charity fund-raising, I recorded a quick preview video at the harbour, with crowds of runners in the background. I was upbeat, both for the race itself but also because of a growing sense that the challenge was in the final stages, that I was going to accomplish what I'd set out to achieve.

Soon we were off. With vocal support from the many people gathered along the boardwalk and out to the road that skirts the beach at the heart of the holiday town, the running throng began to climb the slope that I'd come down earlier en route to the start, passing a succession of hotels and tavernas until we were on the outskirts with glimpses of sea between buildings and through trees to our right. I had anticipated that we'd follow the coast for some distance but we were soon marshalled and signposted left and inland. From this point and for much of the race we followed long straight stretches of road, including a lengthy spell along a ring road, occasionally crossing roundabouts, in the hinterland behind Paphos. The surrounding land was that mix of ochre earth and olive hues, part scrub, part cultivated, that characterises Mediterranean landscapes. Falling into step alongside a Redway Runner, I exchanged comments about the deceptive terrain: "This is an incline, isn't it?" "Yes, it's a sneaky hill." The route was touted as being flat and fast and generally it was true. Even at this particular point the low-level sightlines seemed to reflect that, but there's a rule in running – trust your legs, whatever your eyes are telling you. The exertion level had stepped up. Slowly, steadily, we were heading up a gradient.

Things had also warmed up. Even the breeze had lost its earlier freshness. There's usually a point in a distance race where things begin to feel like an effort and this was my spot. It's also where experience kicks in, where runners with some decent mileage under their belts draw on the tool kit of tricks, the coaching and cajoling techniques we play on ourselves to keep going. Not that I wasn't going to see this one through, I just needed an interior pep talk. The art is to focus on what's already been achieved, the distance already run, the memory of past triumphs of endurance – you've done it before, you will do it again – and a reminder that I'd collected a lot of money in donations for RSVP and Changing Faces already and more people would probably contribute the further I ran. The serious mind-games are more often needed in a full marathon, often around the 16-mile mark – far enough in to feel the exertion and a sense of energy levels beginning to deplete, with the knowledge that there's still another 10 miles to run.

But this was merely a half marathon, a fleeting moment of self-doubt in a couple of hours of running that was easily fixed with each passing kilometre marker as I closed in on the finish at 21K. Running's great for building mental as well as physical resilience. And sometimes I've also been able to flip the self-coaching to cope with stressful work scenarios by drawing strength from running. In these situations where work pressure has just got too much, I've reminded myself that I've successfully faced down a succession of mid-marathon demons during the London, Manchester, Birmingham, Ljubljana and other marathons, and run countless training runs of 16, 18 or 20 miles as well as many actual long-distance races – including the demanding Leicestershire inclines of the Ashby 20 (several times – and I've got the finishers' hoodies to prove it). So in comparison a work blip would be just that – a blip, a passing cloud casting a temporary shadow on my generally sunny outlook. It would clear away. And these personal pep talks are effective. To another person this could all be nonsense, of course, but it works for me.

The Logicom Cyprus Half Marathon finishes where it starts, by the castle overlooking Paphos harbour. The race had re-entered Paphos town, bringing me along with it, back around the seafront, along the boardwalk and under the finish arch. The wind was strong enough to carry the distinctive almost cow-bell like ringing of halyards against masts from the facing marina, adding a layer of audible nautical colour to the blaring Tannoy announcements and the chatter of runners.

Distance runners know that a long time spent out on feet tends both to simplify and to amplify the body's priority signals – eat, drink, breathe. Drinks stations en route had helped me keep topped up with water. Even so, running a half marathon on a warm day builds up a demanding thirst and seconds after crossing the line my body's messaging changed from an immediate command to force air back in my lungs to one of rapid rehydration as I downed a bottle of water in a swift succession of urgent glugs.

I hung around the finish area, regaining my composure as I watched other runners cross the line, their expressions a cocktail of exertion, relief and elation just as mine probably had been a couple of minutes earlier. Eventually I trudged back along the boardwalk, past a long line of race-watchers and café terraces doing a busy trade with late-morning breakfast. Runners continued to stream towards me, now just a couple of hundred metres from the finish as a steady ripple of applause and well-wishing rose from the spectators. A few minutes passed and by now I was climbing the slight rise as the seafront gave way to the now-familiar succession of shops, tourist agencies and holiday apartments. Back briefly at my own lodgings I showered, changed and went straight back out, this time for lunch. After a half marathon of effort I didn't want to go wandering far in the middle of a warm, sunny day merely in search of somewhere different to eat. Yesterday's taverna had been fine and it would be so again today.

And it was. In fact with hunger sharpened – I was ravenous by this point and everything I'd enjoyed the previous day now tasted even better, including a bottle of the local Keo beer. In a more discerning mood I'd seek out something a bit less mainstream or obvious. But after the morning's efforts I was simply refuelling. The taverna wasn't busy and I was served quickly – the manager remembered me from the previous day and my decision to return evidently took my custom and the warmth of service it received in return to an unspoken but subtly higher level. Washed, well-fed and watered, refreshed and with the effect of two Keos inside me only adding to my post-run endorphin rush, I felt on top form. Perhaps this had not been one of the most exciting stages of the challenge but

I'd rarely felt more relaxed as I strolled casually back down to the centre and the waterfront in the afternoon sunshine for a final look around before picking up my bag and heading to the bus station for the short trip to the airport and the journey home. All was well with the world, at least in my part of it. As I took in the sun's rays on the promenade it was a pleasure just to be still and absorb the warmth of early spring in the eastern Mediterranean. One last thing to be done. I opened Facebook and wrote an update:

> **Facebook 17 Mar** "Cyprus half marathon done and dusted. Warm, sunny, strong breeze and a couple of gentle climbs including a steady 2K rise. Good organisation, well supported, water every 3K, decent bling and a truly international participation (Poland, Hungary, Latvia, Germany, Russia) although mainly British runners. I finished in a completely unremarkable 1:57:43. Running Me Running EU Stage 24 complete. Next: Romania, Bulgaria and Luxembourg before finishing in Greece on 29 March."

I'd started on this improbable journey the previous April. There were now just 12 days to go. Less than two weeks. And four countries…

RUNNING: ME RUNNING EU

STAGE 25

Bucharest, Romania A hands-on kind of day, starting with the RoboRun and an exuberant star-jump, and ending in work mode as an award ceremony presenter, trying not to be upstaged but clearly outdressed by my robot co-host Reem-C, resplendent in a traditional Romanian red embroidered waistcoat.

Bucharest photography by kind permission of euRobotics and Corina Radu, Visual Outcasts.

PART 2 | THE ACTUAL RUNNING PART

STAGE 25

Romania and the RoboRun

THURSDAY 21 MARCH – 8 DAYS TO GO

The penultimate week of Running: Me Running EU promised to be both fascinating and hectic. Although I'd effectively taken a sabbatical (the hifalutin' expression for not working for a period of time while doing something a lot more fulfilling) in order to pursue the challenge and get it completed by the deadline, I had kept my links with euRobotics, the European robotics association for which I'd run a series of workshops over the last four years. Thanks to a good working relationship and, presumably, for having run those workshops well, I was now able to combine the challenge with the 'day job'. I would be interviewing some people at the European Robotics Forum in a series of video clips, playing the front man for future promotional video material and hosting an awards presentation ceremony. The latter would possibly be the highlight – if not for the audience then at least for me…

My client knew that she was doing me a favour as well as getting my part of the work covered. I'd struck a deal on the fee in order to secure the work and I would find the lowest cost flight and accommodation in order to meet the event budget.

This was how I discovered Blue Air, a Romanian-owned budget airline with a fleet of 737s that would fly me from Birmingham to Bucharest and back with priority boarding, extra leg room, a hot meal each way and space in the hold for a 32kg suitcase, all for £88.92. Sounded like a good deal that wouldn't break the budget and it was. I don't own 32kg of stuff that I would want to take with me on a holiday for a month, let alone a five-day round trip, but it was a generous baggage allowance. I didn't need the weight limit but the space for a large suitcase was useful. I'd grown used to stuffing meagre belongings for each trip into my Ljubljanski Maraton running holdall which was small enough to stow under the seat. However, appearing on stage and on camera demanded a higher level of sartorial presentation, hence the need to store suits and suchlike with sufficient space to breathe.

Come the morning of the flight and I found myself sitting in seat 1A, the front row, by the window. Best seat in the house apart from the pilot's, I thought. Once up in the air, the meal was served and I exchanged pleasantries about the food and the airline with my front row companion. He said he often flew with Blue Air and asked me about my trip. I gave him the 10-second version (not everyone's interested so best to keep it short, at least at first) but he wanted to know more. He looked a little younger than me but we were near enough in age and I felt comfortable expanding on the story. I asked him about what had brought him to be catching this flight. He was British, ran a division of an international business (hence the travel), married to a Romanian and with a family in Bucharest (hence today's destination) and had just visited his mother in a nursing home in Birmingham. I asked where in Birmingham. Edgbaston... I mentioned Cannon Hill parkrun. He'd run it! The rest of the three hour and 20 minute journey then passed very quickly and we chatted almost without interruption for the rest of the flight.

I mentioned the need to pick up some Romanian currency – something I hadn't made time to do before the trip – and that I would do that once I reached the city centre rather than at the airport. He asked me how I planned to get to central Bucharest. I mentioned a bus service that I'd read about and that I expected to be able to use a card to pay the fare. He told me that I'd need some currency just in case and without hesitation thrust a small wad of fairly worn Romanian lev notes into my hand. There then followed a brief to-and-fro of "It's really kind but I can't accept this" and "It's nothing. Take it..." I gave in and kept the notes. I asked how I could repay him. He repeated that it was nothing, that there was no need. Eventually he said "Maybe if our paths cross again, perhaps at Cannon Hill parkrun you can pay me back then – but only if you really feel you need to." Once we were on the ground and through the formalities at Arrivals, he then took the time to show me where to find the city centre bus. One final act to underscore the goodwill: "Here's my family's phone number in Bucharest. If ever you get stuck. You never know..." And with that we parted company. The kindness of strangers...

Otopeni airport is about 11 miles from central Bucharest and the heavy traffic between them is legendary. It took nearly two hours before I stepped out into the crisp night air and followed Google Map directions to my accommodation, a small, showy (for which read tawdry, borderline tacky), unimpressive hotel that nonetheless had two advantages – it was cheap for central Bucharest (£50 a night; I would be there for three nights) and was within reasonable walking distance of both the conference venue and the park where RoboRun, the event that would enable me to complete Stage 25 of Running: Me Running EU, would take place early on Thursday morning. It was also close to a great monstrosity from the days of the communist regime – the so-called People's Palace, which in its conception had very little to do with 'the people' and a whole lot more to do with the pomp, pretensions and cult of personality of Nikolai Ceaușescu, dictator and president of Romania for a generation before his violent overthrow and unceremonious execution at the fall of communism in 1989.

Meanwhile this was March 2019 and I was in town to work – and run. I made contact with my client, Lavinia, and headed over to the Marriott for dinner and a catch-up about our plans for the week. Architects talk about building cities on a human scale. The planners who created the buildings and infrastructure around Bucharest Sector 5 had another vision entirely. Where once an entire district of homes, factories and monasteries had stood for generations, the area bordering Izvor Park leaves me with a sense of alienation bordering on intimidation with its wide sweeping avenues and huge, imposing structures. Those were certainly my prevailing feelings as I walked, a slowly moving speck in the cold night air, past Izvor's bombastic buildings – the Ministry of National Defence, the People's Palace, the Marriott itself and the People's Salvation Cathedral, under construction since 2010 and destined to become the largest, tallest, highest-domed and apparently the heaviest (how do you weigh a church?) Eastern Orthodox cathedral in the world.

Inside the similarly super-sized Marriott, Lavinia and I made our plans for the next few days with Corina, our talented videographer, photographer and graphic designer – who to interview and where, locations for links. Lavinia also outlined plans for RoboRun, the charity run which I would both race-direct and run in. It would be a low-key unofficial event held in Izvor Park at 7.30am the day after next. Participants would be delegates from the European Robotics Forum who would make a €30 donation to take part. All proceeds would be given to a local charity that encouraged children, especially girls, from disadvantaged parts of Bucharest to go on to study science, technology, engineering or mathematics (STEM) and pursue a future career in one of these fields. The focus on girls is important. Women are very under-represented in STEM subjects and the professional fields that arise from them. It's certainly true in the world of robotics. Representatives of the charity would be with us at the park.

Lavinia explained why the run had to be low-key. The park was next to the People's Palace, which was also Romania's parliament building, in the heart of Bucharest's heavily policed official district, like Whitehall but with a much more visible armed-police presence. Applying for permission to hold an organised race in the park would have taken months, a lot of form-filling and a very uncertain outcome. So they'd reframed the RoboRun effectively as part of the European Robotics Forum's wellness programme, a pre-conference run around the park for a maximum 30 conference participants for just half an hour. Kept at such a low scale, the run (not a race!) would stay below the radar of any passing security patrols. It made sense to me. A few weeks earlier while in run director mode I'd broached the topic of signage, marshals in hi-viz vests around the park and timekeepers on the finish line but had been firmly advised against all of this on the grounds of not attracting the undue attention of officialdom. At the time, this nervousness had seemed odd and out of keeping with my expectations of how a run should be set up. Now I was in situ it made more sense. So be it, then. I would have less to do. My role on the day would essentially be to act like a safety car in Formula 1, leading from the front and moderating the pace as we ran a couple of laps at a sedate speed around the perimeter of Izvor Park. I knew some of the robotics community were keen runners. I would just need to manage their expectations.

I left the bright lights, glitz and warmth of the Marriott and plunged back into the near-zero cold darkness (Cyprus had been a very brief reprieve) for a brisk, hoary-breathed, collar-up walk down the hill and along the edge of the park. I was tempted to walk across it and save a few minutes' walk back to my underwhelming Tawdry Towers of a hotel. I peered into the featureless gloom beyond the first line of trees and decided not to. It was cold but I wasn't *that* desperate. I would be in the park soon enough. The RoboRun was scheduled for 7.30 the next morning.

It felt like an ungodly time to be up and standing in a freezing park, and according to my body clock it was. Romania is two hours ahead of UK time. This meant that in my head it was now just after 5am, whatever the local clocks claimed. On arrival at the park I'd run the paths along the chosen course and checked for ice and other potential hazards (because you never know). Inspection completed, I saw Corina setting up her camera and headed over to her. She was going to film the run and take pictures, too. Two women from the local charity appeared, carrying packs of water bottles. Introductions made, we all did our best to keep warm and waited for the other runners to arrive from the Marriott, where most were staying. Soon a trickle of assorted runners came into view, with just one woman, Nadine, a former national championship swimmer from Germany and now a keen and competitive triathlete. One or two more runners arrived from other directions.

With everyone gathered, and the monumental People's Palace across the road providing a striking if unlikely backdrop, I gave a short briefing about the run. This merely confirmed what they'd already been told – a run, not a race, 30 minutes, water at the end and so on. I pointed out my Running: Me Running EU vest, explained the significance and said that this run would be one of the very last stages in my challenge. There was a round of applause, genuinely unexpected and all the more pleasing because it was spontaneous. With no more to be said, our motley squad of robotics engineers, tech entrepreneurs and me began our moderately-paced run around Izvor Park.

I enjoyed the novelty of the occasion, the quirkiness of taking part in a run for participants at a robotics conference, and the setting, part-exotic (we were in Bucharest, a stone's throw from the former seat of Romania's last dictator) and part-mundane (this was a city park like many others). Finally, and most importantly, this was Stage 25 of Running: Me Running EU. In a matter of days I would cross the final finish line of my year-long challenge. The scale and enormity of completing the challenge had once seemed improbable and yet there it was, just like the People's Palace now in clear view on the other side of National Unity Boulevard. At the end of the run, Corina went into art director mode and we all posed for a series of pictures. One of these features us all jumping, each in our own way, caught in mid-air, hands raised in a mist of icy breath, in a frozen moment of time. It remains one of my favourite images from the entire challenge. Photography complete, cold hands shaken and warm hugs shared, the RoboRun gathering dispersed in the direction of showers, breakfasts, workshops and presentations.

The rest of my day became a blur of mic tests, pieces to camera, fluffed intros, interviews, conversations, time spent dipping in and out of conference presentations, awards ceremony script run-throughs and surprises. Come the evening and I was on stage to host the 2019 euRobotics Awards. I should say, co-hosting. In the past I've double-headed awards ceremonies, working with 'celebrity' presenters, typically familiar faces from TV news. Here at Le Chateau, a heavily ornate extravaganza of a venue with its marble floors and crystal chandeliers, my co-host was Reem-C, a robot wearing a traditional Romanian red embroidered folkloric waistcoat (I'm not making this up) who had been programmed to comment at key points in the proceedings. To say it made the Oscars seem spontaneous would be an understatement. I saw a recording later. Happily, the flesh-and-blood half of this undynamic duo looked less wooden than his metal-and-microchip partner, although from an audience perspective there probably wasn't much more than a few splinters in it. Besides, both man and machine were about to be upstaged and instantly forgotten.

I try to keep on top of the detail of live events when I'm presenting, and to know exactly what will happen, where, when and how. I work on scripts and fine-tune the things I'll say to get the wording and phrasing right, where to put the emphases and when to pause. It may sound like this leaves no room for improvisation but actually the opposite is true. If you're well-versed with a script and fully drilled in an event's running order, it can be easier to ad lib or improvise if necessary or to take an opportunity to be spontaneous if one arises. In a sentence: prepare well but expect the unexpected.

In Bucharest, the unexpected came in the form of a question when I first arrived at the awards venue: "Steve, what time should the traditional Romanian dancers come on stage?" I knew the sequence of events by heart and had everything nailed down to the minute. There was absolutely *nothing* about traditional Romanian dancers in my running order. I guessed it was a wind-up – but it wasn't. With the final award presented I left the stage, my part in the ceremony complete. But there was barely time for a heartbeat before a sudden, frenetic blur of colour and movement as more than 20 costumed dancers filled the stage in a vigorous display of, yes, traditional Romanian dancing.

By this point my head was a mix of elation, adrenalin and fatigue. From the crisp, early morning chill of Izvor Park and RoboRun to these late exuberant scenes at Le Chateau it had been a long and fulfilling day.

There were a few more work-related things to do back at the Marriott the next morning. By the afternoon, though, things were winding down. Sessions were still running but some of the exhibitors were beginning to pack up. With the final interview complete and coffee in hand, I sat and chatted about next steps with Lavinia as a casual stream of people passed nearby: lingering conference delegates, packing crews wheeling large industrial cases big enough to house a robot, and hotel staff with chores to run and places to go. Coming down from the high-stakes, high-energy stress of getting everything done to a demanding schedule the previous day, it was good to relax and feel an inner spring uncoil a little. Just then, as we sat and talked, a robot approached, paused to turn and face a short flight of steps to a mezzanine floor and then slowly began to climb them. We watched. So did a hurrying waiter, steadying a tray of drinks in his hand as he stopped, visibly bemused at this scene. Working in a top hotel he'd probably seen it all – but maybe nothing like this glimpse of the future taking infant steps right there on the first floor of the JW Marriott Hotel in the centre of Bucharest.

Two hours later and I was on the Pegasus minibus crawling out of the city amid the weekend exodus, heading south for the Bulgarian border and the next stage in the adventure. I'd be back in Bucharest soon, but only en route to the airport and home before Luxembourg, the penultimate stage. Meanwhile, I set out to cross one of Europe's great waterways for the third time and discover the border with Bulgaria. Tomorrow was Saturday and at 9am I would be running in another park. But it wouldn't be parkrun. I had a rendezvous with the Runners of Ruse.

PART 2 | THE ACTUAL RUNNING PART

STAGE 26

Another frontier: "What the f*** am I doing in Bulgaria?

SATURDAY 23 MARCH – 6 DAYS TO GO

Before this latest trip I'd spent quite some time checking bus and train options between Bucharest and Bulgaria's two largest cities, Sofia and Varna. To me they were the obvious locations for the Bulgarian stage of RUNNING: ME RUNNING EU. However, the timings simply wouldn't stack up. I'd be working at the robotics forum until Friday afternoon. My flight back home from Bucharest was at 7.40pm the next day. I had barely 24 hours to get from Bucharest to an as-yet unspecified location in Bulgaria, run and get back to Bucharest Otopeni airport in time for the flight, with an uncertain border both ways. So I'd browsed the map to see if there was somewhere else that I could reach to run in just over on the Bulgarian side. Then I noticed that the border towns of Giurgiu in Romania and Ruse in Bulgaria more or less faced each other. I had never heard of either and knew nothing about them but I figured that maybe I could run from one to the other and back. They were only separated by seven miles – and a wide expanse of the Danube. There was a road, rail and pedestrian crossing, the Friendship Bridge, surprisingly one of only two bridges to link Romania and Bulgaria along the entire 300-mile stretch of the Danube that forms the border between them. No doubt there would be border control, too, but I could run with my passport. Surely that could work?

That may sound naïve and overly optimistic but at this time when the challenge was at its peak, my personal optimism and a sheer determination to see it through were among the magic ingredients in the fuel that drove me on. But even though the 'bridge to Bulgaria and back' option sounded feasible, I decided against it for three reasons. Firstly, if it didn't work and I was prevented from crossing the border on the way over to the Bulgarian side the whole plan could come unstuck because the RUNNING: ME RUNNING EU deadline was looming and I wouldn't have time to cobble together another option to run in Bulgaria. Secondly, what if

I successfully crossed over but then had a border control problem when trying to return? I had an aerial-view mental image of myself in running gear, stuck at the wrong end of the bridge and unable to cross back into Romania. Even though a UK passport still conferred full EU privileges at that time and the likelihood was low, the risk of being stranded and running out of time put me off.

Beyond those practical considerations, the third reason was the real decider. I wanted Stage 26 to be about more than just a few brisk footfalls on Bulgarian soil. Once I'd found Ruse on the map and begun to read about it I wanted to spend some time in the city. Maybe Ruse had a running club that I could run with… After a quick search on Google I found the Runners of Ruse. I sent a message on the club's Facebook page to introduce myself and outline the challenge. I said I'd be in Ruse on 23 March if anyone was around and willing to run with me. I thought at the time that there might be a 50-50 chance of getting a reply. In fact I did get one and the enthusiastic response took me by surprise.

> "Wow, what a story! We're delighted you've chosen Ruse as part of your challenge. Most people have never heard of it! It would be an honour to run with you…"

This was more than I could have hoped for and everything I'd wished for at this late stage. It remained to fix some details and a rendezvous. I didn't have long to wait. Next came this message:

> **Facebook 20 Mar** "Hey Steve, this is Deyan from Runners of Ruse! I am excited to meet you and help you with your campaign. Please tell me if you need something in advance. Would it be a good idea to try to invite some media on Saturday? We've already made a public event and there will be more people probably. Tonight we have a runners' party and we will invite everybody to come as well. Please do not hesitate to contact me for anything. I'd be very glad if I could help."

The Runners of Ruse. I liked the name. It had a ring to it, which was appropriate because it reminded me of the Riders of Rohan from Lord of the Rings. I didn't expect to be greeted by flaxen-haired, blue-eyed equestrians from the pages of Tolkien when I met them but I now knew there would at least be some kind of welcome.

Ruse is a small city of around 140,000 people, similar to the size of Dundee and which, like the Scottish city, sits on a wide river. Run along the riverside embankment in Ruse and you look out across a wide expanse of the Danube. On the far bank, clearly visible a mile away, lies Romania. As the crow flies, Ruse lies about 150 miles inland from the Black Sea, although the Danube meanders north and its outlet to the sea is much further away. Even so, the Danube has been Ruse's great economic artery and the city is Bulgaria's largest inland port. The city centre itself is very attractive, much of it pedestrianised, with fine neo-Baroque architecture, avenues, squares and parks all within easy walking distance. It's yet another example of the largely unknown and unsuspected richness that lies beyond Europe's coasts and capitals. And I'd chosen it as the location for the Bulgarian stage of RUNNING: ME RUNNING EU almost by simply putting a pin in the map and because of a minibus run by a company called Pegasus which would get me from Bucharest to Ruse, a journey of barely 50 miles, and directly back to Otopeni airport the next day.

The minibus from Bucharest was late enough for me to wonder if I was standing in the right place, not a bus station as you might imagine but, as advised when I made the booking online, on the pavement outside the Hotel Oroscope. The name was telling. While waiting I imagined a passing fortune-teller: "I see travel – but who knows when…?" Reassuringly several other people were waiting, their demeanour expressing more of a resigned irritation than real anxiety. As flying steeds go, our Pegasus transport had presumably been winged by Bucharest's late Friday afternoon traffic. Eventually it arrived and, cramped with people and half a ton of luggage, was soon nosing its way into the rush hour exodus.

Many European borders are invisible. Think of Irish crossing points or the virtual boundaries between the countries of the EU's border-free Schengen zone and there's almost nothing to tell you that you've passed from one national jurisdiction to another country. You may see a modest roadside plaque quietly telling you that that was Slovenia now this is Italy but blink and you will miss it, especially on a rural road where the terrain on either side of the imaginary line is identical. Occasionally there will be more obvious signs – the dilapidated remains of customs posts and other now-deserted outbuildings and former barrier installations that had once served as part of the firm infrastructure of an international frontier. But the frontier at the Friendship Bridge is a reminder that crossing borders can still be striking, even spectacular.

For a start, this is no notional line, or rather there is an agreed point in the Danube where Romanian territory ends and Bulgarian waters begin, but you will need to navigate a substantial stretch of river before you cross that line. And that's why the Friendship Bridge exists. Built in the 1950s when this was a border between two Soviet-era Eastern bloc countries, the bridge is two tiers of criss-crossed steel, one level for road traffic and foot traffic, the other for trains, with all the paraphernalia of a border crossing at each end. Above the highway a large blue and yellow nameplate announces 'Bulgaria' to southward traffic. Northbound travellers get a little more for their glance ahead, with the name 'Romania' flanked by the 12 stars of the EU and the tricolour of the Romanian flag. From pick-up to drop-off, the journey from Bucharest to Ruse took a little over two hours, well over half an hour of which was spent waiting while first one and then a second set of border control authorities satisfied themselves about our Pegasus taxi-van, its occupants and our documentation. Finally we were through. I tracked the remaining minutes of our journey as we left the heavy industry of the riverside district behind and made our way into the outskirts of Ruse. By now it was dark as we were deposited at a small, unassuming bus station.

Feeling unsure of myself in an unfamiliar city whose language I could not read (Bulgarian script is Cyrillic), let alone speak, I followed Google Maps and made my way towards the centre and the Dunav Plaza, my hotel. Normally I would thrive on the uncertainty of arriving somewhere new but that wasn't how I felt at that moment. Certainly by the next morning I would come to appreciate that Ruse is a city of considerable charm but that evening as I walked along a long straight road of modest housing blocks with few people around, I felt ill at ease. The street names and shop signs were completely indecipherable to me. None of this should have mattered but it was late in the day and dark, I felt cold and tired and while as a linguist I pride myself on being able to understand at least something of the language of whatever country I'm in, here I felt illiterate. This disturbing feeling was crystallised when my eye caught the lights of a shop across the road with the name above it: СУПЕРМАРКЕТ. Actually I could understand it but in that moment it felt to me as if a familiar word had been hideously disfigured.

Thinking back, I realise that it was actually being able to understand what it meant – Supermarket – that had pushed me into what roboticists call the 'uncanny valley'. That's when a humanoid robot bears such a close but not complete resemblance to a human being that feelings of revulsion can arise in the person who sees it. Whether that's a fair diagnosis of my mental state or not, it was at that moment that I said to myself: "What the f*** am I doing in Bulgaria?!" All completely irrational, of course, but it reflected my mood, akin to homesickness and almost the only time I can remember from the entire challenge when I doubted what I was doing and why I was there.

Just over a mile and 25 minutes after leaving the bus station I arrived at the Dunav Plaza, a smart, modern low-rise hotel overlooking a central square. It looked very good online and the rating and reviews were excellent. A four-star hotel, it was more than a cut above the level of accommodation I'd normally allowed myself during the challenge but there were two good reasons for choosing the Dunav Plaza, the location and cost: 86 lev – just £38, breakfast included. Inside, the Dunav Plaza lived up to its kerb appeal, my room was airy, warm and welcoming with a pleasing décor. Suddenly my mood improved.

After the now-familiar ritual of unpacking and putting the following morning's running kit together, I showered, lingering in the luxury of a hot, gently stinging spray. If there was a league for hotel showers taken during my running challenge, the Dunav Plaza would have been a top-3 contender. Refreshed and reinvigorated, I headed out to eat. The central square offered a few options. I was keen to try what Bulgarians might consider as a typical dish and headed into a restaurant that seemed to offer what I was looking for. It was busy and bustling – usually a good sign. Not having a clue about what the menu said was a barrier I would just have to overcome. Inside, I asked if anyone spoke English (or Français, or Deutsch...). Eventually a young woman was summoned from the kitchen. With reasonable school English and a resourceful use of verbal workarounds for items that neither of us understood, she valiantly explained a couple of dishes. Just when I committed to go with her recommendations and looked for a table, I saw people clutching banknotes as they prepared to pay. I had no local currency at that point and I hadn't seen a cash point. I needed to check if I could pay by plastic fantastic before the young woman relayed my order to the waiter. She shook her head when I showed her my credit card: "No card. Only cash."

Disappointed – for me and for her, because she'd made a real effort to claim me as a customer – I left, scanned the square and then decided to keep it simple by eating at the hotel. Normally, that would be an expensive option, one I would only take as a last resort. However, just as with the room rate, the hotel restaurant provided remarkably good value for a diner from a more affluent part of Europe: three tasty, well-prepared courses with a glass (well, two) of decent Bulgarian red, all for the equivalent of just £18. The large, airy dining room had few other diners. Wherever the people of Ruse were eating tonight, it wasn't here. Well-fed, with a gentle glow from the wine's warming effects, I'd now fully recovered from my earlier wobble. Spirits fully restored, I went back to my room to write and rehearse a short introduction for tomorrow's encounter with the Runners of Ruse. I found a few Bulgarian words of greeting and thanks. I would have to rely on my experience of Slovene for hints about pronunciation. It was the only other Slavonic language I knew. Still, I wanted to meet them and they were clearly making an effort to meet me. The will to communicate was there on both sides. It would be enough.

The next morning it took me just a few minutes to run from the hotel to the rendezvous, a nearby park. As I neared the meeting point I saw a small group of about a dozen runners. They weren't hard to spot in their shorts, tops and sports shoes in a rainbow of different colours – the universal garb of runners. A few noticed me approaching. I guess I wasn't hard to spot, either, wearing my own-designed RUNNING: ME RUNNING EU vest. A tall, bearded guy in his mid-30s stepped out to greet me: "Hello, Steve. I am Deyan. Welcome to Ruse!" He introduced me to Ani, his wife, and then gestured to the growing gathering of runners, who by now were a couple of dozen in number. Deyan and Ani wore the distinct green and white club tops of the Runners of Ruse with 'Staff' on the back. Singly or in pairs, a few more people joined the group so that by the time Deyan called everyone to attention and addressed them, around 30 people had turned out to join the welcoming party for this somewhat older Englishman, who had chosen their less well-known city for the Bulgarian stage of his European grand running tour. Deyan spoke to them briefly, switching quickly to easy, fluent English, which seemed to be well-understood by most if not all of the Runners of Ruse who were present. Deyan invited me to speak.

"Good morning everyone. My name is Steve Doswell. I am from Birmingham in Great Britain. Thank you for the welcome. I am happy to be here in Ruse today..." At that point I spared the group from any further commentary in my all-purpose pidgin Slavonic (Slovene masquerading as Bulgarian) and continued in English. I kept it short. In a couple of sentences I outlined what RUNNING: ME RUNNING EU was, mentioned the two charities, confirmed that this was the 26th out of 28 countries and thanked them for joining me. I added that I hoped I would have a chance to speak to everyone and I looked forward to running with them all around Ruse.

And so we ran, 30 Bulgarians and me, on a cool, bright sunny Saturday morning, through city parks, down to the banks of the Danube and along the embankment, looking across the water to Romania on the far bank. It was an easy pace and as we ran I spoke to Deyan, to Ani, to Nina, who came up to introduce herself. Nina had lived and worked in the UK for a few years. Our conversation was unforced and friendly. A couple of the men in the group came up alongside. One asked me about the two charities. To my slight surprise they seemed really interested in the work of RSVP and for the next few minutes I found myself discussing themes of domestic violence and examples of rape as a weapon of war while running in an unfamiliar city with a group of Bulgarian men and women who I'd only met less than an hour earlier. It felt slightly surreal but wholly within the spirit of RUNNING: ME RUNNING EU. The conversation moved on to more anticipated ground. We discussed football allegiances and shared a mutual appreciation of Stilyan Petrov, the great Bulgarian international and decent, modest-mannered character who had been club captain and a stalwart in Aston Villa's midfield during the late noughties before illness curtailed his career.

I realised that I was really enjoying myself. As our running tour of Ruse progressed I experienced another one of those rare, vivid moments of contentment that are hard to describe but that stay in the memory long after many other details are forgotten. I'd discovered Ruse literally by scouring a map, learned of the existence of the Runners of Ruse through a bit of desk research, and made contact by sending them an email. They'd responded positively, and here we were. Everything that we were experiencing that morning had been made possible via a few electronic clicks. I don't really believe in destiny, but increasingly I find myself ascribing to the idea of karma, or at least, to what I understand karma to be. In short, if you do the right things, the right things will probably happen. And here I was in Ruse, Stage 26 of the challenge proceeding as well as I could have hoped. It simply felt... right.

Aware that I was on a tight schedule that morning, Deyan eventually led us back to the park where we'd started. We'd been running for an hour, we'd stopped a couple of times for some pictures and we'd covered just under 10K. Even in that brief time I'd seen enough of Ruse to realise that, just as with Varaždin, Györ and Kaunas, so much of the beauty and fascination of Europe lay beyond its capitals and other tourist hotspots, and above all in its people.

There was time to quench our thirst before I left them. We arrived at a rather ornate café in the park. I told Deyan about the Saturday morning tradition of parkrun at Cannon Hill with steaming mugs of tea that were as much part of the local parkrun experience as the running itself. He smiled politely and produced a clutch of bottled beers instead. OK, I thought, this is how they do it in Ruse. And when in Ruse...

As we downed our beers a steady stream of people from the morning's run came by to say goodbye and wish me well with the final stages of the challenge, until it was my own turn to leave. There was time for a warm embrace for both Deyan and Ani, who'd really made this morning's encounter happen, and then I trotted back along the wide pedestrianised avenue towards the hotel. Back in my room I showered quickly, packed my bag, checked out and walked the mile back up the boulevard in the direction of the bus station with a new-found confidence, in complete contrast to the fleeting negativity I'd felt when I arrived.

At the bus station there was plenty of time to buy a drink and some nuts from the cubbyhole that served as a snackbar. The by-now familiar Pegasus minibus pulled in and before long we were on our way out of the city, up to the highway to the Friendship Bridge. Two international checkpoints and a half an hour later we were back over the Danube and heading north to Bucharest city, onwards to Otopeni airport and, finally, home.

While Romania's own Blue Air had flown me here, the low-cost Hungarian carrier Wizzair would be getting me back. The flight was busy but calm, arriving more or less on time back in Birmingham. After that morning's heady, almost exotic experience of running with the Runners of Ruse came the bathos of arriving at New Street station, then waiting for the number 50 bus to Moseley. Mundane or not, I was home indoors before midnight. Stage 26 was over.

PART 2 | THE ACTUAL RUNNING PART

STAGE 27

Luxembourg: into the ravine, the journey's almost done

WEDNESDAY 27 MARCH – 2 DAYS TO GO

I thought the emotions would come to the surface in Athens. They did, but not as I'd imagined. No, the lump-in-the-throat moment came on the penultimate stage, in Luxembourg. I'd run from Hamm, the quiet suburb where I'd been staying above the Piccolo Mondo, an Italian restaurant, climbed up through trees on a short trail until I reached the beginning of a residential street in Luxembourg City itself. I checked Google Maps (as I did frequently) and navigated my way to one of the main city bridges over the ravine that's one of the city's defining features. Half-way across the bridge I stopped and recorded a short video clip for the Facebook post that had become my standard update. I said whatever I said, something about having made it to Luxembourg, Stage 27, and being happy to find a bridge because I didn't fancy having to descend and ascend the steep sided ravine (cue panning shot to show the ravine), finished, and then felt a short rush of... joy. I had a sense of an audience – supporters, well-wishers, people who were somehow with me while I was pursuing this adventure, friends from London, from Birmingham, and people I'd met in the places I'd run in. I hadn't had this feeling before, although I knew that many Bournville Harriers had been with me from the beginning. This time the support felt almost tangible, as it often does when taking part in a marathon and knowing that people have downloaded the tracking app, know where I am and how far I've come.

With Luxembourg under way and just one more stage to go, flights and accommodation booked, map printed, logistics checked, re-checked and safely detailed in my notebook, I found myself close to brimming with emotion. I knew I was going to finish the challenge. I'd always 'known' that, of course. But now, I *knew*, and in this heightened moment of awareness I had this clear sense that the people who'd supported me knew it too. I decided not to shed any joyful tears into the ravine but tucked my phone back in the trusty running belt that had been such an important part of my kit throughout the challenge and carried on running into the heart of Luxembourg City.

This was the second time I'd actually been to Luxembourg but the first time I'd entered the city proper. The previous time had been to work with the communications team at the European Investment Bank, but running a workshop doesn't count as running! Then, I'd barely managed a hundred paces on Luxembourg soil, straight from the airport into a taxi to an office building in the suburbs and back again. I'd had no sense of Luxembourg's dramatic contours, its architecture, its greenery. This time I was able to appreciate a lot more of Luxembourg's charm.

I made my way to a stone parapet overlooking another fold in the ravine with a narrow waterway at the very bottom, greenery on either side and what looked like the heart of the city across the ravine. A rather striking bridge close by would take me comfortably the few hundred metres over to the other side. But where was the sense of challenge in that? I looked over the edge again. There were paths and steps cut into my side of the ravine. Must be some leading up the other side, too… It was time to embrace the contours of Luxembourg City. I just had to find an opening that would lead me off this promenade and down into the ravine. I trotted past a group of selfie-snapping (I guessed Chinese) tourists – one nodded that acknowledging nod that marks runners who find themselves in civvies but who want to make it clear that they're runners, too. I nodded back in likewise fashion. It's a code. We know it. The steps appeared and down I went. The steps ran out and I continued the descent along a trail path, zig-zagging down the valley side in the shadow of the bridge's dramatic substructure. When I reached the bottom I stopped to take some pictures of the underside of the bridge, all lines and curves in geometric form. Images captured, I kept going. This morning, as so often during the challenge, I had a fairly tight deadline.

On arrival at the hotel-restaurant last night, I'd asked if I could check out at 12 noon instead of the stated time of 11am. I've found hotels are usually amenable to this – any longer, though, and they may refuse or expect to charge a supplement. They'd offered an extra half-hour – until 11.30am – and I'd accepted. By this point I was under the bridge, on the floor of the ravine and it was just after 10am. My flight wasn't until mid-evening so I would have time to come back into the centre to look around and linger. For now, the job was to run, get back to the hotel, clean up and check out. I was about 5K away, with a couple of steep climbs along the way, starting with the ascent up the side of this ravine. Once at the top, I took a few seconds to catch my breath and allow my heart-rate to return to normal, then started to head back. By this point the (possibly Chinese) tourists were filing back onto their luxury coach, no doubt en route to another of Luxembourg's spectacular vantage points.

I found my way back to the ravine, crossed the bridge and then followed the ravine round. The road fell away quite steeply until I reached another crossing, this time at low level. At this point there was a choice of routes ahead, all of them steep. After a pause to check the map, I chose to take a small side road and then to wend my way up the hillside via a steep zig-zagging path. The effort took my breath away and half-way up I had to slow to a walk, my heart pounding. A few further sweat-inducing minutes later and I emerged from the trees opposite a well-secured house – all gates and alarms, it seemed – and onto a refreshingly almost-level path alongside a meadow. I remembered seeing this from a distance when I started the run earlier. By this point I was only a few minutes from Il Piccolo Mondo and the welcome prospect of no longer running. They say that music is not only the sound of the notes but the spaces between them too and that's certainly how I relate to running. The pauses, rests and respites are all part of running.

I ran the final kilometre through the neat suburb of Hamm (my impression, though, was that all of Luxembourg is tidy) towards the finish. By this point I was excited at having almost completed Stage 27 and at looking forward to a shower and food – breakfast had been minimal and hurried because I had to run, get back, clean up and pack before check-out. Once I'd done those things in that order I returned downstairs in the restaurant and treated myself to a coffee and pastry. Part of the rhythm of life as a runner is knowing when to reward yourself and how. I'd seen the patisserie display during breakfast and foregone the delights therein because no one needs a belly full of cream pastry a few minutes before hitting the tarmac.

Now that I'd completed the run, though, a decent slice of tarte aux fraises and a good Americano had been earned and were definitely going to hit the spot. After this reward, I arranged to leave my bag for collection later and set out once more for Luxembourg centre, this time at walking pace. I retraced the route I'd taken earlier on the way back, descending the zig-zag path, crossed the main road alongside the low bridge but this time followed a path that tracked the river at the floor of the ravine. On one side were individual houses and the occasional inn, with meadow stretches by the water's edge. On the other, cut two-thirds of the way up a steep escarpment banked high above the path were the tracks and overhead pantographs of a railway line. A bit further along, a gang of construction workers were busy reinforcing the lower slopes against subsidence, some working in hoists as protection against the near-sheer drop. In contrast, I spotted a heron standing serene and motionless by the water's edge. More to the point for running, although the scenery and terrain are always noteworthy unless running in the gym, all along this path runners were passing me almost every few seconds, singly and in groups, and I realised that I'd happened upon on a popular running route. For a fraction of a second I regretted not having found it and run it earlier. Just as quickly, though, I filed it away as an idea that Luxembourg would be a superb location for a running club tour.

Eventually the ravine curved round to a very attractive collection of traditional inns and houses overlooked by the city proper high above. This level, known locally as Grund, was connected to the central district by a lift, which opened out onto Luxembourg's law courts district. Once at the top, I found a suitable place for lunch and for the next couple of hours I simply strolled around the calm, quietly characterful and very green historic centre of Luxembourg. No trip to a new city is complete for me without a visit to a cathedral, a huge, often Gothic edifice created as a space for reflection and relaxation, a place for mindfulness in stone and stained glass – no app required. My one prior trip to Luxembourg had been for work, a strictly functional airport-office-airport visit with no time to admire the surroundings. Now, with time to spare and feeling relaxed, I wanted to enjoy at my leisure some of what I'd glimpsed during the morning's run. And indeed, nowhere was more peaceful than the interior of Luxembourg's Notre-Dame Cathedral. For a few precious minutes I was one of a bare handful of lone pilgrims from the bustle outside, moving slowly and silently within the great echoey embrace of the nave, which slowed the clocks, muted the city's noise and held it at bay.

Suddenly, the doors opened and in flew a busy swarm of tourists, heavily armed with cameras and selfie sticks, advancing up the aisles, crowding the altar, filling the chapels and feeding an evident desire to comb the interior and capture every conceivable image and angle in a thousand snaps and a hundred flashes. For five frenetic minutes the prevailing mood of slow, solemn, almost soundless reflection was drowned out in what seemed like a touristic supermarket trolley dash as these visitors tore around the cathedral. And then, just as suddenly, they were gone. With the 'flash mob' moment over, I savoured the return of an enveloping stillness for a couple more minutes and then went outside to continue my brief tour of the streets, parks and, inevitably for this railwayman's son, the central railway station of Luxembourg city.

Eventually, lengthening shadows reminded me of the time. I retraced my steps down to the Grund and the floor of the city ravine and followed the course of Luxembourg's river, the Alzette, before the climb back up to the suburb of Hamm and the hotel. There was no one around. I called out. Silence. I called again. No one came. I passed beyond the reception counter feeling as though I were breaking a rule in this small, very orderly country, retrieved my backpack from the room behind and left with a contradictory mix of feelings: a faint twinge of relief that no one had appeared to ask me what I was doing behind the reception desk, yet a slight disappointment there had been no one to say goodbye to at this point of Stage 27, though it hardly mattered. I made my way along the rue des Peupliers (a faint hint of home, there's a Poplar Road a short walk from my house) to the bus stop by the local station, from where I would catch a bus to the airport. I was tempted to walk – it was only 5K – but figured that I'd been on my feet for long enough already.

The bus came, left with me on board, and after initial progress was soon part of a slow-moving log-jam of traffic heading away from the city. Luxembourg has an acknowledged traffic problem and is listed among the world's most congested cities, leading to chronic delays. In its attempt to solve the problem with congestion, Luxembourg had recently announced that it would abolish all train and bus fares as a way of coaxing people out of their cars and onto public transport. This was for the future, though. Meanwhile, we sat in stationary traffic, inching forward at glacial speed. I wasn't worried. In fact I was entirely relaxed, benefiting from a triple whammy of the endorphin effects of running, the euphoria of having completed Stage 27 and having plenty of time before my flight. But it was clear from the growing anxiety of other airport-bound passengers with their tell-tale luggage that they feared the growing prospect of final calls and missed departures. Indeed a couple of them decided to abandon ship (or bus, in this case) and take their chances on foot.

Time-wise I was comfortably in credit and wasn't tempted to follow suit but I did wonder who would be first among us to reach the departure lounge. That particular race probably ended in a draw. By the time the bus was freed from the motorised morass oozing slowly from Luxembourg's outer suburbs and had reached its desired speed the perimeter fence and lights of Luxembourg airport were already in view. Soon I swapped the crowded bus's slightly fuggy interior for the climate-controlled expanse of the airport. Security was uneventful and my final hour in Luxembourg was spent with a beer and a book before the flight and a smooth journey home. I was deeply happy and excited. Thinking back to Mallorca last April and the long adventure since then it was incredible to think but here it was: just one more stage to go.

STAGE 28

The final stage: from Marathon to Athens, following in the footsteps of Pheidippides, at least in my imagination: "The land continued to climb and the road became a stony path up into the hills...The route had become unpredictable and the terrain a lot wilder than I'd anticipated."

PART 2 | THE ACTUAL RUNNING PART

STAGE 28

Greece: Acropolis now

FRIDAY 29 MARCH – DEADLINE DAY

I decided to keep the details of my final run for a surprise reveal until I actually began it so once I'd reached Athens I shared a teaser:

> **Facebook** Steve Doswell is in Athens, Greece.
>
> **March 29, 2019** "Running: Me Running EU. After 12 months, a lot of planes caught, borders crossed, journeys planned and, of course, miles run, it's the final day, 29 March 2019. I wanted today to be a bit special and I think it will be. I'm now on a bus heading out of Athens to my chosen start line. More later…"

There were lots of messages in response – well-wishing, words of encouragement. A couple of people guessed the Marathon connection, although this was not going to be 'a marathon'.

There's a lot to be said for focusing on the pleasure of travel as an end in itself rather than simply fixating on the end-point – the journey, not the destination. All journeys end, of course, unless the whole purpose is aimless wandering. There's something to be said for that, too. My own journey's goal (there were many journeys, milestones too, but one ultimate goal) was set from the start. The location where I would achieve it, though, would only emerge much later, during the final weeks of the challenge. I hadn't started out with Greece as the final stage but once I'd chosen it, the setting for the desired closing scene came quickly to mind. Athens, specifically at the Acropolis, which is practically a shrine for classical European civilisation. Rather like the feeling I had of everything falling into place as soon as I'd coined the name Running: Me Running EU for the challenge, once I had that famous temple on the hill above Athens in mind, it felt right, almost pre-ordained.

The difference was that I'd settled on the name months before I'd set out on that first warm, solo run to the sea and around the coast to Puerto de

Pollensa and back. But it was only during the weeks before the deadline that I had the idea of starting the final leg at the birthplace of the marathon – the town of Marathon itself – and then running back to Athens. But the timing wasn't significant. What did matter was that the final run would be a worthy close to the entire challenge, and a highlight – although there had already been so many of those that I knew it would take something really special to lodge this final effort in the memory above the others.

A run from Marathon to Athens certainly fed the imagination. Legend records that that's exactly what Pheidippides had done some two and a half millennia earlier when the Athenians overcame the Persians in battle. At this point I began to delve further into the story. Did Pheidippides volunteer to take the news of victory back to Athens? Did he draw an ancient Greek equivalent of the short straw? It is said that Pheidippides was a herald, somewhere between a messenger and a professional distance runner, employed for the purpose of delivering information over long distances. As a modern-day communicator delivering information often to remote audiences, I could relate to his job. And as a runner, having run a few marathons of my own, maybe I could even relate to his challenge, although, as tenuous connections go, this one was hanging on by a thread.

The legend of that very first marathon says nothing about a measured course, marshals at key points, cheering crowds or water stations. During his arduous advance over the scrubby stone-strewn hills that separate modern-day Marathon from Athens, did Pheidippides pause to share the good news with solitary goatherds or drop in at isolated farmsteads en route? The legend is hazy on the details. However, his defining run and mine would certainly differ at the end. For Pheidippides, the epic dash over the hills would prove to be among his last moments on Earth. Famously (according to the legend) he delivered his message "Nike! Nike!" (Victory! Victory!) and then collapsed and died from sheer exhaustion. There is another story that just before his final, fateful (and fatal) marathon effort, Pheidippides had just completed a 300 mile out-and-back run between Athens and Sparta to summon help before the battle. As if that colossal mileage wasn't enough, he had then run from Athens to the coastal plain and scene of the sea battle against the Persians before turning round and running back to Athens again with news of the famous victory.

Back-to-back ultras and back-to-back marathons, all on a diet of figs, dried meat, sesame seeds and honey – I can imagine a few of the more nutritionally aware members of the modern-day running community shaking their heads sadly at this point – no wonder he expired after that! So for my own challenge 'following in the footsteps of Pheidippides' would be interpreted very loosely. Some poring over maps was needed, along with some googling about the town of Marathon and how to reach it. For me, there would be no back-to-back ultras to and from Sparta first, and my outward journey to Marathon would be by bus!

There was something else to think about. I'd said at the outset that I wasn't going to run a full marathon as part of the challenge. Maybe I would need to reconsider that. I was reluctant, because I hadn't trained for one. After running several marathons I knew what it took to be fit and ready to run 26.2 miles safely. And as someone who'd entered his seventh decade and with every hope and intention of making it to 80 and beyond in reasonable health, I'd made "You can't blag a marathon" into a personal mantra. I was also conscious of the huge amount of single-mindedness involved in this whole challenge. My family had been cautiously tolerant (and probably sceptical, too, but never openly) when I'd first set out on this quest to run in every country of the EU within one year and by the original date of Brexit. As time passed and I'd pursued the challenge country by country, they'd become increasingly supportive. I owed it to them to look after myself and not take stupid risks (let's draw a discreet veil over the 'Maltese mishap'...), certainly not so close to the end.

Despite these considerations, I admit to checking out the course of the annual Athens marathon and weighing up the pros and cons. In the end the cons proved more persuasive. The official marathon takes place on closed roads. If I ran the same route now, there would be traffic – how heavy I didn't know. It was a bigger risk than I was willing to take. Plus, this was my final stage. I'd come a very long way geographically and in spirit, too. These past weeks I'd been cresting on a sense of fulfilment and I really wanted to enjoy the final miles of RUNNING: ME RUNNING EU. This challenge had become one of the great experiences of my life (so far!) and I planned to finish with a flourish, not an ordeal. I would certainly run from Marathon to Athens but it wouldn't be a marathon. As at so many points over the past 12 months I turned to Google, checked transport options to Marathon and the shortest routes to run back. I found a bus route that would take me all the way to Marathon and then what appeared to be a winding backroad – a lane of sorts that seemed to dwindle to a single line on the map, but a way back nonetheless – that I could follow for the run to Athens.

Lunch in a taverna near the hotel was simple: skewered chicken, pitta, tzatziki with salad and, inevitably, a cool Mythos beer (when in Greece...) – fresh, filling and thoroughly satisfying. After this I was ready to recce where I would catch the bus to Marathon the next day. I set out to walk the mile and a bit. This was early spring but already the daytime temperature in Athens was as high as what typically we would once have called a pleasant June day in southern England. It took half an hour to find the place next to Areos Park. It wasn't a terminal as such, more a series of stops with an ever-changing fleet of buses pulling in or easing out into light traffic.

With no destination board to guide me, I toured the stops, poring over destinations in an unfamiliar alphabet, trying to spot that combination of Greek letters that would tell me I'd found the right stop for the bus to Marathon. I pored in vain and adopted plan B – ask someone. My first attempt produced nothing more specific than a neutral shrug and a pointed finger. Had he understood me? Was he pointing towards the right stop or simply the general direction towards Marathon. I walked further on and soon found a slightly battered information kiosk. It was closed. I began to wonder if this quest might not deliver the result I wanted. Then I spotted a driver who had just parked and stepped off his bus, and approached him. In good English he told me the route number of the buses that could take me to Marathon and their departure time. The journey would take an hour and a half. I skipped the idea of a very early start, a decision that would have consequences the next day. Instead, there were two buses that I could catch before a gap in service in the middle of the day.

Getting to Marathon was settled. Next I returned to the centre and laboured my way up the Acropolis, the steep hill at the centre of Athens on which the Parthenon stood. In my father's familiar phrase, it was a 'fair old climb'. This was my plan: I would take the bus to Marathon, where I would visit the Marathon Museum, surely a place of pilgrimage for anyone who has ever tackled running's iconic 26.2 mile distance. Then I would start my run and find my way back 'overland', over the hills for what looked like a dozen miles until I reached the Greek capital's suburbs, where I'd head for Kifissia, the terminus station on the Athens metro line 1. Then I'd take the metro into the centre until I reached Monastiraki. From there I'd run what I now dubbed 'the final ceremonial kilometre', zig-zagging up the steep Acropolis hillside until I reached the Parthenon. The plan for the last day of RUNNING: ME RUNNING EU was set.

Back at the hotel I made one last arrangement by booking a ticket online to visit the Parthenon. Entry is strictly controlled: it's an historic site, a Greek national monument and a protected UNESCO Heritage Site and I knew the Greeks regarded its artefacts with a fierce national pride. Just how fiercely they guarded this unique seat of Hellenic identity I would discover the following day. Visiting it would set the seal on the final stage. Now that I had a ticket, though, I would have to be mindful of the time tomorrow. The Acropolis closed at 5pm. I would need to make good progress on the run.

The hotel was clean and perfectly comfortable but being within my chosen budget its qualities didn't extend to air-con in the room. After a warm night I prepared a simple day-pack: bread, water, suncream, plasters and space for the shorts and shirt that I'd wear for the journey to Marathon but would remove for running. After a double-check just to make sure I had the essentials but no more, I headed out and made my way across town on foot to the bus stop at Areos Park and waited for the bus. Inevitably there was a brief period of angst (not maranoia this time but definitely Maranoia) as the departure time came but the bus didn't. Had I misunderstood or been given duff information? What were my options now if these no longer included taking the bus? At last it came and the Maranoia melted away.

A small and motley cluster of fellow passengers assembled from wherever they'd been waiting – it certainly hadn't been with me at the bus stop. I paid my fare and told the driver where I wanted to go. "Mara-ton", he confirmed. Once everyone was on board, and a cool, casual 20 minutes behind schedule the bus pulled away from its stand and we were off. It wasn't long before we were passing through some fairly nondescript districts as we moved further and further out from the centre towards the surrounding countryside. Urban Athens began to fragment and let the greenery in. Soon the scene of outlying suburbs had been replaced by a continuous vista of smallholdings, olive trees, stone walls and wayside tavernas. Occasionally we would stop, the odd passenger would step down to the roadside with a brief word of thanks to the driver, shouldering a day bag or knapsack. Occasionally another would join us, almost invariably clutching a basket or plastic bag with (I assumed) a few groceries. Those who used this bus were local people – villagers going home with provisions. As far as I could judge, there were no tourists (and I didn't count myself as one…). I'd had no preconceptions about Marathon as a destination but from this I sensed that there would be no great hordes of visitors. And so it proved.

With the light glinting on the nearby Aegean Sea, the bus made its way across a stretch of coastal plain backdropped by the hills through which I knew I would soon be climbing on foot. At least the start would be flat. Eventually the bus passed the Marathon Town entry sign. It was barely more than a village of one- and two-storey buildings, a languid place of a few thousand souls. It felt out-of-season, as indeed it was. This was March, after all. Houses, a handful of bars, their terraces dotted with customers who had that look of regulars with no other pressure than to fill the time with a coffee, a coke, casual conversation and a drifting curl of cigarette smoke.

I wondered if the scene was deceptive and the Marathon Museum would be the bustling heart of Marathon Town. It wasn't. I had to check that it was open, calling out from a vacant front desk into the interior that seemed full of sunlight and Olympic memorabilia but devoid of life. I heard a voice, then footsteps, finally, a greeting. "Welcome to the Marathon Museum!" A woman, perhaps in her late 30s, all smiles and an apology for the lack of a welcome party, as if this wasn't a museum open to the public and she wasn't expecting visitors. For me this was a kind of pilgrim's Mecca, a Santiago de Compostela, a holy place for runners. I did my best to convey that without overdoing it. I also briefly mentioned RUNNING: ME RUNNING EU, and that after visiting the museum I would be running back to Athens. As I heard myself speaking, I felt a frisson, a reminder that this was the final stage, the end of the challenge. It was exciting. I'd come a very long way to be here on a warm spring Friday in southern Greece, at a very out-of-season Marathon Museum, and about to embark on the run that would bring a year of planning, travelling, running and adventures to a fitting – and, I hoped, memorable – conclusion.

As I spoke, the thought suddenly dawned that a woman who worked front-of-house at this temple of honour for more than a century's worth of modern Olympians was hardly likely to be impressed by my story. But if she wasn't interested, she covered it well. Clearly I was profoundly invested in the challenge so I was no objective observer and in no position to gauge if she was merely feigning interest, but her apparent enthusiasm seemed real enough to me at that moment. She asked if there was anything about my challenge – a memento of some kind – that I could leave with her to display at the museum. I was surprised and felt a childish pride for a moment. All I had was my RUNNING: ME RUNNING EU vest. The thought that it might be displayed along with the vests and memorabilia of the men and women who'd been Olympic Marathon champions was almost too much to imagine. In fact it did seem rather far-fetched (which, having had the vest printed over 2,000 miles away in Stirchley, Birmingham, it literally was!).

I was tempted to leave it with her but chose not to. I wanted to wear it during my final run. I'd visualised wearing it up on the Acropolis. It was part of the challenge, a necessary detail in the final scene. No, the vest would come with me as I headed back to Athens. I enjoyed a moment's indulgence at the thought of the museum woman's kind offer but declined. In any case she was probably just being polite. Warmed by the idea, though, I began to wander through the exhibition, the only visitor at this point.

The museum was fascinating. The story of the marathon was told chronologically from Pheidippides's original run through to the founding of the modern Olympics in 1896 and the place of the marathon within it. There were posters, marathon route maps and other memorabilia from each modern Olympic Games, with pictures of the marathoners. I was drawn in particular to items from the various London Games – 1908, 1948 (the so-called Austerity Olympics, staged just after the end of the Second World War at a time of great scarcity and rationing of food and fuel), and just a few years ago in 2012. There were replicas of winners' medals and running vests worn by various of the victors down the years.

I was there for an hour and could have stayed for several but I had something else to do. By this point other visitors had arrived – I saw a couple, presumably in their 20s, and heard other, younger voices and a few deeper adult tones. I said goodbye to the friendly museum attendant. She acknowledged me with a smile but her attention had already moved on to the new arrivals. I slipped out and found a discreet spot in the museum garden to strip off my outer garments, packing them in the small strap bag with my other remaining essentials – especially water and a cereal bar – to carry on my back while I ran.

I checked Google Maps and turned the corner into a side street, suddenly feeling self-conscious as if I'd broken a local by-law against motion in this seemingly static setting where no other living being appeared to be moving – a tiny town which, if set in a classic Western movie in Arizona, would have one horse... I began to run. Within a couple of minutes I'd passed the last house and was moving steadily past olive orchards and grazing land. The terrain began to climb. There were wild flowers. The landscape was the green of spring in southern Europe before Easter, a temperate season before things really hotted up and the ground became parched.

In just a few months, I knew, this scene would be arid, the ground baked, the colour leeched from all but the hardiest vegetation. I was glad to be running in the relative cool of a March afternoon in Attica, the region of southern Greece that included Athens and Marathon.

Before long the tarmac ended and the road surface became a dusty gravel. Soon this ran out, too. The land continued to climb and the road became a stony path up into the hills. I paused to drink some water – I had one small bottle. I would need to make it last – and looked back towards Marathon, now a toy town down below, and just beyond it from this height, the clear grey-blue of the Aegean Sea. By now there was no path, although Google Maps still showed my way ahead as a dotted line. I now realised that this merely meant that there was a way over the hills to get to Athens, that there was no insurmountable barrier, but that it did not mean that there was a thoroughfare of any kind. By now the going was getting tough. The ground was strewn with large stones and I had to make my way around a steady succession of rocky outcrops, rooted into the landscape like jagged trees. It was barely possible even to jog by this point and before long I had to pick my way over boulders, stretching my legs and swinging my frame from one boulder to another. The incline grew steeper. By now I was on all fours, clambering very cautiously across the stones. Judging by the droppings this was goat territory, although I hadn't seen any since passing the last smallholdings on the edge of Marathon. That had been little more than an hour earlier and yet already it seemed like a very different phase and a long time ago. Lived time was now unravelling at a different pace to the one indicated by my watch. I stopped for more water and reflected on the sudden, unexpected level of difficulty of this run. We talk about running technical routes when they involve negotiating hazards that pose risks of injury, typically a fall or a turned ankle. Well, this was definitely 'technical'. I didn't relish coming a cropper while abroad, and especially not in this suddenly remote location. For a moment I was reminded of stories of people who suffer misfortunes in the Scottish Highlands, slipping down hillsides or crevasses and requiring search teams to put themselves at risk and come to their rescue. Certainly if I did trip and break or sprain something, there was no one within proximity to call on for help. I hadn't seen another soul for a couple of hours.

The only signs of life around me were of the small, round, animal droppings variety, possibly useful for an impromptu camp fire but little else. Anyway, I put the vulnerability narrative on hold and pushed on up the hillside.

Eventually the land levelled. Soon I saw a barbed wire fence, then a path and finally, a building – a house, albeit with no signs of life. The path was wide enough for a car, though, as tyre tracks in the dried and rutted mud confirmed. By now there were a couple of farm buildings. And then, 20-30 metres ahead, I saw the way ahead barred by... what exactly? A moving mass. Sheep! Seemingly an entire flock. Their shepherd and I spotted each other at the same moment. I'm not sure who was more surprised: the 20-something farmhand dressed entirely as you would expect a young farmhand to dress, moving his charges across familiar pastures or the 60-something stranger in shorts, running (slowly). Who's the odd one out? No prizes here – I realised that *I* was the incongruous figure in this rural scene.

There's probably an ingrained mistrust among farmers of any unexpected change in the landscape, especially an uninvited stranger who appears from nowhere. The shepherd shouted gruffly, whether as an admonition or a warning, I didn't know, but they certainly weren't words of welcome. The path ahead was full of sheep, moving en masse in the same direction as me (though I doubted that they were also on their way to Athens). I wasn't going to get past them and I certainly had no intention of wading into their midst. I decided to be patient and wait for the ovine tide to turn, whether left or right, we would see. I'd wondered if there was a dog, too, and there it was, a brown and white sprite of energy darting around the heels of the animals at the back. I followed behind at a short distance. And then they were gone, wheeling off onto a track to the right. The whole encounter must have taken no more than a couple of minutes.

I resumed the run. The path broadened and before long I reached a low wall surrounding a substantial single-storey house with a high-end four-wheel drive parked on a drive at the side of the house. The tarmac began again at the exit gate and from this point on I was on terra firma, a road rather than a track. A substantial fence surrounded the property, which also had an alarm. Another similarly guarded residential pile stood adjacent, then another. A sign fixed to the wall indicated that this road had a name. As I continued, I realised that I had just possibly reached the outermost suburbs at the eastern edge of Athens. A further check of Google Maps confirmed this. I pushed on, increasingly buoyed that the knowledge that I was now on the outskirts of the city where the challenge would end, although still a long way from the end-point itself.

And that was a problem. Time was running out. I'd booked an online ticket to visit the Acropolis – that was where I wanted to finish – and the site would close at 5pm. It was now 3.30pm. By this stage my surroundings were most definitely suburban, mostly residential but with a few shops, too. As I ran, I made a decision. I'd run for just over 10 miles already with an unscheduled added adventure when the route had become unpredictable and the terrain a lot wilder than I'd anticipated. There'd been a moment on the craggy hill-climb, clambering over boulders, when I half-imagined myself running in conditions that Pheidippides himself might have recognised (well, up to a point...). For the last day of RUNNING: ME RUNNING EU it had been a fitting final run already, I owed nothing more to the challenge, to the people who had supported and sponsored me, or to myself.

But I was still in the outer suburbs, somewhere near Athens's equivalent of Bromley or Barnet if you know Greater London, Barnt Green or Burntwood for Brummies (at this point it's tempting to leave a blank space here for readers from elsewhere to write in their own equivalents!). In other words, just at the edge of the urban sprawl but nowhere near the centre, and with the clock ticking. I spotted a bus stop and made a decision. I'd seen on the map that the furthest point on the Athens metro system was a couple of miles away, at a place called Kiffisia, the terminus for line 1. A lifetime of family links with public transport (and simple common sense) told me that a metro terminus in the suburbs was likely to be a local transport hub, so the chances were high that a bus serving this stop would go to Kifissia. I joined a short queue, feeling suddenly conspicuous in my running gear, visibly sweating. I looked at the bus stop for information. Literally and otherwise, it was all Greek to me. I asked a woman in the queue, unsure exactly how to pronounce the name of my destination... "Kifissia?" She smiled, repeated it and nodded. The bus arrived a few minutes later and my journey towards central Athens continued by bus.

After several slightly anxious repeated stares out of the window to make sure I would get off at the right place, I saw the metro sign. This was Kifissia. Off the bus, I was quickly onto the metro platform. The train left soon afterwards. Even so, it took just over 30 tense minutes and 16 intermediate stops before the train finally rattled into Monastiraki. It was 4.35pm. The Acropolis site would close in 25 minutes. I hot-footed it to street level and began to run immediately. This was the final kilometre, although there was nothing remotely ceremonial or stately about it. Evading the armfuls of souvenirs and baubles proffered by street hawkers around the station, I began to zig-zag my way through a mixed throng of sightseers, locals and the occasional figure in uniform, presumably city police – I didn't waste time finding out.

The approach paths to the Acropolis are quite steep and I jogged slowly up the hill with its mix of steps and inclines. I reached the entrance to the Acropolis grounds. It was 4.50pm. I'd made it – just – or so I thought. I pulled out my phone to display my ticket to the woman at the entrance, to be met with a shaking head: "No, you are too late. Last entry is at 4.30pm. It says so clearly on the website." Stunned, I began to burble about my challenge, that I was leaving early the next morning and that I wouldn't get another chance. The attendant was unmoved. I could see the columns of the temple a matter of metres away but couldn't physically reach them. I persisted but she wouldn't budge. This was unfortunate and something new to me – a closed door that simply couldn't be made to open.

Moments later the stalemate was broken when a second Acropolis official came to close the entrance gate. That looked final, but even so I looked for a way in, and studied the perimeter fence to see if I could find a gap. I wasn't thinking rationally and fortunately I was spared the consequences of what would have been a very stupid act by what happened next. Mere minutes after the Acropolis grounds closed for the day an army truck pulled up in front of the gate and out jumped half a dozen soldiers armed with rifles. They formed up, the gate opened again and in they marched to guard this globally-famous UNESCO World Heritage Site and unique symbol of Greek nationhood. I instantly recovered from my micro-tantrum. Risking arrest for trespass was one thing, being shot by a Greek soldier for desecrating a national monument was another. Instead I turned and looked out from the heights of the Acropolis, the hill on which the Parthenon stands, which towers commandingly above the expanse of Athens towards distant hills. My mood changed in an instant.

The sun was low in the sky and at my feet the ground picked up its rays and began to glow with a growing intensity. I felt its warmth. Soon the flagstones were ablaze with honey light. It felt almost spiritual and at that moment I experienced a profound sense of fulfilment. RUNNING: ME RUNNING EU was over. The challenge was complete.

Or almost. I chose a path down the side of the Acropolis that enabled me to reach some of the lower stonework on which the Parthenon stands. If I couldn't stand among the temple's famous columns I would at least touch its foundations. Here there was no one to bar my way and certainly no risk of a bullet. Some early 20-something American tourists were close by. I asked them to take my picture. They agreed and I reciprocated. They seemed friendly so I told them about the challenge.

Enthusiasm comes easily to young Americans and I had no need of approbation but they said the right things and were genuinely positive in their response. I've mentioned before that 'seven seconds of nirvana' feeling, a transient higher state of mind and body, a sense of oneness, that all is well, the world is firmly on its axis and at that exact moment, everything is as it should be. I felt it again as I came down (in both senses) from the Acropolis. Returning to my hotel, I showered, packed, then went out to eat, returning to sit up on the hotel's modest roof terrace with a beer and a view to the Acropolis, now shrouded in darkness under the night sky. Back in my room I rested for a while – sleep was impossible and not needed as I replayed the day's twists and turns in my mind and savoured the enormity of what I'd just completed.

A little after 1am I headed down to reception, and said goodbye to the night duty manager, who was startled to find a guest checking out at this unusual time. I walked the 20 minutes to Syntagma Square and the airport bus stop. It was late but as expected, the street was busy. Athens isn't a city that settles down early, if at all. The X95 bus arrived and left with me on it. Leaving Athens was uneventful, as was the flight. Shortly before 9am I was on the tarmac on a cool March morning at Stansted. The adventure was over. I couldn't do anything about Brexit, but at least I was able to run about it. And I had. Soon it would be time to tell the story...

Athens, Greece Savouring that 'seven seconds of nirvana' feeling that all is well, the world is firmly on its axis and at that exact moment, everything is as it should be. The challenge was complete.

Postscript

I've already said that optimism and determination were among the 'magic ingredients' in the fuel mix that enabled me to pursue and complete the challenge. But clearly that wasn't all I relied on. By my own modest standards it was an adventure – but a thoroughly modern one, enabled by a whole kit of tools that didn't exist for the true adventurers of the past. There's no shame in that – we all use the tools at our disposal at the time and in my case I had a specific purpose and a unique challenge and I used whatever I had to achieve these. I'm thankful to live in a world of smartphones, search engines and online maps. Between them, Google and Wikipedia told me much of what I needed to know about the places I would visit, and helped me find obscure half marathons and running clubs in less well-known cities. Thanks to the convenience of Booking.com and Airbnb I always knew where I was going to sleep and how to do so with the best balance of cost and comfort.

A variety of mainly low-cost air carriers got me out to many starting points across Europe and back again, while FlixBus, Pegasus and other international bus companies took me across various borders during the most intense stages of the challenge, especially during Baltic Week and the 'Habsburg Tour' (five countries in five days). Without Facebook, how else could I have kept on telling the story in real time to the growing number of people who I discovered were following my progress, especially as the challenge approached its conclusion? Those posts and the responses people made at the time gave me a vital online diary to check details and fill in some blanks in my memory. It also proved to be a really useful archive searchable month by month which I referred to repeatedly while trying to summon elusive moments and details for this story.

So much for the practical tools. Throughout the entire year I was enormously grateful for the support of a few individuals, none more so than Lisa Thompson, CEO at RSVP, one of the two charities I supported, who was my constant cheerleader from start to finish. I also offer my sincere thanks to Peter Moran who went out of his way to look after me during my visit to Ireland. Thank you to everyone who liked my posts and who commented with such unfailing positivity. Each of your likes and mentions administered a tiny dose of dopamine that helped keep me happy in the knowledge that I was doing something worthwhile.

Thanks also to the Free Athletes Nantes (FR), Gent Running Team (BE), Urbani Tekači in Ljubljana (SI), Hamburger Lauflåden (DE), the Riga Marathon training group (LT), Newbridge AC (IE), the European Robotics Week charity runners in Bucharest (RO) and the Runners of Ruse (BG), all running clubs and groups whose welcoming members I ran, trained and sometimes drank coffee or other beverages with (sometimes all three but clearly not all at the same time) either by design or by very happy chance, at different points during the year.

Thank you to my running family at Bournville Harriers for taking the challenge seriously from the outset and also by giving it added recognition by naming me Member of the Month once I'd completed it.

Heartfelt thanks to the very welcoming parkrun event teams at Amager Fælled (DK), Malmö Ribersborg (SK), Naas (IE), Katowice (PL) and Helsinki Tokoinranta (FI). Thank you also to everyone who supported my chosen charities by sponsoring me.

It took a few months first to conceive the idea of the challenge and then to fashion it into the form it finally took as RUNNING: ME RUNNING EU. As everyone who has read this far knows by now, I gave myself one year to complete the challenge. I knew long before Athens, though, that once the adventure was over I would eventually write the whole thing down. Inevitably it took me a while to get started and then a further four years spent drafting, pausing, progressing, revising and pausing again. Then one day in 2023 during what proved to be the last of several 'pauses' Bernd Liepert asked me how the book was going, before making a simple, practical and generous suggestion that gave me the renewed motivation, and most importantly, a deadline to complete it. I am truly grateful to Bernd for believing in the book at a time when I most needed that added spur to action.

It was then almost unnerving yet exciting to entrust a finished draft to my beta readers Paul Anderson, Claire Daniels, Stacey Marston, Steve Partridge and Steve Thompson, all busy with their lives and yet as generous, constructive and encouraging with their feedback as I could reasonably have expected.

Thank you to Liz Dexter for bringing a professional book editor's unblinking eye to the text, suggesting countless small improvements that I would otherwise have been too close to see. Her being a fellow runner also helped.

If this edition can be judged favourably by its outward appearance then the credit goes to the talented cover designer Spencer Roberts. Far from least, the fact that the book now finally exists in its physical form is due to Peter Erftemeijer of Mot Juste, the publisher. Thank you both.

Finally, I am grateful for the support of my children, Gemma and Luke and my wife Liz, a realist who (quite reasonably) was probably sceptical at first about what had all the signs of being just another of my short-term enthusiasms, but whose backing grew the further I progressed. Thank you.

About the author

Stephen Doswell is a corporate communication specialist and a linguist. His short story Vinjeta Vignettes *was published in 2023 in English and Slovene as part of a collection to mark 30 years of diplomatic relations between the UK and Slovenia. He grew up in south London and has a strong emotional attachment to his 'ancestral homeland' south of the Thames. He lives in Birmingham and is an active member of the city's running community.* Running: Me Running EU *is his first full-length published book.*

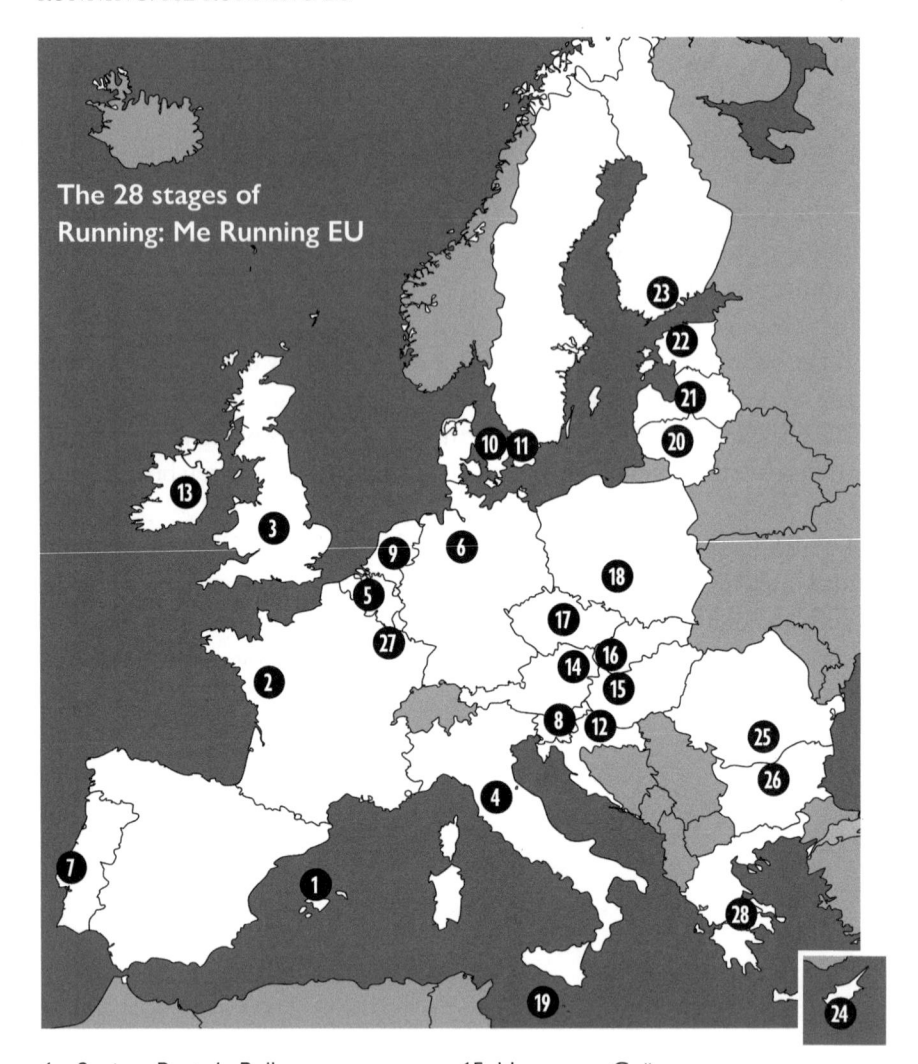

RUNNING: ME RUNNING EU

The 28 stages of Running: Me Running EU

1 Spain – Port de Pollença	15 Hungary – Győr
2 France – Nantes	16 Slovakia – Bratislava
3 United Kingdom – Catton Park	17 Czechia – Brno
4 Italy – Tuscan Hills	18 Poland – Katowice
5 Belgium – Ghent	19 Malta – Sliema
6 Germany – Hamburg	20 Lithuania – Kaunus
7 Portugal – Lisbon	21 Latvia – Riga
8 Slovenia – Ljubljana	22 Estonia – Tallinn
9 The Netherlands – Nijmegen	23 Finland – Helsinki
10 Denmark – Copenhagen	24 Cyprus – Paphos
11 Sweden – Malmö	25 Romania – Bucharest
12 Croatia – Varaždin	26 Bulgaria – Ruse
13 Ireland – Newbridge	27 Luxembourg – Luxembourg City
14 Austria – Vienna	28 Greece – Athens